Readings in Child Development

Readings in Child Development

Nancy Lauter-Klatell

Wheelock College

Mayfield Publishing Company
Mountain View, California
London • Toronto

To my daughters, Jenna and Devon, who make my life rich.

Library of Congress Cataloging-in-Publication Data

Readings in child development / [compiled by] Nancy Lauter-Klatell
    p. cm.
    Includes bibliographical references and index.
    ISBN 1-87484-942-X
    1. Child Development. I. Lauter-Klatell, Nancy.
HQ767.9.R42 1991
305.23′1—dc20   90-46200
                                   CIP

Manufactured in the United States of America
10 9 8 7 6 5 4 3 2 1

Mayfield Publishing Company
1240 Villa Street
Mountain View, California

Sponsoring Editor, Janet M. Beatty; production management, The
Book Company; copy editor, Linda Purrington; text designer,
Wendy Calmenson; cover designer, Joan Greenfield; cover
photographer, Mimi Cotter; photograph hand tinted by Lissa
Jones. The text was set in 10/12 Palatino by Harrison Typesetting,
Inc. and printed on 50# Glatfelter Spring Forge by Bawden
Printing, Inc.

Preface

The study of human development is grounded in strong theoretical foundations, yet individuals develop in ways that can be unpredictable. We must view development through the lens of theoretical principles, but with sensitivity to the surprises and inconsistencies that exist. The environment, for example, has a significant influence on behavioral outcomes, yet some children from the most unfortunate and limited circumstances become successful and well-functioning human beings. What makes the difference?

The aim of this book of readings is to help students grasp the principles and also understand the complex inconsistencies of human development as they begin their study of the relationships between theory and reality. The articles have been chosen to provide diverse insights into development as it is played out in our daily lives. How do our actions, background, and genetic dispositions influence others? And how are we influenced by the people, ideas, and attitudes around us? The selection is governed by a view of human development that is:

- *Comprehensive.* Balanced attention is given to each area of development: physical, cognitive, linguistic, social, and emotional. The child is seen as playing an active, competent role in establishing and maintaining certain patterns of development.

- *Interactive.* Development of the individual is considered within the context of interpersonal relationships and interactions with the environment (family, school, community, country, and world).

- *Continuous.* What comes before influences what follows, yet individuals have a tremendous capacity to adapt and change.

Most of the readings clearly reflect a social-ecological orientation to development which assumes that behaviors cannot be isolated from the social, political, and cultural environment in which the individual grows. A child raised in a congested urban area will have different ideas and behaviors than a child raised in a remote rural community. If a child's parents are divorced or a sibling has died, environmental influences in that child's life are different from those of a friend whose life includes neither of these conditions. These differences should be discussed, valued, and used to modify some of our assumptions about development. Moreover, society and science have offered social scientists powerful tools to examine and influence human experiences, and with some of these technological advances come new ethical dilemmas which force us to make decisions about a range of human issues. This text focuses on some of the most current topics in the field of child development. Attention is paid to:

- changes in today's society that particularly affect families,

- the continuum of normality and exceptionality,

- cross-cultural and multicultural perspectives,

- ethical dilemmas presented in research practices and advanced technologies, and

- the need to translate research (what we know) into practice and policy.

The readings are organized into six sections. The first is an orientation to influences on development. What do different perspectives reveal about the course of human life? What are the influences? Which ones are most powerful—for whom? How do different theorists and researchers explain patterns of behavior? The following five sections are arranged in chronological order beginning with pregnancy and birth and ending with adolescence. Each section highlights the range of developmental areas and incorporates social context issues. The Cross Reference Chart at the front of the book will assist the reader in finding articles according to the age of development and specific developmental topics they cover: cognitive, language, social-emotional, parent and child relationships, peer interactions, and social/political/cultural influences.

In the selection of articles, special attention was given to articles which would be especially interesting to students interested in human services and the application of developmental principles. When an acceptable article could not be found on a topic of interest, original manuscripts were written by experts in the field. Five original readings present the very latest information on high-risk infants, parent-child separation issues, early interactions between peers, development of literacy skills, and mathematical thinking during the middle years.

Finally, a special feature of this reader is a two-part appendix, Reading For Meaning and Strategies For Writing Assignments. This resource helps students understand how to read human development articles and gives practical advice on how to write a clear and meaningful class paper based upon a reading assignment.

ACKNOWLEDGEMENTS

It was a treat for me to review the most current literature on human development issues. I want to thank Frank Graham for guiding me through the process of selecting articles and refining the format, and Judith Schickedanz for creating this opportunity. I also want to acknowledge the many authors and journal editors who I contacted regarding the use of articles. In most cases, professionals were more than willing to share their good ideas. Finally, I want to thank my colleagues who wrote original manuscripts; Jean Cole, Kimberly DiCero, Mieko Kamii, Susan McBride, and Judith Schickedanz. Their expertise and their patience was appreciated.

I am grateful to the following reviewers of the text for their many excellent suggestions: Janet Gonzalez-Mena, Napa Valley College; Patricia Major, State University of New York, College at Oneonta; Mary Ann McLaughlin, Clarion University of Pennsylvania; Philip Mohan, University of Idaho; Grace Nunn, Eastern Illinois University.

Cross Reference for Content of Readings

Each article in this text was chosen, in part, for its "wholistic" approach to development. Therefore, many of the readings encompass more than one isolated dimension of development. The chart below indicates areas emphasized in each article. For example, if you are looking for information on social and emotional development, refer to the articles which have an "x" in the column marked **SO-EMO**. This chart may be used to focus attention on specific areas of development or to select articles which highlight the interaction between different areas.

COG	Cognitive development
LAN	Language development and communication strategies
SO-EMO	Social and emotional development
PAR-CH	Parent and child interactions and influences
PEER	Peer interactions and influences
SOC/POL/CUL	Social, political, cultural, economic interactions and influences on development—the impact of "world view"

AUTHOR	COG	LAN	SO-EMO	PAR-CH	PEER	SOC/POL/CUL
Part I						
Skinner	X			X		X
Werner			X	X		X
Kagan/Greenspan	X	X	X	X		
Scherer	X					X
Ryan				X		X
Crooks				X		X
Cole	X		X	X		X
Part II						
Acredolo/Goodwyn	X	X		X		
Lewis	X	X	X			
Honig			X	X		
McBride/DiCero			X	X		X
Lauter-Klatell		X	X		X	
Wingert/ Kantrowitz			X	X		X
Part III						
Bruner	X	X		X		
Flavell	X					
Schickedanz	X	X		X		X
Roedell	X		X		X	
deYoung	X		X			X
Part IV						
Kamii	X					
Schwartzberg			X		X	
Postman			X	X		X
Norwood			X	X		X
Grant			X		X	X
Part V						
Petersen			X		X	
Blyth/Traeger	X		X			
Elkind			X	X	X	X
Bronfenbrenner			X	X		X
Sung			X	X	X	X
Williams			X		X	X

Contents

Part One

INFLUENCES ON DEVELOPMENT

How do we decide what factors affect the development of any particular child? Is development driven by biological endowment, so that some infants are born to become great leaders, while others will never amount to much? Or does environment (the settings, interpersonal relationships, cultural values, and experiences of daily life) shape if and when a child will be successful? Is development continuous, so that skills and behavioral patterns developed early in life remain? Or is it discontinuous: can behaviors not acquired early (such as an ability to form relationships with others) be learned later in life? Can a preschooler whose language development is delayed later become captain of the high school debating team?

There are many questions, and few simple answers. Human development is a complex series of interactions between an individual (including his or her previous experiences and present view of events) and the environment. Theories of development, research, and the current world view allow us to generate new questions and help us reach toward answers that explain the intricacies of human behavior.

Theories are sets of assumptions about events, why they occur, and what happens before and after their occurrence. Explorers of theory, driven by a specific interpretation of how development unfolds, carry out a research agenda (ask certain questions) that responds to selected assumptions. Research is a systematic attempt to document the descriptive, explanatory, and predictive qualities of events (what does aggression "look like," why does it occur, and how can it be changed?). And, "a worldview" is the interaction of social, cultural, political, moral, and economic forces that shape ideas about environment during a specific time in history. Theories, research, and "worldview" govern what we know about human development, the questions we ask, and (to some extent) what we expect or hope to find out.

The interaction among theory, research, and worldview is well played out in the nature-versus-nurture debate that continues to generate controversy among human development scientists. Early in this century, the dominant worldview was that inherited factors determined one's role in life. According to this view, if you were born in a poor section of town and your parents were unskilled laborers, that would probably be your place and condition for life. People born to a particular group inherited certain traits that resembled the behavioral patterns of other group members. These assumptions mirrored the class structures of Europe, but conflicted with the U.S. philosophy of individualism and "pulling oneself up by one's bootstraps." The mismatch between theory and worldview pushed the research pendulum from a geneticist view to an extreme environmentalist view, demonstrated by the first article, "Baby in a Box." B. F. Skinner joined Edward Thorndike and John Watson to shape the behaviorist theory of the 1930s and 1940s. However, as we move toward the year 2000, our theories—influenced by the work of Piaget and research by Brazelton, Bruner, and Kagan—are more interactive. Today there is substantial agreement that heredity and environment interact continuously throughout the life span. Each factor influences development. But we still have questions about *how much* influence heredity and environment have on development and *when* each influence is most powerful.

The second and third articles highlight the interplay between heredity (nature) and environment (nurture). "Children of the Garden Island" is an example of longitudinal research that followed one group of children over a thirty-year span. What made the difference for children who were at risk early in life, but in fact became successful, productive adults? Was the cause of their achievements biological or environmental? The article documents that for some children an environmental intervention (a role model) "changed" their lives. But why were these children more receptive to external influences than others? In the next article, "Milestones of Development," Greenspan argues that development is continuous and patterns of interaction that affect later behaviors are developed early. Kagan, however, views development as discontinuous. He believes that dramatic behavioral changes can occur during the course of development. Although Greenspan and Kagan agree on the combined influence of heredity and environment, they disagree on how development progresses over time.

In the fourth article, Howard Gardner introduces a new "theory" of intelligence. His research, carried out at Harvard University, redefines our notion of intelligence to include not two (language and logico-mathematical) but seven domains. Schools and standardized tests have always valued language and logic as the measure of intelligence. Yet there is a growing certainty within the educational community that we short-change children who have other talents and/or learning styles. This hypothesis may be a "theory" that our worldview is ready and willing to accept.

The next three readings focus on environmental factors or interventions that affect the birth and early development of infants. During the past decade, we have witnessed both great success and dismal failure in attempts (or lack of action) to provide optimal condi-

tions for parents and newborns. Any intervention in the lives of individuals is viewed through thick social, political, moral, and cultural lenses. In many cases, new technological advances such as genetic counseling, prenatal surgery to correct genetic defects (see the article by Crooks) and in vitro fertilization have led to healthy infants and delighted parents. In other instances, certain practices have required court decisions on who are the "legitimate" parents (for example, the surrogate mother case of Baby M). In addition, factors such as prenatal and birthing practices (see the article by Ryan), age of the mother, the fetus's exposure to drugs and the AIDS virus in utero (see the Cole article), financial and emotional resources (or lack thereof) available to the family, and the parent's ability to offer a safe and nurturing environment all affect the development of a newborn infant.

Prenatal development is clearly influenced by environmental factors. The presence of any potentially harmful drugs (alcohol, tobacco, cocaine, and so on) or lack of good nutrition affects the unborn infant's growth patterns and possibly the timing of birth (prematurity). In the case of drugs and AIDS, we know very little about how to help afflicted babies whose reaction patterns and organizational abilities show the antithesis of normal development. It is extremely difficult for adults to interact normally with such infants, yet a poor start during the early weeks of life may put an infant and his or her family at a distinct disadvantage for subsequent optimal development. The crucial bonding behaviors that take place between parents and infants are key to later development of attachment, affect, and other cognitive, social, and physical abilities. Combinations of stress factors—prematurity plus need for medical interventions plus lack of family resources—put certain newborns in the high-risk category. Yet research such as the longitudinal study of the Garden Island children gives cause to hope that we can overcome the vulnerable start of some of these at-risk infants. In addition, instruments such as the Brazelton Neonatal Behavior Assessment Scale (see article by Cole) are being developed to provide information on how to modify the early environments of at-risk infants and thereby facilitate optimal development.

Differences between the biological endowment and environmental circumstances of individual children should not cause us to throw our hands up in despair, but to find the nature of those differences so we can respond appropriately and make reasonable changes in the environment. (For example, our country could ensure that every woman has access to good nutrition and prenatal care and thus instantly reduce the number of premature infants and birth defects.)

Differences detrimental to the infant's well-being must be reduced.

There is no doubt that each infant is born with innate abilities. The capacity to learn from birth establishes that some behavioral patterns are innate. In balance, each infant is also born into an environmental context that includes gender, race, culture, economic and political opportunity, and the potential to establish effective and enduring relationships with others. Heredity and environment combine and confront each other as a child's developmental patterns unfold. And people will continue to ask why and how nature and nurture affect our lives.

Baby in a Box

B. F. Skinner

B. F. Skinner, one of the most renowned proponents of behaviorist theory, believes that the environment is the source of all learning. If you want to teach a child a new behavior or maintain the status quo, you must manipulate the environment (by implementing reinforcement or punishment techniques) to achieve your goal.

In the early 1940s, Skinner designed a mechanically responsive box to meet certain needs of his infant daughter and to decrease the amount of child-parent interaction time. When the child cried, the temperature in the box was lowered and crying ceased. When the infant awoke to be fed too early in the morning, the temperature in the box was raised to encourage extended sleeping periods.

The question might be raised, can a change in temperature replace the warm arms of a parent's cuddle?

What do infants need in addition to warmth, food, sleep, and cleanliness? Without question, current research underscores parent (or other human) response to an infant's needs as the foundation of the child's social and cognitive development (see Greenspan's arguments). Skinner, however, is not interested in the interaction between infant and parent (environment). He is only concerned with the action of the environment on the infant. His theory dictates his research and highlights what he expected to find—his daughter was perfectly happy in the box! It is important to remember that theorists of any persuasion conduct research to validate their ideas. Sometimes researchers find what they are looking for, rather than what actually exists.

In that brave new world which science is preparing for the housewife of the future the young mother has apparently been forgotten. Almost nothing has been done to ease her lot by simplifying and improving the care of babies.

When we decided to have another child, my wife and I felt that it was time to apply a little labor-saving invention and design to the problems of the nursery. We began by going over the disheartening schedule of the young mother, step by step. We asked only one question: Is this practice important for the physical and psychological health of the baby? When it was not, we marked it for elimination. Then the "gadgeteering" began.

The result is an inexpensive apparatus in which our baby daughter has now been living for eleven months. Her remarkable good health and happiness and my wife's welcome leisure have exceeded our most optimistic predictions, and we are convinced that a new deal for both mother and baby is at hand.

We tackled first the problem of warmth. The usual solution is to wrap the baby in half-a-dozen layers of cloth—shirt, nightdress, sheet, blankets. This is never completely successful. The baby is likely to be found steaming in its own fluids or lying cold and uncovered. Schemes to prevent uncovering may be dangerous, and in fact they have sometimes even proved to be fatal. Clothing and bedding also interfere with normal exercise and growth and keep the baby from taking comfortable postures or changing posture during sleep. They also encourage rashes and sores. Nothing can be said for the system on the score of convenience, because frequent changes and launderings are necessary.

Why not, we thought, dispense with clothing altogether—except for the diaper, which serves another purpose—and warm the space in which the baby lives? This should be a simple technical problem in the modern home. Our solution is a closed compartment about as spacious as a standard crib. The walls are well insulated, and one side, which can be raised like a window, is a large pane of safety glass. The heating is electrical, and special precautions have been taken to ensure accurate control.

After a little experimentation we found that our baby, when first home from the hospital, was completely comfortable and relaxed without benefit of clothing at about 86°F. As she grew older, it was possible to lower the temperature by easy stages. Now, at eleven months, we are operating at about 78°, with a relative humidity of 50 percent.

Raising or lowering the temperature by more than a degree or two will produce a surprising change in the baby's condition and behavior. This response is so sensitive that we wonder how a comfortable temperature is ever reached with clothing and blankets.

The discovery that pleased us most was that crying and fussing could almost always be stopped by slightly lowering the temperature. During the first three months, it is true, the baby would also cry when wet or hungry, but in that case she would stop when changed or fed. During the past six months she has not cried at all except for a moment or two when injured or sharply distressed—for example, when inoculated. The "lung exercise" which is so often appealed to to reassure the mother of a baby that cries a good deal takes the much pleasanter form of shouts and gurgles.

How much of this sustained cheerfulness is due to the temperature is hard to say, because the baby enjoys many other kinds of comfort. She sleeps in curious postures, not half of which would be possible under securely fastened blankets.

When awake, she exercises almost constantly and often with surprising violence. Her leg, stomach and back muscles are especially active and have become strong and hard. It is necessary to watch this performance for only a few minutes to realize how severely restrained the average baby is, and how much energy must be diverted into the only remaining channel—crying.

A wider range and variety of behavior are also encouraged by the freedom from clothing. For example, our baby acquired an amusing, almost apelike skill in the use of her feet. We have devised a number of toys which are occasionally suspended from the ceiling of the compartment. She often plays with these with her feet alone and with her hands and feet in close co-operation.

One toy is a ring suspended from a modified music box. A note can be played by pulling the ring downward, and a series of rapid jerks will produce Three Blind Mice. At seven months our baby would grasp the ring in her toes, stretch out her leg and play the tune with a rhythmic movement of her foot.

We are not especially interested in developing skills of this sort, but they are valuable for the baby because they arouse and hold her interest. Many babies seem to cry from sheer boredom—their behavior is restrained and they have nothing else to do. In our compartment, the waking hours are invariably active and happy ones.

Freedom from clothes and bedding is especially important for the older baby who plays and falls asleep off and on during the day. Unless the mother is constantly on the alert, it is hard to cover the baby promptly when it falls asleep and to remove and arrange sheets and blankets as soon as it is ready to play. All this is now unnecessary.

Remember that these advantages for the baby do not mean additional labor or attention on the part of the mother. On the contrary, there is an almost unbelievable saving in time and effort. For one thing, there is no bed to be made or changed. The "mattress" is a tightly stretched canvas, which is kept dry by warm air. A single bottom sheet operates like a roller towel. It is stored on a spool outside the compartment at one end and passes into a wire hamper at the other. It is ten yards long and lasts a week. A clean section can be locked into place in a few seconds. The time which is usually spent in changing clothes is also saved. This is especially important in the early months. When we take the baby up for feeding or play, she is wrapped in a small blanket or a simple nightdress. Occasionally she is dressed up "for fun" or for her play period. But that is all. The wrapping blanket, roller sheet and the usual diapers are the only laundry actually required.

Time and labor are also saved because the air which passes through the compartment is thoroughly filtered. The baby's eyes, ears and nostrils remain fresh and clean. A weekly bath is enough, provided the face and diaper region are frequently washed. These little attentions are easy because the compartment is at waist level.

It takes about one and one half hours each day to feed, change and otherwise care for the baby. This includes everything except washing diapers and preparing formula. We are not interested in reducing the time any farther. As a baby grows older, it needs a certain amount of social stimulation. And after all, when unnecessary chores have been eliminated, taking care of a baby is fun.

An unforeseen dividend has been the contribution to the baby's good health. Our pediatrician readily approved the plan before the baby was born, and he has followed the results enthusiastically from month to month. Here are some points on the health score: When the baby was only ten days old, we could place her in the preferred face-down position without danger of smothering, and she has slept that way ever since, with the usual advantages. She has always enjoyed deep and extended sleep, and her feeding and eliminative habits have been extraordinarily regular. She has never had a stomach upset, and she has never missed a daily bowel movement.

The compartment is relatively free of spray and air-borne infection, as well as dust and allergic substances. Although there have been colds in the family, it has been easy to avoid contagion, and the baby has completely escaped. The neighborhood children troop in to see her, but they see her through glass and keep their school-age diseases to themselves. She has never had a diaper rash.

We have also enjoyed the advantages of a fixed daily routine. Child specialists are still not agreed as to whether the mother should watch the baby or the clock, but no one denies that a strict schedule saves time. The mother can plan her day in advance and find time for relaxation or freedom for other activities. The trouble is that a routine acceptable to the baby often conflicts with the schedule of the household. Our compartment helps out here in two ways. Even in crowded living quarters it can be kept free of unwanted lights and sounds. The insulated walls muffle all ordinary noises, and a curtain can be drawn down over the window. The result is that, in the space taken by a standard crib, the baby has in effect a separate room. We are never concerned lest the doorbell, telephone, piano or children at play wake the baby, and we can therefore let her set up any routine she likes.

But a more interesting possibility is that her routine may be changed to suit our convenience.

A good example of this occurred when we dropped her schedule from four to three meals per day. The baby began to wake up in the morning about an hour before we wanted to feed her. This annoying habit, once established, may persist for months. However, by slightly raising the temperature during the night, we were able to postpone her demand for breakfast. The explanation is simple. The evening meal is used by the baby mainly to keep itself warm during the night. How long it lasts will depend in part upon how fast heat is absorbed by the surrounding air.

One advantage not to be overlooked is that the soundproofing also protects the family from the baby! Our intentions in this direction were misunderstood by some of our friends. We were never put to the test, because there was no crying to contend with, but it was never our policy to use the compartment in order to let the baby "cry it out."

Every effort should be made to discover just why a baby cries. But if the condition cannot be remedied, there is no reason why the family, and perhaps the neighborhood as well, must suffer. (Such a compartment, by the way, might persuade many a landlord to drop a "no babies" rule, since other tenants can be completely protected.)

Before the baby was born, when we were still building the apparatus, some of the friends and acquaintances who had heard about what we proposed to do were rather shocked. Mechanical dishwashers, garbage disposers, air cleaners and other labor-saving devices were all very fine, but a mechanical baby tender—that was carrying science too far! However, all the specific objections that were raised against the plan have faded away in the bright light of our results. A very brief acquaintance with the scheme in operation is enough to resolve all doubts. Some of the toughest skeptics have become our most enthusiastic supporters.

One of the commonest objections was that we were going to raise a "softie" who would be unprepared for the real world. But instead of becoming hypersensitive, our baby has acquired a surprisingly serene tolerance for annoyances. She is not bothered by the clothes she wears at playtime, she is not frightened by loud or sudden noises, she is not frustrated by toys out of reach, and she takes a lot of pommeling from her older sister like a good sport. It is possible that she will have to learn to sleep in a noisy room, but adjustments of that sort are always necessary. A tolerance for annoyance can be built up by administering it in controlled dosages, rather than in the usual accidental way. Certainly there is no reason to annoy the child throughout the whole of its infancy, merely to prepare it for later childhood.

It is not, of course, the favorable conditions to which people object, but the fact that in our compartment they are "artificial." All of them occur naturally in one favorable environment or another, where the same objection should apply but is never raised. It is quite in the spirit of the "world of the future" to make favorable conditions available everywhere through simple mechanical means.

A few critics have objected that they would not like to live in such a compartment themselves—they feel that it would stifle them or give them claustrophobia. The baby obviously does not share in this opinion. The compartment is well ventilated and much more spacious than a Pullman berth, considering the size of the occupant. The baby cannot get out, of course, but that is true of a crib as well. There is less actual restraint in the compartment because the baby is freer to move about. The plain fact is that she is perfectly happy. She has never tried to get out nor resisted being put back in, and that seems to be the final test.

Another early objection was that the baby would be socially starved and robbed of the affection and mother love that she needs. This has simply not been true. The compartment does not ostracize the baby. The large window is no more of a social barrier than the bars of a crib. The baby follows what is going on in the room, smiles at passers-by, plays "peek-a-boo" games, and obviously delights in company. And she is handled, talked to and played with whenever she is changed or fed, and each afternoon during a play period which is becoming longer as she grows older.

The fact is that a baby will probably get more love and affection when it is easily cared for, because the mother is not so likely to feel overworked and resentful of the demands made upon her. She will express her love in a practical way and give the baby genuinely affectionate care.

It is common practice to advise the troubled mother to be patient and tender and to enjoy her baby. And, of course, that is what any baby needs. But it is the exceptional mother who can fill this prescription upon demand, especially if there are other children in the family and she has no help. We need to go one step further and treat the mother with affection also. Simplified child care will give mother love a chance.

A similar complaint was that such an apparatus would encourage neglect. But easier care is sure to be better care. The mother will resist the temptation to put the baby back into a damp bed if she can conjure up a dry one in five seconds. She may very well spend less time with her baby, but babies do not suffer from being left alone, only from the discomforts which arise from being left alone in the ordinary crib.

How long do we intend to keep the baby in the compartment? The baby will answer that in time, but almost certainly until she is two years old, or perhaps three. After the first year, of course, she will spend a fair part of each day in a play pen or out-of-doors. The compartment takes the place of a crib and will get about the same use. Eventually it will serve as sleeping quarters only.

We cannot, of course, guarantee that every baby raised in this way will thrive so successfully. But there is a plausible connection between health and happiness and the surroundings we have provided, and I am quite sure that our success is not an accident. The experiment should, of course, be repeated again and again with different babies and different parents. One case is enough, however, to disprove the flat assertion that it can't be done. At least we have shown that a moderate and inexpensive mechanization of baby care will yield a tremendous saving in time and trouble, without harm to the child and probably to its lasting advantage. . . .

FURTHER COMMENTS (1977)

The word "box" was put in my title by the editors of the *Journal* and it led to endless confusion because I had used another box in the study of operant conditioning. Many of those who had not read the article assumed that I was experimenting on our daughter as if she were a rat or pigeon. Those who read it, however, viewed it quite favorably. Hundreds of people wrote to say that they wanted to raise their babies in the same way. I sent out mimeographed instructions to help those who proposed to build boxes for themselves. My contacts with potential manufacturers were disappointing but eventually an enterprising man, John Gray, organized the Aircrib Corporation and began production on a modest scale. He contributed much of his own time without remuneration, and when he died his son was unable to carry on. Second-hand Aircribs are now in demand.

Our daughter continued to use the Aircrib for sleeping and naps until she was two and a half, and during that time we all profited from it. The long sheet and canvas "mattress" were replaced by a tightly stretched woven plastic, with the texture of linen, which could be washed and dried instantly, and once her bowel-movement pattern was established she slept nude. Urine was collected in a pan beneath the plastic. Predictions that she would be a bed-wetter were not confirmed. She learned to keep dry in her clothing during the day and when she started to sleep in a regular bed she treated it like clothing. Except for one night when we had been traveling and were all rather tired, she has never wet a bed. She proved remarkably resistant to colds and other infections.

Possibly through confusion with the other box, the venture began to be misunderstood. Stories circulated about the dire consequences of raising a baby in any such way. It was said that our daughter had committed suicide, become psychotic, and (more recently), was suing me. The fact is that she is a successful artist living in London with her husband, Dr. Barry Buzan, who teaches in the field of international studies. My older daughter, Dr. Julie Vargas, used an Aircrib with her two daughters, and she and many others have confirmed the results we reported.

The Aircrib has many advantages for both child and parents. For the child it offers greater comfort, safety, freedom of movement, and an opportunity for the earliest possible development of motor and perceptual skills. For the parent it saves labor and gives a sense of security about the baby's well being. There is no danger of being strangled by bedclothes or becoming uncovered on a cold night. It is somewhat more expensive than an ordinary crib, even including mattress, sheets, blankets and laundry, but the resale value is high. It can often save money by saving space.

By drawing a curtain over the window at night it can be closed off from the rest of the room, making it possible for a young couple to stay for another year or two in a one-room apartment or to let a baby share a room with an older child.

I do not expect to see Aircribs widely used in the near future. It is not the kind of thing that appeals to American business. It is impossible to convince a Board of Directors that there is a market that justifies tooling up for mass production to keep the price down, and so long as the price remains high a market will not develop.

Nevertheless, the first two or three years are the most important years in a child's life, and I am sure that much more will eventually be done to make them more enjoyable and productive.

Children of the Garden Island

Emmy E. Werner

One way to decipher the nature-versus-nurture formula is to study the same children over many years. Researchers could then compare the biological and environmental risks with the behavioral outcomes of children. This article traces the development of many children over a thirty-year span. We might assume that if biological factors are the predominant influences for child outcomes, then those children born with any mental or physical disability or those who experience complications during pregnancy, labor, or delivery (prenatal and perinatal stress) would be the least successful in adulthood. But this was not the case. If environmental influences hold sway over developmental outcomes, then those who were raised in the least optimal environments

would be least successful as adults. This was not the case, either. Different combinations of biological and environmental factors determined outcomes.

Some of the children who were most vulnerable due to both inherited and environmental stresses (that is, moderate to severe perinatal stress, chronic poverty, parents lacking education, families troubled by divorce, discord, parental alcoholism, or mental illness) became successful adults. Why were these "resilient" children able to succeed when others were not? This study documents both the innate and environmental influences that made a difference for individual children in overcoming sizable odds.

Kauai, the Garden Island, lies at the northwest end of the Hawaiian chain, 100 miles and a half-hour flight from Honolulu. Its 555 square miles encompass mountains, cliffs, canyons, rain forests and sandy beaches washed by pounding surf. The first Polynesians who crossed the Pacific to settle there in the eighth century were charmed by its beauty, as were the generations of sojourners who visited there after Captain James Cook "discovered" the island in 1778.

The 45,000 inhabitants of Kauai are for the most part descendants of immigrants from Southeast Asia and Europe who came to the island to work on the sugar plantations with the hope of finding a better life for their children. Thanks to the islanders' unique

spirit of cooperation, my colleagues Jessie M. Bierman and Fern E. French of the University of California at Berkeley, Ruth S. Smith, a clinical psychologist on Kauai, and I have been able to carry out a longitudinal study on Kauai that has lasted for more than three decades. The study has had two principal goals: to assess the long-term consequences of prenatal and perinatal stress and to document the effects of adverse early rearing conditions on children's physical, cognitive, and psychosocial development.

The Kauai Longitudinal Study began at a time when the systematic examination of the development of children exposed to biological and psychosocial risk factors was still a bit of a rarity. Investigators attempted to reconstruct the events that led to physical or psychological problems by studying the history of individuals in whom such problems had already surfaced. This retrospective approach can create the impression that the outcome is inevitable, since it takes into account only the "casualties," not the "survivors." We hoped to avoid that impression by monitoring the development of all the children born in a given period in an entire community.

We began our study in 1954 with an assessment of the reproductive histories of all the women in the community. Altogether 2,203 pregnancies were reported by the women of Kauai in 1954, 1955 and 1956; there were 240 fetal deaths and 1,963 live births. We chose to study the cohort of 698 infants born on Kauai in 1955, and we followed the development of these individuals at 1, 2, 10, 18 and 31 or 32 years of age. The majority of the individuals in the birth cohort—422 in all—were born without complications, following uneventful pregnancies, and grew up in supportive environments.

But as our study progressed we began to take a special interest in certain "high risk" children who, in spite of exposure to reproductive stress, discordant and impoverished home lives and uneducated, alcoholic or mentally disturbed parents, went on to develop healthy personalities, stable careers and strong interpersonal relations. We decided to try to identify the protective factors that contributed to the resilience of these children.

Finding a community that is willing or able to cooperate in such an effort is not an easy task. We chose Kauai for a number of reasons, not the least of which was the receptivity of the island population to our endeavors. Coverage by medical, public health, educational and social services on the island was comparable to what one would find in communities of similar size on the U.S. mainland at that time. Furthermore, our study would take into account a variety of cultural influences on childbearing and child rearing, since the population of Kauai includes individuals of Japanese, Philipino, Portuguese, Chinese, Korean and northern European as well as of Hawaiian descent.

We also thought the population's low mobility would make it easier to keep track of the study's participants and their families. The promise of a stable sample proved to be justified. At the time of the two-year follow-up, 96 percent of the living children were still on Kauai and available for study. We were able to find 90 percent of the children who were still alive for the ten-year follow-up, and for the eighteen-year follow-up we found 88 percent of the cohort.

In order to elicit the cooperation of the island's residents, we needed to get to know them and to introduce our study as well. In doing so we relied on the skills of a number of dedicated professionals from the University of California's Berkeley and Davis campuses, from the University of Hawaii and from the island of Kauai itself. At the beginning of the study five nurses and one social worker, all residents of Kauai, took a census of all households on the island, listing the occupants of each dwelling and recording demographic information, including a reproductive history of all women 12 years old or older. The interviewers asked the women if they were pregnant; if a woman was not, a card with a postage-free envelope was left with the request that she mail it to the Kauai Department of Health as soon as she thought she was pregnant.

Local physicians were asked to submit a monthly list of the women who were coming to them for prenatal care. Community organizers spoke to women's groups, church gatherings, the county medical society, and community leaders. The visits by the census takers were backed up with letters, and milk cartons were delivered with a printed message urging mothers to cooperate. We advertised in newspapers, organized radio talks, gave slide shows, and distributed posters.

Public health nurses interviewed the pregnant women who joined our study in each trimester of pregnancy, noting any exposure to physical or emotional trauma. Physicians monitored any complications during the prenatal period, labor, delivery, and the neonatal period. Nurses and social workers interviewed the mothers in the postpartum period and when the children were 1 and 10 years old; the interactions between parents and offspring in the home were also observed. Pediatricians and psychologists independently examined the children at 2 and 10 years of age, assessing their physical, intellectual, and social development and noting any handicaps or behavior problems. Teachers evaluated the children's academic progress and their behavior in the classroom.

From the outset of the study we recorded information about the material, intellectual and emotional aspects of the family environment, including stressful life events that resulted in discord or disruption of the family unit. With the parents' permission, we also were given access to the records of public health, educational, and social service agencies and to the files of the local police and the family court. My collaborators and I also administered a wide range of aptitude, achievement and personality tests in the elementary grades and in high school. Last but not least, we gained the perspectives of the young people themselves by interviewing them at the age of 18 and then again when they were in their early thirties.

Of the 698 children in the 1955 cohort, 69 were exposed to moderate prenatal or perinatal stress; that is, complications during pregnancy, labor or delivery. About 3 percent of the cohort—23 individuals in all— suffered severe prenatal or perinatal stress; only 14 infants in this group lived to the age of 2. Indeed, 9 of the 12 children in our study who died before reaching 2 years of age had suffered severe perinatal complications.

Some of the surviving children became "casualties" of a kind in the next two decades of life. One out of every 6 children (116 children in all) had physical or intellectual handicaps of perinatal or neonatal origin that were diagnosed between birth and the age of 2 and that required long-term specialized medical, educational, or custodial care. About 1 out of every 5 children (142 in all) developed serious learning or behavior problems in the first decade of life that required more than six months of remedial work. By the time the children were 10 years old, twice as many children needed some form of mental health service or remedial education (usually for problems associated with reading) as were in need of medical care.

By the age of 18, 15 percent of the young people had delinquency records and 10 percent had mental health problems requiring either in- or outpatient care. There was some overlap among these groups. By the time they were 10, all twenty-five of the children with long-term mental health problems had learning problems as well. Of the seventy children who had mental health problems at 18, fifteen also had a record of repeated delinquencies.

As we followed these children from birth to the age of 18 we noted two trends: the impact of reproductive stress diminished with time, and the developmental outcome of virtually every biological risk condition was dependent on the quality of the rearing environment. We did find some correlation between moderate to severe degrees of perinatal trauma and major physical handicaps of the central nervous system and of the musculoskeletal and sensory systems; perinatal trauma was also correlated with mental retardation, serious learning disabilities, and chronic mental health problems such as schizophrenia that arose in late adolescence and young adulthood.

But overall rearing conditions were more powerful determinants of outcome than perinatal trauma. The better the quality of the home environment was, the more competence the children displayed. This could already be seen when the children were just 2 years old: toddlers who had experienced severe perinatal stress but lived in middle-class homes or in stable family settings did nearly as well on development tests of sensory-motor and verbal skills as toddlers who had experienced no such stress.

Prenatal and perinatal complications were consistently related to impairment of physical and psychological development at the ages of 10 and 18 only when they were combined with chronic poverty, family discord, parental mental illness, or other persistently poor rearing conditions. Children who were raised in middle-class homes, in a stable family environment and by a mother who had finished high school showed few if any lasting effects of reproductive stress later in their lives.

How many children could count on such a favorable environment? A sizable minority could not. We designated 201 individuals—30 percent of the surviving children in this study population—as being high-risk children because they had experienced moderate to severe perinatal stress, grew up in chronic poverty, were reared by parents with no more than eight grades of formal education or lived in a family environment troubled by discord, divorce, parental alcoholism, or mental illness. We termed the children "vulnerable" if they encountered four or more such risk factors before their second birthday. And indeed, two-thirds of these children (129 in all) did develop serious learning or behavior problems by the age of 10 or had delinquency records, mental health problems, or pregnancies by the time they were 18.

Yet one out of three of these high-risk children—seventy-two individuals altogether—grew into competent young adults who loved well, worked well, and played well. None developed serious learning or behavior problems in childhood or adolescence. As far as we could tell from interviews and from their record in the community, they succeeded in school, managed home and social life well, and set realistic educational and vocational goals and expectations for themselves when they finished high school. By the end of their second decade of life, they had developed into competent, confident, and caring people who expressed a strong desire to take advantage of whatever opportunity came their way to improve themselves.

They were children such as Michael, a boy for whom the odds on paper did not seem very promising. The son of teenage parents, Michael was born prematurely, weighing 4 pounds 5 ounces. He spent his first three weeks of life in a hospital, separated from his mother. Immediately after his birth his father was sent with the U.S. Army to Southeast Asia, where he remained for two years. By the time Michael was 8 years old he had three siblings and his parents were divorced. His mother had deserted the family and had no further contact with her children. His father raised Michael and his siblings with the help of their aging grandparents.

Then there was Mary, born after twenty hours of labor to an overweight mother who had experienced several miscarriages before that pregnancy. Her father was an unskilled farm laborer with four years of formal education. Between Mary's fifth and tenth birthdays, her mother was hospitalized several times for repeated bouts of mental illness, after having inflicted both physical and emotional abuse on her daughter.

Surprisingly, by the age of 18 both Michael and Mary were individuals with high self-esteem and sound values who cared about others and were liked by their peers. They were successful in school and looked forward to the future. We looked back at the lives of these two youngsters and the seventy other resilient individuals who had triumphed over their circumstances and compared their behavioral characteristics and the features of the environment with those of the other high-risk youth who developed serious and persistent problems in childhood and adolescence.

We identified a number of protective factors in the families, outside the family circle and within the resilient children themselves that enabled them to resist stress. Some sources of resilience seem to be constitutional: resilient children such as Mary and Michael tend to have characteristics of temperament that elicit positive responses from family members and strangers alike. We noted these same qualities in adulthood. They include a fairly high activity level, a low degree of excitability and distress, and a high degree of sociability. Even as infants the resilient individuals were described by their parents as "active," "affectionate," "cuddly," "easygoing," and "even-tempered." They had no eating or sleeping habits that were distressing to those who took care of them.

The pediatricians and psychologists who examined the resilient children at 20 months noted their alertness and responsiveness, their vigorous play, and their tendency to seek out novel experiences and to ask for help when they needed it. When they entered elementary school, their classroom teachers observed their ability to concentrate on their assignments and noted their problem-solving and reading skills. Although they were not particularly gifted, these children used whatever talents they had effectively. Usually they had a special hobby they could share with a friend. These interests were not narrowly sex-typed; we found that girls and boys alike excelled at such activities as fishing, swimming, horseback riding, and hula dancing.

We could also identify environmental factors that contributed to these children's ability to withstand stress. The resilient youngsters tended to come from families having four or fewer children, with a space of two years or more between themselves and the next sibling. In spite of poverty, family discord or parental mental illness, they had the opportunity to establish a close bond with at least one caretaker from whom they received positive attention during the first years of life.

The nurturing might come from substitute parents within the family (such as grandparents, older siblings, aunts, or uncles) or from the ranks of regular babysitters. As the resilient children grew older, they seemed to be particularly adept at recruiting such surrogate parents when a biological parent was unavailable (as in the case of an absent father) or incapacitated (as in the case of a mentally ill mother who was frequently hospitalized).

Maternal employment and the need to take care of younger siblings apparently contributed to the pronounced autonomy and sense of responsibility noted among the resilient girls, particularly in households where the father had died or was permanently absent because of desertion or divorce. Resilient boys, on the other hand, were often firstborn sons who did not have to share their parents' attention with many additional children in the household. They also had some male in the family who could serve as a role model (if not the father, then a grandfather or an uncle). Structure and rules in the household and assigned chores were part of the daily routine for these boys during childhood and adolescence.

Resilient children also seemed to find a great deal of emotional support outside their immediate family. They tended to be well liked by their classmates and had at least one close friend, and usually several. They relied on an informal network of neighbors, peers and elders for counsel and support in times of crisis and transition. They seem to have made school a home away from home, a refuge from a disordered household. When we interviewed them at 18, many resilient youths mentioned a favorite teacher who had become a role model, friend and confidant and was particularly supportive at times when their own family was beset by discord or threatened with dissolution.

For others, emotional support came from a church group, a youth leader in the YMCA or YWCA or a favorite minister. Participation in extracurricular activities—such as 4-H, the school band, or a cheerleading team, which allowed them to be part of a cooperative enterprise—was also an important source of emotional support for those children who succeeded against the odds.

With the help of these support networks, the resilient children developed a sense of meaning in their lives and a belief that they could control their fate. Their experience in effectively coping with and mastering stressful life events built an attitude of hopefulness that contrasted starkly with the feelings of helplessness and futility that were expressed by their troubled peers.

In 1985, twelve years after the 1955 birth cohort had finished high school, we embarked on a search for

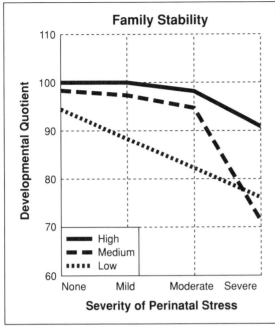

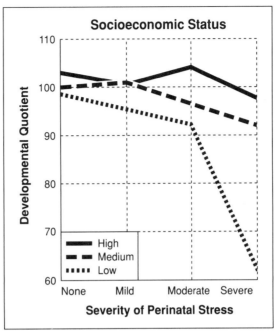

Figure 1. Influence of environmental factors such as family stability (left) or socioeconomic status (right) appears in infancy. The "developmental quotients" derived from tests given at 20 months show that the rearing environment can buffer or worsen the stress of perinatal complications. Children who had suffered severe perinatal stress but lived in stable, middle-class families scored as well as or better than children in poor, unstable households who had not experienced such stress.

the members of our study group. We managed to find 545 individuals—80 percent of the cohort—through parents or other relatives, friends, former classmates, local telephone books, city directories and circuit court, voter registration, and motor vehicle registration records, and marriage certificates filed with the State Department of Health in Honolulu. Most of the young men and women still lived on Kauai, but 10 percent had moved to other islands and 10 percent lived on the mainland; 2 percent had gone abroad.

We found sixty-two of the seventy-two young people we had characterized as "resilient" at the age of 18. They had finished high school at the height of the energy crisis and joined the work force during the worst U.S. recession since the Great Depression. Yet these 30-year-old men and women seemed to be handling the demands of adulthood well. Three out of four (46 individuals) had received some college education and were satisfied with their performance in school. All but four worked full time, and three out of four said they were satisfied with their jobs.

Indeed, compared with their low-risk peers from the same cohort, a significantly higher proportion of high-risk resilient individuals described themselves as being happy with their current life circumstances (44 percent versus 10 percent). The resilient men and women did, however, report a significantly higher

number of health problems than their peers in low-risk comparison groups (46 percent versus 15 percent). The men's problems seemed to be brought on by stress: back problems, dizziness and fainting spells, weight gain, and ulcers. Women's health problems were largely related to pregnancy and childbirth. And although 82 percent of the women were married, only 48 percent of the men were. Those who were married had strong commitments to intimacy and sharing with their partners and children. Personal competence and determination, support from a spouse or mate, and a strong religious faith were the shared qualities that we found characterized resilient children as adults.

We were also pleasantly surprised to find that many high-risk children who had problems in their teens were able to rebound in their twenties and early thirties. We were able to contact twenty-six (90 percent) of the teenage mothers, fifty-six (80 percent) of the individuals with mental health problems and seventy-four (75 percent) of the former delinquents who were still alive at the age of 30.

Almost all the teenage mothers we interviewed were better off in their early thirties than they had been at 18. About 60 percent (sixteen individuals) had gone on to additional schooling, and about 90 percent (twenty-four individuals) were employed. Of the delinquent youths, three-fourths (fifty-six individuals) were still in need of mental health services in their early thirties. Among the critical turning points in the lives of these individuals were entry into military service, marriage, parenthood, and active participation in a church group. In adulthood, as in their youth, most of these individuals relied on informal rather than formal sources of support: kith and kin rather than mental health professionals and social service agencies.

Our findings appear to provide a more hopeful perspective than can be had from reading the extensive literature on "problem" children that come to the attention of therapists, special educators, and social service agencies. Risk factors and stressful environments do not inevitably lead to poor adaptation. It seems clear that, at each stage in an individual's development from birth to maturity, there is a shifting balance between stressful events that heighten vulnerability and protective factors that enhance resilience.

As long as the balance between stressful life events and protective factors is favorable, successful adaptation is possible. When stressful events outweight the protective factors, however, even the most resilient child can have problems. It may be possible to shift the balance from vulnerability to resilience through intervention, either by decreasing exposure to risk factors or stressful events or by increasing the number of protective factors and sources of support that are available.

It seems clear from our identification of risk and protective factors that some of the most critical determinants of outcome are present when a child is very young. And it is obvious that there are large individual differences among high-risk children in their responses to both negative and positive circumstances in their care-giving environment. The very fact of individual variation among children who live in adverse conditions suggests the need for greater assistance to some than to others.

If early intervention cannot be extended to every child at risk, priorities must be established for choosing who should receive help. Early-intervention programs need to focus on infants and young children who appear most vulnerable because they lack—permanently or temporarily—some of the essential social bonds that appear to buffer stress. Such children may be survivors of neonatal intensive care, hospitalized children who are separated from their families for extended periods of time, the young offspring of addicted or mentally ill parents, infants and toddlers whose mothers work full time and do not have access

to stable child care, the babies of single or teenage parents who have no other adult in the household and migrant, and refugee children without permanent roots in a community.

Assessment and diagnosis, the initial steps in any early intervention, need to focus not only on the risk factors in the lives of the children but also on the protective factors. These include competencies and informal sources of support that already exist and that can be utilized to enlarge a young child's communication and problem-solving skills and to enhance his or her self-esteem. Our research on resilient children has shown that other people in a child's life—grandparents, older siblings, day-care providers or teachers—can play a supportive role if a parent is incapacitated or unavailable. In many situations it might make better sense and be less costly as well to strengthen such available informal ties to kin and community than it would to introduce additional layers of bureaucracy into delivery of services.

Finally, in order for any intervention program to be effective, a young child needs enough consistent nurturing to trust in its availability. The resilient children in our study had at least one person in their lives who accepted them unconditionally, regardless of temperamental idiosyncracies or physical or mental handicaps. All children can be helped to become more resilient if adults in their lives encourage their independence, teach them appropriate communication and self-help skills and model as well as reward acts of helpfulness and caring.

Thanks to the efforts of many people, several community action and educational programs for high-risk children have been established on Kauai since our study began. Partly as a result of our findings, the legislature of the State of Hawaii has funded special mental health teams to provide services for troubled children and youths. In addition the State Health Department established the Kauai Children's Services, a coordinated effort to provide services related to child development, disabilities, mental retardation, and rehabilitation in a single facility.

The evaluation of such intervention programs can in turn illuminate the process by which a chain of protective factors is forged that affords vulnerable children an escape from adversity. The life stories of the resilient individuals on the Garden Island have taught us that competence, confidence and caring can flourish even under adverse circumstances if young children encounter people in their lives who provide them with a secure basis for the development of trust, autonomy, and initiative.

Milestones of Development: A Dialogue Between Jerome Kagan and Stanley I. Greenspan

Jerome Kagan is a famous researcher of child development who teaches at Harvard University. He has studied infant development in other cultures, and he is presently examining how temperament (shyness, assertiveness) affects behavior and development. Stanley Greenspan is a clinical psychiatrist who works with infants and families experiencing stress in the parent-child relationship. Greenspan is interested in the social and emotional development of the parent-infant relationship.

These two accomplished researchers agree that both nature and nurture play roles in human development. But they do not agree completely on how much nature or nurture affects developmental outcomes for a specific child. In this dialogue, Kagan and Greenspan use data on specific developmental milestones such as stranger anxiety, memory, and self-awareness to support their respective views on continuity versus discontinuity and the patterns of biological and environmental influences.

Jerome Kagan: I am pleased to be here and with only fifteen minutes, have no time for preliminaries. I do not think there will be a serious fight between Stanley and me. We disagree on important details, rather than on deep premises. I believe that all phenomena in human development are influenced by complementary forces. In order to understand the phenomena, we have to attend to both influences. However, during any one historical period, scholars focus on one of the complementary themes and ignore the other. I want to use my time to talk about two such complementary themes. The first is whether one views the development of the qualities of a child as a continuous process, or as composed of discrete stages of organization.

J. Kagan and S. Greenspan. (1986, June). Milestones of development: A dialogue, *Zero to Three*, 6 (5), 1–9. (Portions of the original manuscript have been deleted. Permission for some clarifying inserts granted.)

Many developmentalists want to see the qualities of the infant growing continuously, as seventeenth-century naturalists saw in the fertilized egg all of the qualities of a human being. The embryo was believed to be fully formed, and with time it increased in size as it grew. The complementary idea is that the growth from fertilized egg to blastula to gastrula to fetus has discontinuities. A few months later, it has all its major organs.

Suppose all of us were transported to a time several hundred million years ago when the highest animal forms were insects. Standing on that landscape, one could not have predicted the rise of primates while looking at a butterfly. I believe that there is insufficient attention to major stages of reorganization that occur in the early years. One of the consequences of attending to stages of reorganization is that some words that are used to characterize 5- and 10-year-olds are inappropriate for the young baby. Words like *intelligent, sad, angry*, or *curious* are applied to older children and adults, and I wish to raise your consciousness about the possibility that, because of major changes in the central nervous system and in cognitive competences, those words are not appropriate for infants. Infants cannot possess those qualities in the same way that 10-year-olds do.

I now want to describe two milestones that define stages of organization. The first is very important in the development of primates. It is the *enhancement of retrieval memory* between 8 and 12 months of age. It is not an accident that Piaget claimed that the object concept emerges at 8 to 12 months. The research of many scientists, both in Europe and the United States, reveals a major improvement in the child's ability to remember the past in the months before the first birthday. That fact means that a baby under 7 or 8 months has great difficulty reaching back and retrieving events that happened in the past. If a baby exposed to a novel event is unable, for maturational reasons, to retrieve the familiar schemes of event, there is no basis for fearfulness.

Separation anxiety is not only an index of the quality of the prior relationship between the infant and the mother; it is partly due to the fact that when the mother leaves, the infant is able to "reach back" and remember that she was present moments ago. Being unable to resolve the difference between the memory of her former presence and her absence now, the child grows anxious, as you and I would if we heard a jet engine that sounded odd and retrieved our schemata of how the engine normally sounds.

There is a good reason why object permanence and separation anxiety occur at about 8 months: this is a special time in the growth of the central nervous system.

One implication of those findings is that experiences that occur prior to 8 months may be of less relevance than experiences after 8 months because of the young infant's inability to retrieve past experiences.

A second important stage of organization, which is probably unique to humans, occurs between 16 and 24 months. There is a great deal of research to support the suggestions of nineteenth-century observers that two qualities emerge in the last half of the second year.

First, the child develops a moral sense, an initial sense of right and wrong. I agree with Hume, Kant, and the nineteenth-century observers that an appreciation of good and bad is an innate capacity of human beings, as innate as the ability to speak, to understand language or to crawl, stand, and walk. A child does not have to be taught this idea. The child does have to be taught what specific acts are right and wrong—good or bad. Those of you who work with young children know that by 18 months children become concerned with flawed objects—a tiny thread is loose in their pajamas and the child says, "Mommy, bad. Mommy, fix." Children will now point out to their mother or day-care teacher that another child did something "bad."

The second year is also the time when a child first becomes self-aware. Observers from many cultures report that the child will use words like *I, mine,* and *me.* Now the child will point to its nose when it sees a reflection of the nose with rouge on it in a mirror. If an adult poses an imitation problem, the child will become anxious if the problem is too difficult. Why should a child begin to cry if a woman models some act in front of him or her? One way to explain the distress is to assume the child is "aware of its inability to complete the act." That phrase requires the positing of a self-concept. It is the earliest foundation upon which a self-concept will be built over the next decade.

I believe that this self-awareness is also like singing and talking. It, too, is an innate quality of our species, and will develop in all normal children. This is important because once a child has a sense of self he or she begins to relate experiences to that concept. Now the rules change. Experiences are related not only to how pleasant or how painful they are, but how relevant they are to one's gender, size, or perception of the parents.

That is one reason why it is difficult to make fixed predictions about the effects of environments. The child is now transducing the environment. He or she is not reacting, as an invertebrate would, only to the pleasure or pain in the experience, but rather to his or her interpretation of it. This means he or she relates the experience to his or her standards and sense of self.

A second complementary theme—the first was continuous growth versus discrete stages—contrasts endogenous and exogenous processes. I hope you will agree that one can't explain animal evolution without attending to both mutation, which is an internal process, and natural selection, an external process. Similarly, one can't understand a child's development unless one looks at both its experience and the internal biological characteristics—what many call temperament.

We will not be able to understand development until we acknowledge the child's psychobiological characteristics, or temperament....

There are children who, by the middle of the second year, are fearful, shy, timid, and vigilant, and those who are outgoing, sociable, and hard to frighten. The two types come from similar families. Because our culture values the sociable child, when we observed these children at school age, we found that only 10 percent of the uninhibited, fearless children had become fearful, while half of the fearful ones had become much less uninhibited and timid.

There is a positive message in these data. Even though a quality is biologically based, in this case a vulnerability to becoming timid and fearful, the environment can change this tendency. There is no rigid biological determinism in the system. If half of the children who are temperamentally fearful can be socialized to overcome this quality, then surely anyone who argues that the events of infancy constrain the child in a serious way should be questioned.

I believe that there are a small number of structures and functions that are slow to change, and might be preserved for a relatively long time, as well as a complementary set that is easily changed. Developmental scientists and educators must now discover the members of those two classes. But our progress will be slow if we continue to be bothered by change and discontinuity in development and only concerned with defending the limitless power of early experience to set the direction of growth for some indefinite time.

Stanley Greenspan: I would like to focus on indepth emotional development. Indepth emotional development is qualitatively different from motor development; from cognition, including memory; and even from the expression of discrete affects.

Let me just give two examples. An 8-month-old can learn cause and effect, as Piaget so well described, in the impersonal sphere by banging a toy on the floor. The toy makes a noise. To learn cause and effect in the emotional, interpersonal sphere, however, depends on a sensitive, loving human partner (e.g., to learn that a smile leads to a smile, or more importantly, that feeling love leads to being loved). In terms of memory we see 3- and 4-month-olds, if abused enough, become fearful and hypervigilant at a very early age. Is this conditioning? Is this retrieval memory? If it is memory, we wonder what this suggests about the role of emotion in memory, in the context of the suggestion by Dr. Kagan that we think of memory in terms of data based on experiments in cognition that do not vary the intensity of emotion to any great degree and do not necessarily look at emotionally relevant experiences (and I should add, in experiments that depend on motor skills and motor planning capacities for inferences about memory).

These are questions that need to be answered, but certainly we can't cross over and generalize from experiments in one realm, that of memory in relatively cognitive terms or even superficial emotional terms, to the realm of indepth emotional development, where we are talking about love, dependency, dealing with aggression and the like. To stress the importance of emotional development, indepth emotional development involves core areas of adaptive functioning, many of which, remarkably, are learned or not learned

in the first three or four years of life. For example, by age 3 or 4, children are learning to be intimate and comfortable with dependency, or are learning to be suspicious and aloof. They are learning one or the other. They are learning how to regulate behavior and emotion, or they are learning to be impulsive and destructive. Our clinical work with infants suggests that if the family's emotional environment is compromised enough, a tendency to treat people as things may begin in the first eighteen months of life and may be well established by age 2. [Contrary to Dr. Kagan's statement that an initial sense of morality is innate,] this observation suggests that the emotional tone of the family environment plays a significant role in the early learning of morality.

In the first three or four years, too, children are learning positive self-esteem or they are learning to be sad and have negative self-images. They are learning to create emotional ideas and conduct emotional thinking (e.g., have an image of mother hugging them when they are away from mother, or have an image of kicking their little brother so they don't have to actually kick their little brother). Or they are learning to be concrete and use only behavioral discharge. They are learning also, by 3 or 4, to shift between the demands of reality and the wonderful world of fantasy. Or they are learning to be lost in the world of "make believe," having difficulty adjusting to the demands of group behavior and later school life.

. . . In normal development, a baby progresses from the first stage of homeostasis regulation and interest in the world, to the second stage of attachment, falling in love with the human world, where intimacy and joy and pleasure seem to be developing from the affective expressions of the baby. For example, one sees babies calming down just with visual experience, a look from the mother. One sees a mutual vocalization, obvious pleasure, and synchrony of motor movements and vocal movements between mother and infant (as many investigators have shown). This synchronous joyfulness illustrates the profound emotional interaction a 3-week-old is capable of. Will an infant remember this, and are there different levels of organization of affective memory? Jerry and I will debate that in a few minutes.

I would now like to describe [an] example of an infant who was born physically fine, but who had many constitutional vulnerabilities. He was overreactive to sight, to sounds and even to touch. He looked away rather than toward the human world from his earliest days. He rocked himself, stared off into space, regurgitated his feedings, and often held his body in extension rigidity. At 4 months he would not look at any human face. Mother intermittently overstimulated him and then withdrew. The quality of his emotion was quite clear, exemplified by the extension rigidity in his arms and his attempt to pull away from the human world.

Our therapeutic team worked intensively with both mother and baby, paying attention to his individual differences. It was essential to titrate sensory and affective experience to help him find the human world pleasurable. At the same time the team worked on cross-sensory integration and motor relaxation exercises. Within two months he became an engaging, outgoing infant. He could even "seduce" Mommy and help her come out of her depression. By the time he was 18 months old, both he and his mother had made a major recovery.

It is of interest that at 18 months (in light of the question of memory) this mother and child chose to play out in "make-believe" a scene of mutual rejection. What had been a stark reality in the first few months of life became played out at the level of emotional symbolism. The two were now emotionally relating to one another and had learned not only how to be pleasurable to one another but be purposeful and organized as well.

In this example, we see how the infant's constitutional vulnerability creates an opportunity for preventive therapeutic work. In intervening with an infant, one must pay attention to what Jerry Kagan is saying about the constitutional differences. But there is a second point that Dr. Kagan does not emphasize. The environmental input geared to the infant's individual differences may be the determining factor in how that youngster develops emotionally. There is enormous variation in expression of constitutional differences. Infants like this baby can become trusting and outgoing even though they were withdrawn and cautious at the beginning. Dr. Kagan emphasizes the importance of experience in altering temperament but then, curiously, states that the early months are not especially important (this is probably because of his belief that retrieval memory is not developed until 8–10 months of life). In cases like this, however, we observe that patterns of affective interaction build on one another, and chronic patterns of avoidance can certainly interfere with availability for subsequent learning.

In the few minutes I have remaining, let me highlight the issues where Dr. Kagan and I differ. I think we agree on many but we have to pull our differences out to an extreme to make this dialogue interesting.

In the extreme I think people misinterpret Dr. Kagan's viewpoint, as either genetic determinism or as a statement that the early years don't count. Many people debate these issues and try to evolve public policy or clinical perspectives from them.

While these positions are of academic interest, from a practical point of view neither of these positions is relevant to the way we clinically approach infants and children. Most children who grow up in a high-risk environment do not experience the environment as changing. You haven't got the experiment which answers the question: if there is a bad environment for the first six months and a good environment for the second six months, will the child recover? In fact, multirisk families more often than not remain multirisk unless there is intervention. So in our culture, from a clinical point of view, it is critical to intervene as early as possible to try to facilitate appropriate caregiver and family functioning and deal with the infant's individual differences. Also, from a clinical point of view, it is important to emphasize, indepth emotional development is qualitatively different from impersonal cognitive, impersonal memory, and other functions. We cannot generalize from limited experimental research on impersonal cognition to the world of "human passion."

Dr. Kagan, as indicated, also raises important academic questions about early experience. Is there a difference between deprivation the first year versus deprivation the second year, versus deprivation the third year? Is the first year more important than second, the second more important than the third? We cannot do the experiment to answer these questions. We would have to deprive one baby (or a group) in Year 1, another in Year 2, another in Year 3. In the alternate year, we would need to give them good experiences. We would then ask: did the baby who was deprived in Year 1 do worse than the baby who was deprived in Year 2, or Year 3?

We can't and shouldn't do that experiment.

To move to another point, I would also like to add that certain temperamental features are very, very important. We are trying not only to study them as Dr. Kagan is, but to figure out which sensory pathways determine specific temperamental differences. But I would like to further add that we have to be very, very cautious in generalizing. We must not jump to genetic determinism because we find some interesting individual differences in constitutional patterns.

For example, how much of the variance in overall adaptive functioning does a difference in shyness versus outgoingness account for? How much do these characteristics relate to the more important personality characteristics such as ability to love and be intimate, to integrate and tolerate mixed feelings toward your spouse when you are about to have a fight? Or to feel and endure loss without becoming depressed? How much do these temperamental characteristics play into the core human drama as we know it?

Jerome Kagan: I think I now see where we agree. We agree that if an infant is showing anomalous development, therapeutic intervention can be helpful. That is absolutely right; we should intervene. We also agree that the environment of the young child is important. But let me note where we disagree. I am not claiming to be correct, but no one has the evidence to prove either of us is right on this next issue.

We disagree on the degree to which early experience constrains the child's development. I believe it is less important than Dr. Greenspan claims. An observer gathers evidence in a narrow slice of time. You watch an infant behave. Will that structure, emotion, ability, mother-child interaction, or form of attachment that you note last for a short or long time?

As you look at those tea leaves, you may nod yes. I look at the same tea leaves and am more dubious. The reason I am dubious is because we don't have sufficiently rich longitudinal data to show that babies living in a malevolent environment will show a certain psychological profile at age 6, 12, and 18 years.

In parts of the Fijian chain in the Pacific, a mother who is pregnant is asked by her cousin, "May I have your baby?" That is a most flattering request. And at weaning, the baby goes with the cousin to another atoll and may never see the mother again.

We call that event *abuse* in the United States. But if that practice, which has been going on for generations in the Fijian Islands, were maladaptive, the Fijian society would have stopped practicing. Apparently it does not hurt all babies. Puritan parents did not play with their infants in the same way modern American mothers do. There is no good evidence to show that the Puritan rearing regimen harmed infants. Those qualities that one sees in the sixth month of the infant's life may not be sustained because there will be siblings, kind aunts, cruel peers, success or failure in school, and varied traumata in the future. That's why I like an evolutionary analogy. You can't be sure of the future. The most securely attached child from a middle-class home that values school success may fail in school, and if so, the child will become anxious.

I am not asking you to give up your optimism regarding the importance and relevance of clinical intervention with children who have problems.

I am asking you to reflect a little on the history of our species and practices in other cultures. There are no guarantees in development.

Stanley Greenspan: I think Dr. Kagan has two points that he's made in the past that I agree with. He wants to make the point which we all agree with, that it is never too late to help children, that children have tremendous resilience and tremendous recovery power. In our own work with very worrisome multirisk families

we saw this capacity for recovery. In some cases mothers would not come regularly until the child was 2— and by working intensively for two years, we were able to help the children back on a path of adaptive development. I would certainly applaud the interest in never giving up. It's never too late.

But to go from that point to the point of suggesting that early experiences are less relevant is not warranted. Dr. Kagan has said there are no definitive data one way or the other. And depending on which sets of data you use, either Dr. Kagan can make a good case, or I can make a good case. In the absence of definitive data, I think we have to take a conservative and cautious viewpoint and pay attention to common sense and certain traditions.

There are, as you know, the observations of institutionalized babies, many of whom were so deprived that they had no chance of recovery. Annette Yaker recently studied institutionalized babies in Algeria. These babies were put in relatively good homes after the deprivation of the first couple of years. Many of them are psychotic, and have remained psychotic, even though they have improved marginally with intervention. The lesson of the institutionalized babies does not leave us. Dr. Kagan agrees that extreme situations are different, and that they can devastate a baby. In animal work, if you socially deprive an animal sufficiently, the size of the brain, the neuronal connections within the brain, are not as great [as] at age 3.

Dr. Kagan often makes the point, "In the middle-class family, the average family, isn't it really the temperament that will determine most of the variance in the functioning (or dysfunctioning) rather than the environment?" To that I answer, I don't see this ideal middle-class family where the temperament will determine later behavior. How many marital fights before you say it is not an average middle-class family? How aloof does the Daddy have to be and how angry and frustrated does the Mommy have to be before you say there is family tension? Where do you draw the boundaries? There is no average expectable family. Every one is different, and every one relates to their babies differently. There is a range of stresses and strains.

The important question does not concern the Mommy who, at six months, adores her little baby (who is engaged in a wonderful mutual smile and gaze) but becomes upset that her 15-month-old baby is independent and therefore undermines and overcontrols her baby, leading to negative and rebellious behavior. The real question concerns how patterns at one stage relate to patterns at another. The relationships are not necessarily obvious. But there are relationships.

Certain indepth emotional patterns, I would suggest, are preconditions for another more complete pattern. For example, if you experience intimacy in the first four months, you then value human relationships, and then you have *an opportunity* to learn "cause and effect" in that human relationship. If you haven't connected to the human world, how are you going to learn emotional causality? You can't learn emotional causality relating to "If I love you I will be loved back" unless you have a loving partner. When you reach out, you have to have a valued human object who responds. Pulling a string to ring a bell will teach you about causality but not about the emotional causality relating to dependency, assertiveness, or aggression.

This doesn't mean you can't learn to love at 10 months. You can. But why play catch up? Certain in-depth emotional functions have a line of development where Step 1 is *a precondition* for the next, even though it's not a guarantee that the next step is going to occur.

Jerome Kagan: We are coming closer together.

I want to make one last point. It is a delicate one because I do not want it to be interpreted as opposing Stanley's suggestion, with which I agree, that an emotionally joyful, loving interaction between parents and infants is not only one of the great experiences in our brief lives, but also a beneficial one.

Here is the problem. We live in a society with some very serious problems. One of the most serious is that the gap in psychological potency and talent between the privileged and the less privileged is growing.

Our society, always eager for simple solutions, is waiting for its scholars to tell it what the best solutions are. When I was a graduate student, the poor school performance of black children was attributed to protein malnutrition. The government spent millions of dollars on this idea because it would have been an easy solution. Give the children steak and eggs, and we will not have to do anything more painful, like the sharing of wealth.

I do not question the power of love. But if you assume that the primary reason for success in school, good character, and ability to love is established in the parent-child interaction, you will ignore many significant influences outside the family, tied to class, neighborhood, and school, and you will blame economically disadvantaged mothers, who love their children, for their child's adaptive failures.

I am not saying that the early infant-parent relation is unimportant, only that in our zeal to celebrate it as the only factor, we can do harm to the society because legislators and administrators who want easy solutions will not have to grapple with the serious changes that must be made.

Stanley Greenspan: I think Jerry Kagan and I are in complete agreement on the importance of attending to all the factors—the larger socioeconomic factors, the

stressful environments that many of our families grow up in, as well as the more microcosmic factors that portray and characterize the subtleties of the infant-caregiver relationship, and the family relationships within which our chidren grow.

All of these are important. But I would like to suggest—and I would like to tell Jerry—that his very convincing and seductive arguments are more frequently misinterpreted by policymakers than interpreted as he intends them. They tend to use his arguments concretely to support the importance of biology and ignore the real complexity of early development. A narrow definition of memory, for example, rather than a broader one that includes behavioral and affective tendencies, can mislead rather than inform policymakers.

The best way to have policymakers support societal changes and provide necessary help to families as well as develop the technology needed to understand individual differences in babies so that each baby can have an environment which helps that baby learn to trust and elaborate feelings and eventually create ideas, test reality and moderate moods and impulses is to pay attention to the first three years of life. To realize that the core personality functions that have to do with the essence of humanity are all learned, or not learned, in the early years.

Don't have our kids playing catch-up, trying to learn the basic personality functions for the first time at age 4. Don't be seduced by cross-cultural studies, because as Jerry knows from his own Guatemala study, when you look at the culture closely, you see that people are doing things you didn't think they were doing when you came in as a distrusted outsider, and only observed part of the day. When you live with them for two and three years you see very, very different things. Many cultures also have their own culturally specific catch-up mechanisms. But, more importantly, look at our own society and see what is happening to children in the first three years of life. In our culture, many children experience successive developmental failures at each stage of early development. We cannot afford to ignore the early months when the foundations for core personality functions relating to the capacities for closeness and warmth in relationships, emotional intentionality, and the control of impulses and behavior are first learned. We have a number of challenges, including care for the handicapped, care for environmentally at-risk families, and facilitating the availability of appropriate day-care environments for working families.

While Jerry and I are in agreement, I think, on the basic message, we have different emphases. We hope you will carry both of them with you, for we all must be working together to improve the lives of our infants and young children.

How Many Ways Is a Child Intelligent? An Interview With Howard Gardner

Marge Scherer

Did you ever wonder why IQ tests are not interested in measuring your ability to be president of the class or your talent for organizing scrap metal into sculpture? The mainstream definition of "intelligence" has always been limited to language and math (logic). Howard Gardner proposes that it's time to broaden our definition of intelligence to include music, kinesthetics, and interpersonal and intrapersonal relations. Different people are intelligent in different ways. What they learn and how they learn may be tempered by their areas of strength.

Gardner also suggests that we alter our system of testing to assessment. Assessment focuses on a child's strengths—finds out what a child is good at and encourages those abilities—rather than on weaknesses. Tests, on the contrary, use a deficit model: Their purpose is to find out what a child doesn't know. A broader definition of intelligence might lead more children toward success along a variety of pathways.

Pretend there are two Martians just landed on Earth who are curious about the human mind. One wanders into the education school of a great university and asks an educational psychologist about the mental powers of *Homo sapiens*. He is told that the key to the mind is intelligence and that an IQ test can measure this quality as well as predict who will do well in school and, quite possibly, in life.

"What sort of things do you have to know?" the Martian asks. Oh, what the word *belfry* means, who wrote the *Iliad*, how to multiply 8×3, what a mountain and a lake have in common. "So that's intelligence," says the first Martian.

The second Martian, an independent soul, goes looking for himself for the key to the human mind. He crawls back into the spacecraft and orbits the globe. He sees amazing spectacles: sailors on the South Seas, dancers in Bali, yogas in India, computer programmers, tennis players, concert pianists, productive peasants, and productive presidents. He tries to figure out what makes them operate successfully in their society and he decides that people on this planet have a variety of mental processes—maybe even different kinds of minds. Not knowing English well, he coins a new word—*intelligences*.

Howard Gardner uses that anecdote to introduce his theory of multiple intelligences. Just like his first Martian, Gardner says that at one time he believed that intelligence was a single quality that could be measured on a paper-and-pencil test; that measuring intelligence was a worthwhile thing to do; and that for the most part the IQ scores could tell us "who was smart and who was not."

Research has carried Gardner, a neuropsychologist at Harvard University, away from those beliefs. In his most recent book, *Frames of Mind*, he argues that the definition of an intelligence should be "the ability to solve problems or to create products which are valued in one or more cultural settings." He suggests that there are at least seven intelligences, and that competence in any one does not predict competence in any of the others.

Although the IQ test measures the *linguistic* and *logical-mathematical* intelligences, it does not account for at least five more: the *kinesthetic* intelligence (seen in the dancer, athlete, craftsman, surgeon); the *musical* (as in a composer, singer, musician); the *spatial* (what sculptors and surveyors need); the *interpersonal* (that needed to detect moods in others, to motivate, and to lead); and the *intrapersonal* (that shown by those who understand their own feelings and use knowledge of self in productive ways).

At two conferences for educators this summer, the first called the Coming Education Explosion, at Tarrytown, New York, and the second, the International Conference on Thinking, at Harvard, Gardner described these intelligences and explained his theory. Later, in an interview for INSTRUCTOR readers, he elaborated on the implications for elementary teachers. Here are some of his remarks.

Dr. Gardner, would you talk a bit about the work with children and with brain-damaged adults that led you to your theory?
I am by profession a research psychologist. In the morning I work at the Veterans Hospital in Boston with brain-damaged patients, people who have suffered strokes or other kinds of traumas and have lost the ability to carry out certain kinds of functions. In the afternoon, I go to Project Zero at Harvard, where I work with normal and gifted children trying to understand how their cognitive and artistic abilities develop. . . .

I've become convinced that mental processes can exist in a variety of forms and that these forms are independent of one another. A brain-damaged person can become totally aphasic as a result of damage to the left hemisphere, can hardly speak or understand, yet that same patient may be able to draw very well, sing very well. Some aphasic patients have been able to continue composing music. It gives pause to any attempt to argue that the same mental processes are involved in the same way in language or music or drawing or many other things. By the same token, in my work with children we often see children who have a gift in one area like drawing, that in no way predicts their ability with language, logic, or dealing with other people.

There is a much greater plurality of mind than is usually acknowledged by educators and psychologists. . . . Evidence about the brain strongly supports the theory of mutiple intelligences. There are hundreds and thousands of kinds of columns in the brain, each of which processes different kinds of information. One has to beware of being too facile in thinking the brain only does two things.

How does your theory of multiple intelligences differ from more traditional views, for instance, Piaget's?
Piaget believed the mind was capable of different kinds of operations—sensorimotor, concrete, and formal—and that those operations applied to any kind of material equally well. If you reached a concrete operational level, you used concrete operations no matter what subjects you were dealing with. Now the theory of multiple intelligences is tied to content. It says that the brain is so wired that when it runs into certain kinds of sounds, it will analyze them linguistically or musically.

Traditionally it's been assumed that faculties like perception, learning, memory, can be applied to any content, that memory behaves the same way with pictures, songs, words, numbers. But multiple intelligence theory says that with each intelligence there is a characteristic form of perception, memory, and learning. A person could have a good memory for learning languages, but that doesn't predict anything about his memory for music, people, or how to find his way around.

Another way my theory differs is in its attention to cultural roles. Over the years humans have evolved to do many things very well, and at least seven independent of each other. Most theories are designed for predicting who will do well in school; I'm really interested in people who can find a niche in society once they get out of school. . . . Cross-cultural research shows that humans develop different competencies when their cultures value different intelligences. It's only our Westist and testist bias that puts language and logic at the top of the mountain. . . .

My theory is developmentally grounded, too. The seven intelligences don't exist in the same forms from infancy to old age. Some develop quite quickly and also decline quite quickly—logical-mathematical intelligence is an example. Others develop more gradually and have a longer life—interpersonal, for instance. Individuals differ in the extent to which they are at promise and at risk for different intelligences.

Describe some of the assessment techniques for telling whether a person is at risk or at promise in these areas.
In the next four years David Feldman and I have a grant to discover ways to assess the intellectual propensities of gifted and normal 3- and 4-year-olds at a preschool in Boston. We'll be trying to create experiences that will illuminate strengths and weaknesses.

We'll use testing materials that relate to the intelligences themselves. In case of music, we'll study children's pitch and rhythm, how well they remember melodies. To measure spatial intelligence, we'll have children find their way around an area, observe how they build with blocks.

There are no shortcuts; no multiple-choice tests can tell you about interpersonal or bodily intelligence. Of course, we'll build on tests that already exist in the language-logic area, but even then we'll be trying to move toward products rather than short answers. Can the child tell a story? We might show a silent movie and have kids make up a story of their own. We'll look at how kids do puzzles, and so on. What we hope to do is be able to help individuals discover particular intellectual profiles, the combination of intelligences that are really closest to them.

Aren't you just substituting a whole range of new tests for the old IQ tests? Won't you be running into the same dangers?
I'd like to say *assess* instead of *test*. When you say *test*, it lights up all sorts of bulbs. Scores say either you're dumb or you're smart or you have to take another course. But *assess* means asking, Does the child have abilities in this area that can be further encouraged? Or does the child have a problem in an area? Those are important questions to ask. It's malpractice to ignore them.

The kind of assessment we hope to develop will be open-ended, product-oriented, and take place over a long period of time.

Another point is that we're much more interested in the relative strengths of different intelligences than in the absolutes. I would hope our reporting would give children a chance to address a particular combination of strengths and weaknesses rather than compare themselves with others.

Can an elementary teacher tell whether a child shows signs of being at promise or at risk in these intelligences without these assessments? Could you give some examples?
Yes, teachers can do a lot to recognize these children. I think beginning to think in this way is the first step. As teachers tend to be linguistic, they usually know if a child is good in language. If the child is writing well, has the ability to remember language well, or hear a story and repeat it back, you don't need to have my theory to tell he or she has linguistic intelligence. Now children with spatial intelligence can build a mental model of the spatial terrain. They are able to perceive the similarities of shapes and positions.

You can see logical-mathematical ability in kids who can follow through on a long chain of reasoning. If you're explaining something, and that prompts a question and the answer prompts another, that shows logic. Of course, some kids are peppy with all the questions but don't get the connection between them.

A child who is interpersonally skilled seems to carry around a theory of behavior about the other kids with whom he's playing. He adapts his behavior, makes it appropriate to each of the other children. Or he might be a good bluffer in games because he has the ability of knowing what other kids are going to do. Now that's a good example of how an intelligence can be used in a positive or negative way. Bluffing could be a useful skill if you're trying to survive and a hostile skill if you're trying to take advantage of someone. No intelligence is good or bad. It's the use you make of it.

Are there any children with well-developed intrapersonal intelligence, or does that come with maturity?
No, there are kids who have an uncanny sense of themselves. There are those who could come into an empty classroom and know what kind of activity they want to do while other kids wait for something to happen. When trying to do something hard, children with intrapersonal intelligence won't give up right away, but when they aren't getting anywhere, they'll ask for help. They seem to have models of themselves that they continually revise as their experience grows and their knowledge about what they can do and cannot do increases. The intelligence is present very young in some cases. There are people who are very good in other realms but have zero sense of themselves. Yet others have an unerring sense of their strengths. As for weaknesses, they can be called artful dodgers. They know how to avoid problems they can't handle.

Would you say that sense of self comes from being accepted by a loving family who gives the child a sense of security?
No, if anything I really think we don't know. It helps having people around who have a sense of where they came from and where they are going. But having a model doesn't always mean the child will have a particular intelligence. Children without such a background could just as easily show it.

What about musical and kinesthetic intelligences?
Whether a child's musical and kinesthetic intelligences are developed often depends on whether or not the family emphasizes them. Some families are interested in music or engage in a lot of physical activity. But similarly every parent has blind spots. The child might be terrific in spatial activities, but if the parents aren't oriented that way, they might not do anything to encourage that gift. At school teachers might be aware that a child is gifted in interpersonal intelligence, but they might never realize that that intelligence could be trained and developed.

Once aware of these intelligences, how can a teacher enrich the classroom?

If I were a classroom teacher I would keep in my head or in a file box a list of activities, places to go, games to buy, individuals in the community or in the school who could help a child. Offer suggestions for activities that relate to a child's set of strengths or that relate to areas where the child is not terribly good but might want to be. Often a push in the right direction is enough to help someone with a profile of strengths that no one in his environment has known how to respond to.

Another thing, teachers can make it possible for a child to have what I call crystallizing experiences. These are times when a child is ripe to discover an affinity between himself and some material, an affinity that was not known until that time. Most people who find their niche in life do it through a crystallizing experience, whether accidental or engineered. . . .

The decision of when to downplay a weakness or teach more in that area is one where a knowledge of developmental psychology is helpful. You have to have a sense of where normal developmental milestones are. If a child is not promising in an area, you put more energy into it. That may be enough to help the child catch up. But if you put a lot of energy in, and there is little progress, it may not be a good place to keep pushing. You don't write it off, but you put it on the back burner. Of course, if the child can't read, you can't say we're going to drop this. You try a different approach.

How big of a role should schools play in developing these intelligences?
It's absurd to say to schools to teach all seven intelligences when we have a hard enough time teaching the two we are geared to teaching now. But schools could be better assessors of a child's abilities. They are uniquely qualified to serve as brokers—agencies that can collect information from schoolwork, assessments, tests, parent reports, and combine them to make concrete suggestions about what kids can do in the community, at home, in clubs, or as interns and apprentices in offices and factories.

In what directions are schools headed? Are they beginning to recognize more or fewer of the intelligences?
Modern schools diminish the importance of linguistic intelligence, raise logical-mathematical to a significant extent, and reduce interpersonal intelligence. In today's school it's less important that you have a successful relationship with the teacher or other students—you can still do well if you don't, partly because of tests that are blind to interpersonal dimensions.

In the school of the future built around computers, linguistic intelligence becomes less imporant and logical-mathematical more important. One interesting prediction is that intrapersonal intelligence will be-

come more important. Finding out what you can do with the computer, the kinds of programming at your disposal, will be very important in successfully negotiating a computational environment.

There is a tendency toward appreciation of various intelligences, however. We have more and more specialty schools. Society is beginning to realize that kids do have different strengths. This is happening in totalitarian schools, too. At an early age children with strengths in gymnastics are sent to a school where they can focus on that. It's antidemocratic, and I am not in favor of that. It's part of being part of a democratic society to learn its history and literature, not just gymnastics.

How long do you think it will be before the assessments you are advocating will be put into practice in the schools?
Well, the odds are, a long time. Intelligence testing has developed over years, and billions of dollars are spent on it. To change, it would take a lot of time and a lot of people working together.

Many people are becoming aware of how important finished products are, however. Even the Educational Testing Service now has people writing essays and doing drawings, not simply picking one answer out of four.

Is there anything else you would like to say to teachers?
To those who have been teaching for a while, I would urge them to use the knowledge they have about what happens to kids over several years. Unless teachers are in an environment with a huge change of population, they can see what a child is like in second grade and what he is like in fifth. Teachers need to be thinking all the time about what happens to kids, about how kids present themselves, about when they have been fooled by kids, when they have had a sense of misassessing a child, and when they have had a sense of where the child was at. This knowledge is often more valuable than what tests have to say. Many teachers are intimidated by what experts have to tell them, and they don't draw enough on their own experiences.

The other thing is that teachers should not be afraid to talk to parents, to other kids, and to kids themselves about a child's area of strength and weakness. Parents are struck by very different things from teachers. If you ask a child, What do you like to do? What do you find hard? What are you doing about it? What subjects would you take along on a vacation? the answers might surprise you. We have to demystify testing, and do it in a more sensitive way. We should approach it as a common problem-solving exercise where together we try to decide what is good for the child.

Ideally, what is it that you hope your theory of multiple intelligences will accomplish?

I have two dreams. The first is that the need for testing would fade away and that we would do assessments of children in a more natural way. The second is that we might build a society where a full range of intelligences is recognized. We have too many compelling problems that threaten our survival for us to put all our money on one or even two intelligences.

Giving Birth in America

Kenneth J. Ryan

The prenatal and birthing experiences of mothers in the United States are beset with contradictions. Medical science has made advances in safe deliveries, overcoming infertility, and prenatal diagnosis of fetal difficulties. Yet there are more malpractice suits against obstetricians and greater discontent than ever before with the rising numbers of cesarean sections. And, although we can offer "million-dollar," sophisticated care to premature infants, we have done little to ensure fewer premature births. In fact, more infants are born prematurely today and a disproportionate number of them are black. We know that the effects of smoking, alcohol, drugs, and poverty during pregancy lead to prematurity and often infant mortality. Yet we tolerate these conditions unabated.

Have we taken one step forward and two steps back in guaranteeing successful birthing experiences and healthy infants? Have some medical advances been more harmful than advantageous? Can our society find ways to overcome the social, political, and economic forces that have prevented us from saving babies?

INTRODUCTION

As I began to write this article, I experienced two somewhat conflicting reactions. . . . I thought it would be easy and upbeat to report on the improved prospects for the childless woman to become pregnant and for the pregnant woman to have a happy outcome for both herself and her infant, all because of advances in medical science and technology. On the other hand, I was quickly challenged by some contradictions in this seemingly rosy state of affairs: Why, in the face of such medical successes, is there a professional liability crisis for obstetricians that is driving many of them out of practice? How could we have succeeded so well in the very costly treatment of infertility, pregnancy complications, and prematurity and at the same time have been so unsuccessful in the cost-effective prevention of these conditions? Why, when we have so many unintended pregnancies that are the accidents of "natural" but careless sex, is there so much concern about the morality of in vitro fertilization for the childless, a technology that results in pregnancies that are, at the very least, truly wanted? These questions should bedevil the public and our policymakers, for while our obstetric and infertility outcomes are good, they could be much better, and while medical services reach many in need, they could reach many more.

RAISED EXPECTATIONS AND MALPRACTICE

A wag has suggested that ours is the safest of all times for a woman to have a baby and the most hazardous for her obstetrician. The comment contrasts the vanishingly low level of maternal mortality and the re-

K. J. Ryan (1988). "Giving Birth in America, 1988," *Family Planning Perspectives*, 20 (6), 298–301. ©The Alan Guttmacher Institute.

markable achievements of neonatal medicine, on the one hand, with the dramatic rise in the number of malpractice claims against physicians and the large sums involved on the other. Malpractice premiums have soared to over $100,000 per year in some areas. By 1987, 71 percent of U.S. obstetricians had been sued at least once.[1] Although there are indeed some bad obstetricians and there is undoubtedly some malpractice, the tort liability system appears to be a poor discriminator.

Ironically, the so-called malpractice crisis is an outgrowth of a medical success story. The outcome of obstetric care is generally so good and patients' expectations so great that even an unavoidable "maloccurrence" is likely to be probed for physician error. Because of advances in newborn care, some infants who previously would have succumbed are now surviving. For some of these premature newborns, the price of survival is life with a handicap, a situation that can evoke sympathy from a jury regardless of whether the outcome was preventable. The cost of raising and caring for a handicapped child is enormous, and this can be translated into high malpractice awards or out-of-court settlements. The largest numbers of claims with the highest awards involve brain-damaged or neurologically handicapped infants. In most instances, the cause of the neurological defect is unknown, but too often the presumption is that the physician did something wrong.

There have been changes in the legal process that aid plaintiffs' attorneys in building their cases. For example, the level of care against which a physician's performance is judged and held accountable is now a national one. The expected quality of practice is higher and the scrutiny of physician performance is more stringent now than at any other time in our medical history. At the same time, members of the legal profession now specialize in specific areas of malpractice, and attorneys' efficiency in pursuing cases has improved.

It is also ironic that at a time when "natural" childbirth (or at least minimal technical intervention by the obstetrician during labor and delivery) has been growing in popularity and has become widely accepted, the fear of being sued has resulted in more fetal monitoring, a greater number of cesarean sections, and less willingness to accede to the patient's preferences.

As if all of that were not bad enough, the availability of obstetricians seems to be declining, with obstetricians retiring earlier, limiting the number of babies they deliver, and lessening their exposure to claims by more readily referring complicated cases to subspecialists.[2] There is no doubt that many obstetricians find the practice of their specialty less enjoyable than they once did. I expect that for an indeterminate period, there will be a shortage of obstetricians and of family physicians willing to practice obstetrics. It will be more difficult to find an individual physician who will provide continuity of care; people are already relying more for obstetric services on health maintenance organizations (HMOs), group practices, and hospital-based physicians than on obstetricians with a solo practice. The liability problem is being attacked through experimentation with no-fault systems, legislative limits on noneconomic damages, improved licensing-board surveillance of physician competence, and the development of professional standards of practice; it is likely, however, to be a long time before the current state of affairs is altered.

OBSTETRIC CARE AND PERINATAL OUTCOME

There are many heartening aspects of current obstetric care. According to projections for 1990 from the National Center for Health Statistics (NCHS), the rate of neonatal mortality will be below the target of 6.5 per 1,000 set for that year.[3] In almost half of the vaginal deliveries in our large urban hospital in Boston, no anesthesia (or only local anesthesia) is required, and a birthing room for labor, delivery, and recovery is used instead of a conventional delivery room. It is standard for the father or a companion to be present for labor and delivery, even in the case of cesarean section. Seventy percent of patients breastfeed their infants on discharge from the hospital.

On the other hand, a constant effort to shorten the length of the hospital stay for financial reasons shifts the emphasis to services that can be delivered at home or on an ambulatory basis; the result is to make the hospital experience less restful and to place additional pressure on doctor and patient alike, all in the name of economy.

NCHS projections indicate that rates of prematurity will not meet the 1990 target of 5 percent.[4] Prematurity remains a major cause of perinatal morbidity and mortality; although the United States leads in the successful care of the small premature newborn, we have a higher rate of such cases than other developed countries.[5] Hence, overall perinatal mortality data for the United States do not compare favorably with those of many other developed nations.

The excess of infant and maternal mortality in the black population when compared with such mortality among whites remains particularly disquieting. In a recent study of risk factors accounting for premature birth, our research group identified four predictors; women who are under 20 years of age, are unmarried, receive welfare, or have less than a high school education are at increased risk for having a premature infant. Among women with none of these risk factors, the prematurity rate was 4.6 percent; among those with one risk factor, 7.0 percent, and among those with two or more such characteristics, 11.2 percent. The four factors explained much of the difference in the incidence of prematurity between blacks and whites; in addition, low hematocrit was also associated with preterm birth, and was found more often among blacks.[6]

Although socioeconomic differences may be intractable, it is hoped that interventions during prenatal care may make a difference. Programs have been devised to identify patients at increased risk for prematurity, to try to modify risk factors such as poor nutrition, smoking, and stress. An effort has also been made to anticipate premature labor and treat it early if it occurs. These approaches have thus far been promising, but they have been tried in only a handful of centers and have not yet been confirmed by adequately controlled clinical trials.[7] Unfortunately, almost 25 percent of pregnant women in the United States do not receive prenatal care during the first trimester,[8] which limits what can be accomplished.

There is little hope that we can greatly improve obstetric outcome in our society without also reducing smoking, alcohol consumption, and drug use during pregnancy and without improving the living conditions of those in poverty. Further improvements in our prematurity rate will probably depend as much on good nutrition and decent living conditions as on attempts to manage premature labor when it occurs. It has been calculated that if the prematurity rate in the United States could be reduced by half, the savings in the cost of intensive neonatal hospital care could be as much as $3.38 billion nationwide.[9] This should be a powerful incentive for the establishment of universal health insurance for all pregnant women.

CESAREANS AND A FAILED TECHNOLOGY

The cesarean section rate in the United States climbed from approximately 5 percent in 1970 to 20 percent or more in the 1980s.[10] Initially, cesarean sections were performed largely to protect the life of the mother in cases of uncontrollable bleeding, obstructed labor, maternal diabetes, or toxemia, all of which require prompt delivery. These indications have not changed in frequency during the last two decades, and thus have not contributed to the increased use of this procedure. Rather, the procedure is now performed under a variety of additional circumstances—including prolonged labor, fetal distress, and breech presentation—to improve fetal outcome, and these have tended to dominate as justifications for cesarean section.[11]

In addition, the rate increased rapidly because a cesarean section was in the past always followed by a cesarean in a subsequent pregnancy. This increase in cesarean sections has resulted in an enormous increment in maternal morbidity during the postpartum period, a marginal increase in maternal mortality, increased use of health care facilities, and, obviously, an enormous rise in health care costs.

Since perinatal morbidity and mortality have improved as the cesarean section rate has been rising, a cause-and-effect relationship was presumed. (In other words, a high cesarean section rate could be justified by a better outcome for the infant.) However, comparison with other countries where perinatal outcome similarly improved while the cesarean section rate remained low belies this assumption.[12]

Because the improvement seen in perinatal outcome cannot be attributed exclusively, or predominantly, to increased reliance on cesarean section, the rationale for the procedure is undergoing close scrutiny. In the near future, we will see attempts to limit the use of cesarean section through reducing reliance on electronic fetal monitoring, avoiding admittance of women to the delivery suite too early during the early stages of labor, and turning babies that present in the breech position to the vertex position before the start of labor. In addition, obstetricians will encourage more women to try vaginal delivery after a prior cesarean section, an approach that has been shown to be quite safe.[13] Such efforts will require certain tradeoffs, both in the conduct of labor and in a willingness to accept the increased risk to the infant that can result from less reliance on monitoring and from longer labors.[14]

The trend toward cesarean section was associated with the laudable achievements of reducing reliance on difficult forceps deliveries and reducing the use of oxytocin (a hormone that causes the uterus to contract). Ironically, although the more liberal use of oxytocin is deplored by many enthusiasts of natural childbirth, its administration is a key practice by which obstetricians in other countries (such as Ireland) have kept the cesarean section rate low.

There is no argument that as long as the course of labor proceeds normally, the less intervention the better, for both mother and infant. The outcome when a healthy woman delivers a term infant is generally excellent. The challenge is to be able to identify the one woman in a thousand who needs help, without intervening inappropriately in too many cases in which the woman would otherwise do fine.

It was once widely believed in the obstetric community that electronic fetal monitoring could reliably identify, in utero, fetal problems that would require intervention. However, as a result of the findings of several large, well-controlled studies, most obstetricians now agree that this is not the case.[15] Although a normal fetal monitoring record is reassuring, abnormal patterns do not necessarily predict bad outcomes; selecting cesarean delivery in all of these cases can result in an excess of cesarean sections. Let us hope that in the future we will have the sense to test our technology more thoroughly before allowing it to enter into routine use. The practical consequences of the introduction of this flawed technology are that it will be both difficult to give up completely in the absence of a substitute and difficult to use wisely when the required risk tradeoffs remain uncertain. Other obstetric technologies, including ultrasound, other prenatal diagnostic approaches, and intrauterine therapies, will undoubtedly be more carefully scrutinized in the future as a result of this experience.

In sum, it is clear that we have too high a cesarean section rate, which must be reduced without jeopardizing the gains made in infant survival; in electronic fetal monitoring, we have a failed technology that is so ingrained in practice and culture that it will take time to retrain physicians and the public in its limitations. In the meantime, a better method for evaluating fetal health is needed.

CHOICE IN CONCEPTION AND CHILDBEARING

While the range of options in obstetric care has narrowed and the field's technology has become suspect, the choices for infertility care have proliferated as a result of technical innovation.[16] The combination of in vitro fertilization and embryo transfer makes it possible to overcome infertility caused by tubal obstruction, abnormal sperm count or function and even infertility of unknown causes. With this technique, a woman can donate an egg (or eggs) for in vitro fertilization; the fertilized egg can then be implanted in a woman with no ovaries or eggs but whose uterus has been artificially prepared for pregnancy with exogenous hormones. For the first time, a female analogy to the donation of sperm for artificial insemination has been realized.

These possibilities have triggered a good deal of adverse commentary about the bypassing of nature and the potential for skirting the traditional social arrangements for having children. On the other hand, people have been circumventing social tradition for years without the benefit of any technology, by means of out-of-wedlock sex and procreation. At least with couples who use infertility services and technology, unintended or unwanted pregnancies are seldom an issue.

When the technique of in vitro fertilization was being developed, a strong moral objection was made on the basis that since one could not determine the risk of the procedure for the child so conceived, it should never be tried in the first place. In addition, antiabortion groups were concerned that some fertilized eggs might be discarded in the process, although in fact most are either transferred for implantation or frozen for possible future use. These two points turned out to be a strong impediment to government funding for research on this subject in the United States. In England, however, Patrick Steptoe and Robert Edwards, operating from a different moral perspective and with the encouragement of childless couples, persisted in their work, and in 1978 achieved the first successful birth as a result of in vitro fertilization.[17] Since then, 5,000 successful pregnancies have been achieved worldwide, with no evidence of a significant risk to infants much different from the risks normally associated with natural reproduction.[18]

With the safety issue largely dismissed, the major moral objection to in vitro fertilization remains the potential for its application to individuals or couples outside the traditional marital relationship. Of course, the Vatican Doctrinal Statement on Human Reproduction, which was issued in March 1987, would allow only those medical interventions that facilitate the conjugal act or remedy the causes of infertility.[19] In vitro fertilization is morally illicit according to this doctrine, but in our secular, pluralistic society most couples will make up their own minds on the subject. In fact, there now appears to be a broad societal consensus on in vitro fertilization: Most commissions and committees in the United States and abroad that have reviewed the procedure have found it morally acceptable.[20]

Some have held the mistaken notion that the rapid advance of technology was itself largely responsible for shifts in social practices and moral confusion about reproduction. While technology may have made it easier for a single person to have a child, it has not contributed much to out-of-wedlock childbearing and teenage pregnancy, which occur much too readily as a result of natural sexual behavior. In fact, the "new" reproductive practice most troubling to society has been the least technological—the use of a surrogate gestational mother, which can be achieved with "low-tech" artificial insemination techniques first used over 200 years ago.

The saga of Baby M, whose gestational mother tried to retain the child born under a surrogacy contract to a married couple, raised a number of moral and legal questions. For example, are generally more wealthy and privileged childless couples exploiting the predominantly poor, less-educated women who become involved in these surrogacy arrangements? Should surrogacy contracts allow for the surrogate to change her mind and keep the child? Should a couple be allowed to seek surrogacy when the wife of the contracting couple could bear a child but does not want to, for less-than-compelling reasons? The current trend seems to be for legislatures to make surrogacy contracts unenforceable and noncommercial rather than to attempt to ban the practice completely.

CONCLUSION

The professional liability crisis will effect changes in obstetric practice and care before its financial and emotional burden is lifted. National professional standards of care and quality assurance will improve accountability and performance, but fewer physicians will elect to practice obstetrics or function as solo practitioners. HMOs and other institutionalized services will replace individuals as providers of care and, for a time, obstetric services will be restricted in some communities. Maternal and infant outcomes will continue to improve, reaching the point at which the patient's social and economic characteristics and lifestyle are more important than what medicine can offer. We are almost at that point, but will not reach it without universal health insurance entitlement for pregnancy and newborn care. Cesarean section rates have already reached levels that will induce considerable pressure for change from within the medical profession itself. The demand for new reproductive technologies will continue and expand as infertility services become covered by health insurance policies and social concerns about the safety and propriety of such technologies diminish.

However, we are still treating the symptoms of "diseases" rather than treating or preventing the "diseases" themselves. We have not been successful in preventing prematurity and pregnancy complications because the biological causes of these conditions have their roots in the associated social factors of poverty, welfare dependence, and limited education. Changing these social factors, or at least understanding how they influence biological function, has been more difficult than improving perinatal and obstetric care. Similarly, many causes of infertility are social factors that defy easy resolution—for example, delayed childbearing for career reasons, sexual behavior that spreads sexually transmitted diseases, and the psychological pressures of demanding work and urban life. We have been less successful in influencing lifestyles than in advancing the new reproductive technologies. For the next twenty years, dealing with this social agenda should be a top priority.

Healing the Unborn

Cheryl Crooks

For many parents, advances in prenatal interventions have meant "miracles in the making." Fetal surgery, along with diagnostic tools such as ultrasound, has literally changed the life course of some infants and their families. Doctors are growing more confident that they can make a majority of diagnoses for fetuses in utero. Even when no appropriate intervention can be performed prenatally, a newborn thus diagnosed has a better chance of survival because the doctor knows what to expect following the birth.

Increased information about the unborn child elicits a variety of responses from parents. They may experience grief, fear, and—most certainly—doubt. Their knowledge changes the way they anticipate the birthing and their expectations for the infant. If you knew that your child would be born with a heart defect that must be corrected soon after birth, how would your attitudes, feelings, and behaviors toward your child differ from those of an uninformed parent?

Greg Elie is playing catch with his father, Joe, and his older brother, Brian, on the enclosed patio of his home in Playa del Rey, California. Like any 5-year-old just learning to catch a ball, Greg misses the throws from his father one, two, three times before successfully closing his hands around the ball on the fourth try. He shrieks, delighted at his accomplishment. For most people, watching this blond-haired, blue-eyed boy at play would be like watching any other youngster his age having a good time. But to his parents, Cindy and Joe Elie, it is watching a miracle.

Greg has hydrocephalus, a condition in which excess fluid builds up in the ventricles of the brain. Unless the fluid is continually drained off, brain damage can result.

Cindy heard the diagnosis of her son's condition when she was twenty-seven weeks pregnant, follow-

C. Crooks. (1988, June). Healing the unborn, *Parents*, 63: 138–143. (Portions of the original article have been deleted.)

ing an ultrasound scan. Her doctors had ordered the scan as a follow-up to earlier screenings that showed the fetus's head was large for its estimated stage of development. Possibly, they thought, Cindy was further along in her pregnancy than originally believed. From the follow-up scan, they determined that instead the fetus had hydrocephalus. Cindy's obstetrician referred her to the UCLA Medical Center for further tests. That was the beginning of what seemed to the Elies to be "a nightmare."

The UCLA doctors confirmed the diagnosis and gave the Elies a choice of their next step: Doctors could deliver the baby right away, but at twenty-seven weeks, the fetus's lungs were not fully developed, and the premature birth would mean serious respiratory complications for the newborn. Carrying the baby to term would allow the lungs to mature, but the head would likely continue to swell, and brain damage might result. Or, doctors said, they could operate on the fetus in utero, in order to place a catheter, or shunt, in the unborn baby's head that would drain off the fluid into the amniotic sac. The surgery had been attempted only a few times in the world, never in California, and without encouraging results. But UCLA's doctors would try it if the Elies were willing.

That day, following the appointment at UCLA, Cindy and Joe talked over lunch about what they should do. "I'm going to do it, Joe," Cindy said determinedly. Looking back, she recalls, "I had no choice. I wanted to do whatever I had to do to give this baby the best chance for a life."

One week after her initial visit to UCLA, Cindy was wheeled into the operating room, where ten green-gowned doctors had gathered to observe and participate in the procedure. Joe stood at Cindy's head throughout the surgery, tightly holding her hand and telling her what was happening as doctors explained the procedure to him.

The doctors made three tiny incisions, about the width of a pencil, in Cindy's abdomen before getting close enough to the moving baby. While watching the ultrasound monitor, doctors guided a thin-walled needle, about 2 millimeters in diameter, through the incision, into the amniotic cavity, and through the baby's cranium to the enlarged ventricle. Once the needle was in position, the stylet inside the needle, similar to the point and cartridge of a ballpoint pen, was withdrawn, and a catheter was threaded through the hollow needle. The other end of the catheter was left in the amniotic cavity.

An hour and fifteen minutes later it was finished. The doctors seemed pleased but did not celebrate yet. The next morning, doctors studying the fetus's ultrasound image could find no shunt. The baby, they suspected, had pulled it out. They would have to try again.

The catheter stayed in the second time. The Elies and the doctors monitored the fetus's progress through the ultrasound images. "It was wonderful," says Cindy. "Every day I could see the head get smaller and smaller and smaller."

Eight weeks after the surgery, the 7-pound, 2-ounce Greg was delivered by cesarean section.

"We didn't know what to expect," says Cindy of her son's development since birth. His motor skills developed more slowly than other babies his age. He was 1 year old when he first sat up by himself and was 2 before he walked. "The only thing he did on time," Joe says, "was talk." Greg still has some gross and fine motor skill problems and lags about one year behind the other children in his preschool. There have been other physical problems as well: strabismus (cross-eye) and amblyopia (lazy eye) were both corrected, and his vision is fine now. He also has a profound hearing loss in his left ear, which is slightly deformed.

Mentally, Greg has progressed normally. In fact, an evaluation at 3½ years showed him to have the mental age of a 5-year-old.

Soon after Greg's birth, a new shunt was placed that extended from the ventricles of the brain and ran under the skin behind the ear, down the neck, chest, and abdomen and drained into his abdominal cavity. There the fluid could be safely absorbed by the body. Since then, in order to keep pace with Greg's growth, three additional operations have been performed to place longer lengths of shunt. Another operation is planned for July, with the aim of placing in his abdominal cavity a coil of tubing long enough to be sufficient for the rest of Greg's life; the tubing will uncoil as he grows.

Fetal surgery, such as Greg experienced, is part of the exciting field of fetal medicine. Though still in an early stage of development, fetal medicine is bringing new hope and solutions to expectant parents. It has caused doctors everywhere to reconsider their attitudes about prenatal care and how they medically treat the fetus.

"Over the last couple of years, we've been able to learn so much more about the fetus," says John C. Hobbins, M.D., director of obstetrics at Yale New Haven Hospital. "Ultrasound has made the difference in our ability to look at the fetus and its structure."

Although ultrasound has been in use since the early 1970s, medical professionals' skill at interpreting ultrasound images has improved with experience, and advances in technology have produced better images. As these skills and technologies have progressed, so has doctors' ability to assess a baby's health prior to birth—and to do so increasingly early in the pregnancy.

Besides ultrasound, now ordered for nearly 60 percent of all expectant mothers, there are now other tests that allow doctors to detect and diagnose problems more precisely. For example, the alpha fetoprotein test, which has become widely accepted during the last two years, can help detect neural tube defects. This simple test measures the amount of alpha fetoprotein, an antigen made by a growing fetus, in the woman's blood. Above-normal levels of the substance may indicate a defect.

Much of the emphasis in fetal medicine today is, in fact, on prenatal diagnosis. "There aren't too many diagnoses that we can't make now in utero," explains Yale's Hobbins. Many problems detected through these early diagnoses can be treated medically before birth.

In the past four years, for example, doctors have begun to treat fetal cardiac dysrhythmia, irregularities or disturbances in the heart rate. A too-rapid beating of a fetal heart can be treated by giving the medication digitalis to the mother, either orally or by injection in a dosage that does not affect the mother's heart.

Some birth defects requiring surgical attention, such as spina bifida, gastrointestinal obstructions, and heart defects, can still best be treated after birth. But an early prenatal diagnosis can enhance the newborn's chances for healthy survival because doctors know ahead of time what to expect and can arrange for any special care necessary.

In a very few cases, surgery before birth may be the only way to help or save a fetus. "No one knows precisely how many babies are in this category," says Michael R. Harrison, M.D., co-director of the Fetal Treatment Program at the University of California, San Francisco (UCSF), School of Medicine. But for those few cases, fetal surgery gives parents, and their unborn infants, a potentially lifesaving option.

Fetal treatment through intervention began in the early 1960s when a doctor in New Zealand attempted to treat Rh hemolytic disease, caused when antibodies in the blood of a pregnant woman who is Rh negative attack the blood cells of a fetus whose blood is Rh positive. The physician transfused blood that was compatible with the mother's into the fetus by depositing it in the fetus's belly, in hope that it would be absorbed into the fetal bloodstream. The procedure became standard for treating Rh disease, but results varied. Complicating treatment was the fact that a fetus with Rh disease is likely to be hydropic, or to accumulate fluid in its body cavities, because its heart is failing.

Just two years ago, according to Dr. Hobbins, a hydropic fetus had only a 30 percent chance of survival. Today, in Hobbins's experience, the rate has nearly tripled to 85 percent because doctors, guided by an ultrasound scanner, can insert a needle into the umbilical vein and feed the blood directly into the bloodstream. Besides Hobbins and his colleagues at Yale, very few other fetal medicine centers in this country are experienced in the procedure.

The success of the Hobbins team was encouraging to Barbara and Nick Pignatelli. The Pignatellis' unborn baby underwent a fetal transfusion when Barbara was in her seventh month of pregnancy. Through a routine blood test, Barbara's obstetrician had discovered that Barbara's blood, typed Kell negative, contained antibodies that were killing her fetus's Kell positive blood cells and jeopardizing the fetus's survival. The Kell blood group is one of the human blood group systems, as is the Rhesus (Rh) system. A follow-up ultrasound scan revealed that the fetus was also hydropic and that its overworked heart was beginning to fail.

The Pignatellis immediately headed for Yale New Haven Hospital, where Hobbins and his team were waiting. The next morning, Hobbins, with ultrasound scanning to guide him, carefully inserted a needle through Barbara's abdomen and into the umbilical vein. Her fetus was severely anemic. Its red blood cell concentration was only 9 percent, compared to the 40 percent value expected for a 6-month-old fetus. Hobbins pumped new blood, Kell negative like Barbara's, into the fetus for thirty minutes.

Barbara returned for three subsequent fetal transfusions, at two-week intervals, until 90 percent of the baby's blood had been exchanged. Then, at thirty-five weeks, doctors delivered, by cesarean section, the Pignatellis' 5-pound, 5-ounce daughter. "I took one look at her and thought to myself, 'I can't believe she looks this good after all she's been through,'" says Barbara. Baby Sarah, born May 1, 1987, is thriving and needed only one additional transfusion after birth.

Emily Williams is doing equally well. Emily (a pseudonym) underwent open fetal surgery at UCSF, when she was just an 18-week-old fetus, for an obstruction in her urinary tract. The blockage had caused a backup of urine in her renal system, which, untreated, would have led to the deterioration of her kidneys, a fatal condition known as hydronephrosis. The surgical procedure was pioneered by UCSF's fetal treatment team in 1981 and had been performed only three times prior to Emily's operation in 1986. The first baby's kidneys never recovered, and the baby died of lung failure shortly after birth; the two other babies survived.

During the surgery, doctors actually lifted tiny Emily by her ankles halfway out of her mother's uterus, as far as necessary to make an incision in her lower abdomen and create an external opening between the bladder and the lower abdomen so that the bladder could drain into the amniotic fluid. The procedure, known as *vesicotomy*, is commonly done after birth on babies with bladder blockage problems. Emily, however, would not have survived in the womb because her kidneys would not have made enough amniotic fluid, making it impossible for the fetus to develop properly.

Today, Emily is a strong, playful baby, 14 months old, and her renal system is functioning fine.

"If I hadn't done this, Emily wouldn't be here, and if the doctors hadn't found the problem as early as they did, she would have died," says Emily's mother.

Choosing the right candidate is critical to the outcome of any of these new procedures. Not all fetuses may need medical intervention, and some may even be harmed by it. It is a risky guessing game for the doctors, but they are improving the means of fetal patient selection. In cases of fetal hydronephrosis, for example, the UCSF fetal treatment team has developed a method of extracting a sample of the fetus's urine from the bladder and testing it to determine the extent of the damage to the baby's kidneys and whether or not they will be able to recover if the doctors operate.

Methods of selecting which fetuses with hydrocephalus, such as Greg Elie, should have surgery are not as advanced. And it can be difficult for doctors to assess, when a child has had the surgery, the extent of the benefits of prenatal therapy. Therefore, doctors in the United States have generally discontinued prenatal surgery to place shunts for hydrocephalus until more is learned through research and until it is clearly demonstrated that in utero treatment is more effective than surgical treatment immediately after birth.

But no matter how difficult the choice for the doctors, it is even more difficult for parents who must ultimately decide what to do. Often, they must quickly make a life-or-death decision at a time when one or both of them are still in shock from the news that their unborn child is in trouble. "It all happens so fast, you don't have complete control of yourself," remembers Joe Elie.

In addition, doctors can seldom provide clear-cut answers to the parents' many questions because frequently the doctors themselves simply don't know. In that case, "I put a burden on them," says Lawrence Platt, M.D., professor of obstetrics and gynecology at the University of Southern California School of Medicine. "It's very tough sometimes. All we can do is simply inform the parents. The more information we have, the more we can tell the parents so that they can make their decision."

"It was very frustrating for me," says Patricia Moller. "I kept asking what I could expect. I wasn't looking for answers, just discussion, but people didn't want to discuss it because they didn't want to plant false hopes in my head."

Patricia's doctor had discovered that the blood vessels of the twins she was carrying were connected in the placenta, causing one baby to bleed into the other. One fetus was receiving more blood than needed and the other not enough. (This condition is extremely rare and occurs only with identical twins.)

When she was twenty-seven weeks pregnant, Patricia underwent an unusual operation in which one of the fetal twins was removed from the womb. Doctors hoped that by delivering one baby and allowing the other to remain, one or both would live. "It was the only way to break the cycle and to stop the blood from going from one to another," says Khalil Tabsh, M.D., associate professor of maternal-fetal medicine at UCLA's School of Medicine and the doctor who performed the surgery.

The Mollers were told beforehand that the operation had never been done before, but that without it,

their babies had little chance of surviving. "Pat was committed to do whatever she had to do to give our babies the best chance to live," recalls her husband, Randy Moller. "She was the one who wanted to go through whatever it took. When I understood that, the only option that made sense was the surgery."

Unfortunately, the first twin, Daniel, was so underdeveloped from the lack of nourishment in the womb that he survived only two days before dying of respiratory failure. The second twin, David, was born twelve days later and is today a happy, bright-eyed 18-month-old.

The risks in undergoing any of these procedures are considerable, say the doctors. Before okaying any sort of fetal surgery, parents should seek out the best care possible in their area (almost every state now has a major fetal center, according to Yale's Hobbins), should not be afraid to ask for a second opinion, and should question the physicians involved about their own experience in this area as well as the overall experience of others in the particular procedure being considered.

Even then, doctors advise parents to approach with caution. "The fundamental thing to consider is the safety of the mother, because she has to take a risk when there's no benefit to her other than the possible benefits to the fetus," warns Harrison. "Any risk to her or her reproductive system would be unacceptable." So far, no such damage has resulted in the procedures Harrison has done, and mothers who have undergone fetal surgery have borne subsequent children. Still, parents should think about the number of children they already have, the circumstances surrounding the pregnancy, and the possible consequences, financial or otherwise, should the surgery be unsuccessful or should other physical problems result.

The primary risk, whatever the procedure, is that of preterm labor. Fortunately, this risk can be controlled to a great extent with drugs to suppress preterm labor. Also, doctors have learned that the likelihood of a woman's going into preterm labor is less if the fetal surgery is performed early in a fetus's gestation.

Any sort of fetal medicine procedure places enormous emotional stress on the couple and family involved. Though all may go well, they cannot be fully relieved until the baby is born, perhaps months afterward. But couples who have lived through the experience say that it has actually strengthened their relationships with one another and their families. Prior to the birth of their son, David, the Mollers were both insurance agents, competing with each other. Now, they own a hobby shop and lead a less frantic life. "We were at odds with one another before, but now our relationship is better," says Patricia. "Life is too short to go through all stressed out."

The Elies say they are more sensitive to handicapped children and adults and are active in fundraising for the Special Preventive Research, Intervention, and New Technology for Children program at UCLA, a program dedicated to improving prenatal diagnosis as well as treatment and follow-up care for children with congenital abnormalities or developmental problems. "My new group of friends are mothers of handicapped kids, most of whom have handicaps so much more severe than Greg's that sometimes I feel guilty he's so normal," says Cindy.

For these parents, the endings to their stories have been happy ones. But the field of fetal medicine has raised complicated new ethical and medical issues, such as the question of who should make decisions for the fetus about in utero treatment, what the rights of the mother and the fetus are, how and when to intervene in a fetus's development, and whether such therapies help or make the problem worse.

However, you have only to watch Greg Elie learning to catch a ball, Sarah Pignatelli sitting up by herself, Emily Williams as she stacks blocks, or David Moller speaking his first words to realize that for these children, at least, fetal medicine has been a great advantage.

High-Risk Infants: Prenatal Drug Exposure (PDE), Prematurity, and AIDS

Jean G. Cole

Although high-cost medical and technological advances have improved the survival rate of some infants, the rising incidence of prematurity, drug addiction, and, most recently, AIDS work against the development of healthy and competent infants. Our society has done a poor job of realizing the holistic and continuous nature of nurturing new lives. The birth of an infant is a transitional process—what came before and what will follow are of paramount importance. Good prenatal care is essential for all pregnant mothers, and a physically sustaining and emotionally strong environment is equally necessary after an infant's birth. However, in our country it is not unusual for a hospital to spend thousands of dollars (state or insurance monies) on keeping a premature infant alive and then to send the child and mother home with no resources to provide for the physical and emotional health of mother and infant.

Infants at risk often differ dramatically from full-term infants in their ability to interact with the outside world. Parents of high-risk infants need good information about their infant's capabilities and extensive emotional and physical support for themselves. As described in this article, tools such as the Brazelton Neonatal Behavioral Assessment Scale highlight response differences between infants. If parents and other caregivers understand the at-risk infant's behaviors, they can adjust the environment to meet that child's specific needs. First parents must be convinced that they will become competent in their parenting roles. Then they must find interaction patterns that fit them and their baby. If we cannot help parents establish positive relationships with their at-risk infants early on, the prognosis for these children and our society will be extremely poor.

O ver the past decade, a tremendous amount of information has been published about the capabilities of newborn infants. Initially it was thought that newborns functioned at a brain-stem level and were

J. Cole. (1990). High risk infants: Prematurity, prenatal drug exposure, and AIDS. Original manuscript, Boston City Hospital, Boston, Massachusetts. Jean Cole, M.S. is a Master Trainer in the BNBAS at the Child Development Unit, Children's Hospital, Boston, and an Infant Development Specialist, Department of Neonatology, Boston City Hospital.

merely a mass of reflexes. Now we know newborn infants are complex organisms, capable of defending themselves from stimulation in their environment and capable of communicating with us via their behavior (Klaus, 1986). Understanding the behavior of the healthy full-term infant is crucial in helping us understand the behavior of the infant at risk.

The Brazelton Neonatal Behavioral Assessment Scale (BNBAS) helps us to understand the unique capabilities of the newborn infant (Brazelton, 1984). With this assessment, we can observe infants' behavior as they respond to a series of maneuvers that replicate the kind of stimulation infants experience in the extra-uterine environment; that is, how they respond to light, sound, handling and movement. The infants' responses to the assessment provide the examiner with a behavioral profile of the infants' capabilities as they defend themselves from stimulation and seek to maintain organizational balance, or homeostasis. Homeostasis is the major agenda of the human organism. The behavioral profile of an at-risk infant is often very different from that of a "normal" child.

The Brazelton scale is administered during the neonatal period, the first 28 days of life. The first exam is normally done on Day 3. By this time, the infant has usually recovered from the trauma of labor and delivery and from medication the mother may have taken. The Brazelton assessment is administered in a quiet room where lighting and temperature can be controlled in order to elicit the best performance. The infant is examined between feedings so that the need to feed or a recent feeding do not interfere.

The exam generally begins with the infant asleep so that his or her ability to habituate can be assessed. Habituation is the ability to inhibit a response to a repeated stimulus, something adults do well as we screen out extraneous noise while attending to an interesting event. To test the infant's ability to habituate to a visual stimulus during sleep, a flash of light is shined across the infant's closed eyes for a maximum of 10 presentations or until the infant habituates—stops responding. Most healthy three-day-old infants habituate after a few sweeps of the light, responding initially with strong blinking or body movement and then going back to sleep. They respond similarly to the sound of a rattle and a bell. The ability to habituate helps conserve energy and calories, maintains temperature control, and protects the infant from the environment. It is the first learned behavior of normal newborn infants (Nugent, 1981).

In contrast, high-risk infants may be unable to habituate and are then very much at the mercy of the environment. Such infants respond to every sound and visual stimulus in the environment. They sleep poorly and tend to be irritable and difficult to care for. The inability to habituate can lead to chronic distractibility and poor self-regulation (poorly using a variety of coping strategies to maintain organizational balance or homeostasis).

Assessing the reflexes of the infant provides us with information about how he or she deals with being handled, from very light tactile stimulation to more massive, vestibular stimuli (reaction to being moved up and down and sideways). For example, testing the Moro reflex, a startle as the result of being moved suddenly, the infant will extend his arms out then in

again to the body. It also provides the examiner with information about the infant's neurological integrity, and how well his or her nervous system is functioning (Prechtl, 1968). With the high-risk infant, we are alerted to problems in the integrity of the central nervous system (CNS) by the infant's aversive reaction to touch and movement and sometimes by the presence of abnormal reflexes.

The infant's states of consciousness are observed closely because they will influence all the responses. For example, reflex response will be low if the infant is asleep, and brisk if he or she is crying. Six states of consciousness have been identified in the newborn: deep sleep, light sleep, drowsy, awake-alert, fussing, and crying (Prechtl, 1968; Wolf, 1974). How the infant moves through these states provides important information and reflects the degree of stability of the infant's states of consciousness. Most newborns can make smooth transitions through all six states of consciousness and states are easy to define. But high-risk infants often have difficulty maintaining a stable state of consciousness, instead fluctuating from one state to another. In addition, states are often difficult to define.

The infant's motor abilities are assessed by observing quality of movement: smooth versus jerky movement, range of motion, and smooth flexion and extension with moderate tone, versus limited movement with high tone or floppy tone. For most healthy, full-term infants, we expect to see smooth, well-integrated movement with a good range of motion and moderate tone. High-risk infants often show jerky, uncoordinated movement patterns, with high tone predominating and range of motion restricted.

During the exam, if the infant becomes awake and alert, his or her ability to interact with the examiner is assessed. This aspect is called *the ability to orient*: animate and inanimate interaction are tested. *Animate* entails having the infant focus on the examiner's face and voice and tracking them horizontally and vertically. It also entails having the infant turn to the sound of the voice and search for the source of the sound. *Inanimate* interaction entails the infant tracking a red ball horizontally and vertically in a coordinated pattern. The infant's head and eyes follow the ball smoothly. Then the infant turns toward the sound of a rattle shaken out of his or her line of vision and searches for the source of the sound. Most infants two to three days old can accomplish this behavior quite well. Inanimate stimuli are less complex and not as stimulating as animate stimuli for a newborn infant.

The visual system of the newborn infant is not fully developed until about six months of age (Haith, 1980). At 6 months the visual acuity of an infant is comparable to that of an adult with 20/20 vision. At birth, visual acuity is about 20/500, and at 2 months,

20/200. The visual system of the infant is protected from too much stimulation by this slow process of development. However, the baby can see and responds best to items presented 10–12 inches from his or her face. He or she responds best to items with high contrast, black and white, and strong primary colors, especially red. The infant focuses on the stimulus and tracks it smoothly.

The auditory system of the infant is fully functional from 5 months gestational age onwards, which means the infant has the ability to hear in utero. This system, however, is also protected from overstimulation and newborn infants have a high threshold for sound, which decreases gradually over the first year of life (Klaus, 1986). Fetuses of 5 months gestational age hear intrauterine sounds as well as extrauterine sounds. They can recognize familiar voices once they are born, and respond to those voices in preference to that of a stranger. So although newborn infants hear quite well, they process sound slowly as a result of their high threshold to sound. High-risk infants are often hyperreactive to sound. They respond to sound immediately and then appear to be overstimulated by it, turning away and fussing. They too recognize a familiar voice, but do not sustain the initial response, searching for the source of the sound as a healthy newborn infant does. High-risk infants present negative feedback to caregivers by this behavior, much to the caregiver's consternation.

Newborn infants also have a sophisticated ability to defend themselves from overstimulation. They turn away from overstimulating visual or auditory stimuli. They also change their states by fussing or going to sleep to protect themselves from overstimulation. This behavior is the infant's way of communicating with us and is the language of the newborn. When we acknowledge signs of overstimulation and provide the infant with "time out," a quiet time to recover, the infant then returns and resets the intensity of the interaction at a lower level, building up gradually, then disengaging when he or she needs to. Some researchers have called this interaction pattern a "waltz" with caregivers, a sensitive reciprocity that is a delight to observe (Klaus, 1986). Sensitive caregivers respond appropriately to the infant's cues and behaviors, taking turns and eliciting impressive responses from the infant, and all this in the first few days of life! When an infant is born prematurely, drug exposed, or infected with AIDS, it is exceedingly more difficult to begin and maintain the "waltz" as these infants are easily overstimulated and react adversely to the caregiver's interaction by turning away, fussing, or going to sleep.

HIGH-RISK INFANT—PREMATURITY

Infants are considered "term" when they reach 38 weeks gestation. Most term infants are born at 38–42 weeks, with 40 weeks the average gestational age at birth. Infants born at 37 weeks or less are considered premature or preterm. The viability age of the preterm infant, the age at which the infant can survive outside the womb, is 26 weeks. Although some infants as premature as 24 weeks gestational age, born 16 weeks too early, are now surviving, the quality of survival remains in question and these 24-week infants are very much at risk for severe developmental consequences such as cerebral palsy and chronic lung disease (Illsley, 1984). Preterm infants are also amazingly competent although the degree of prematurity and medical complications can seriously affect their developmental outcome. Preterm infants, due to the fragility of their developing central nervous systems (CNS), are very much at the mercy of the environment and need much protection from environmental stimulation. It is impossible to replicate the protective environment of the womb where it is warm and dark and relatively quiet. The amniotic sac provides a cutaneous boundary for the infant, providing containment and maintaining him or her in flexion, the posture that predominates in utero. The amniotic fluid bathes the infant's body, providing developmentally appropriate tactile stimulation. The movement and sleeping-waking cycles of the mother provide kinesthetic (movement) and diurnal (day-night) experiences, and all the infant's systems are protected and stimulated at age-appropriate levels (Als, 1982). The fetus will respond to a light placed on the mother's abdomen, but for the most part, the environment is dark, protecting the gradually developing visual system. The fetus can hear when he or she is 5 months gestational age, but auditory input in utero is at an appropriate level for the infant's stage of development.

When infants arrive prematurely, they find themselves in an environment for which they are not yet ready. They are "displaced fetuses," attempting to adapt to very stimulating environments with lots of noise, bright lights, much handling, and very little protection for the fragile infant—some weigh as little as 1 pound (Als, 1983). Researchers and nursing-medical staff are now attempting to change the intensive care nursery environment, making it more supportive for these fragile infants through a program of dimmed lights, limited handling, supportive positioning, and noise reduction (Cole, 1989; Tronick, 1987).

The dilemma for parents of preterm infants is that all the normal, intuitive responses they would use with a healthy, full-term infant are too overstimulating for most preterm infants. Stroking and touching (tactile stimulation) are often too overstimulating. Movement in space (kinesthetic stimulation) can often be too much for such infants, and simple rocking could send cardiac and respiratory rates fluctuating wildly! Because of a fragile CNS, a preterm infant often can deal with only one sensory modality at a time. He or she may be able to look at a visual stimulus, but if an auditory component is added (e.g., voice), it is too stimulating and can cause distress. Then the infant will either "shut down" (go to sleep) or become very agitated. This behavior can continue until term age and can be very difficult for parents unless they understand the infant's behavior, realizing that this is the way such infants communicate signs of overstimulation.

Preterm infants progress from visual gazing at a black and white decal, to gazing at a mobile and *then* finally interacting with the caregiver. This developmental sequence needs to be adhered to, otherwise the infants are constantly overstimulated, which can deplete their energies as well as affect other developing systems (Turkewitz, 1985). Parents and other caregivers need to learn to read the infant's behavioral signs of overstimulation and to provide a more modulated approach; for example, when interacting use a less animated facial expression and a softer voice or no voice at all, a visual input only. Some parents state that they feel rejected by their infants who can't sustain eye contact with them. They may say the infant doesn't like them, because he or she keeps looking away. Once they realize that turning away (visual or auditory averting) is a coping strategy that infants use when overstimulated, parents begin to see this behavior as a strength and not a deficit. Parents change their perception of the behavior and begin to respond more appropriately (Cole, 1985).

Preterm infants also have very unstable states of consciousness and it is often very difficult to know if they are awake or asleep, especially in the early days of their recovery when states are very diffuse and unclear. They are frequently hypertonic and become agitated easily, losing tone and smooth motor patterns. Flailing and extended limbs add to the consternation of their parents, who unwittingly overstimulate the infants in their attempts to console them. Preterm infants need a different approach, with "time out," a quiet time to recover and swaddling of limbs by the caregiver's hands or wrapping in a blanket to help regain flexion. Interaction needs to be withdrawn and then proceed at a much lower level of intensity, in a quiet, low-keyed manner, with perhaps only one sensory modality at a time.

Physiologically, preterm infants respond to stress rather dramatically with color change: paling or flushing, or cyanosis (duskiness). They exhibit rapid breathing, increased cardiac rates, tremors, startles and sometimes visceral responses with spit-ups and hiccups. All this reactivity is the result of an immature CNS affected by prematurity.

Researchers are now beginning to realize that preterm infants never really do catch up developmentally, and correction for degree of prematurity needs to be made when estimating developmental age, especially during the first two years of life. After three years, the differences are not that dramatic in terms of developmental delay, but coping style may always have to be considered because the brain organization of the child born prematurely is irreversibly altered by premature birth (Als, 1983). An infant who is chronologically 6 months of age but who was born 12 weeks prematurely (at 28 weeks gestational age) is only able to function developmentally at a three-month level. Preterm infants require superb parenting and endless patience, as they are very demanding infants. About 15 percent will need some form of special education as they are at high risk for developmental delay, depending on degree of prematurity and severity of medical complications (Illsley, 1984).

HIGH-RISK INFANTS—PRENATAL DRUG EXPOSURE

Over the past five years, there has been an alarming increase in the number of infants born exposed to drugs. They are born to drug-abusing women. Drugs that the mother takes during her pregnancy cross the placental barrier and cause many problems for the baby, especially during the first trimester of pregnancy (the first three months), when the infant's CNS is developing and the infant is most vulnerable. Babies who have been exposed to narcotics such as heroin and methadone are born addicted and experience drug withdrawal, exhibiting tremors, sweating, extreme irritability, poor sleep states, limited alertness, and visceral upsets such as diarrhea and poor feeding. All babies with prenatal drug exposure (PDE) tend to have a lower birthweight, smaller head circumference, and are small for their gestational age. These are all factors that place them at risk for less than optimal development (Fulroth, 1989). They are also at risk for infant crib death, or sudden infant death syndrome (SIDS), because the drugs depress the central nervous system, putting the infant at much risk. All these conditions are exacerbated when the mother has engaged in polydrug abuse as opposed to use of one drug only. Marijuana and alcohol are included in substance abuse statistics. A small percentage of the infants are born prematurely, but the average age of birth is 38 weeks gestation (Chasnoff, 1989).

Drug-exposed and addicted babies are very difficult to care for. They are excessively irritable, easily over-stimulated, and difficult to console. They have very few self-regulatory abilities—the strategies that normal infants use when they are over-stimulated. In many ways they are as reactive as premature infants. Both have fragile central nervous systems, but for different reasons: preterm infants because of prematurity and drug-exposed babies because of the effects drugs have had on their CNS.

Narcotic-addicted babies have poorly maintained sleep states and are very easily aroused. They lose control quickly and are difficult to comfort. Their agitation exacerbates their tone, and they frequently are hypertonic, jittery, and tremulous. They frequently need tight swaddling (wrapped in a blanket) to help them get under control. They need shielding from environmental stimuli (light and noise) to help them sleep quietly.

Addicted babies have difficulty sustaining interaction with their caregivers. They avert their gaze (look away) frequently, unable to deal with the stimulation of eye contact. They have a hypersensitivity to sound, reacting immediately and then fussing and turning away from the source of the sound. They appear not to have the auditory protection of normal newborn infants. Even when they are detoxified (treated with medication for their addiction), their interaction at one month of age is poorer in quality than the interaction of a healthy full-term newborn infant three days old. Studies have shown abnormal electroencephalograph (EEG) activity, suggesting that we need to be concerned about developmental outcome (Brown, 1989). Researchers feel that these addicted infants will show behavioral disorders and attentional deficits as they grow and mature. Parents often state that the baby "doesn't like them" or is blind, because of impaired social interaction. Such parents need help in understanding the infant's behavior and how to read the behavioral cues more appropriately. For drug abusing women with low self-esteem and psychosocial problems, the infant's worrisome and negative feedback behavior can disastrously affect the interactional bond between the mother and child. A high percentage of these infants suffers from neglect and abuse and may fail to thrive (Chasnoff, 1989).

Many addicts switch from other drugs to cocaine when pregnant, believing cocaine will be less harmful to the fetus. Actually it is a most insidious drug. It is now believed to be more harmful to the fetus than any other drug, heroin included, and irrevocably affects the infant's brain chemistry, altering the neurochemical transmitters in the brain and putting the infant at terrible risk both for his or her life and developmental outcome (Mirochnick, 1990).

Unlike narcotic exposure, cocaine does not cause addiction in the infant. Nor does the cocaine-exposed infant experience withdrawal symptoms. However, cocaine does depress the CNS of the infant, and causes a drowsy "shut down" behavior, sometimes described as hypersomnolence. The cocaine-exposed infant's responses to stimuli are delayed, then once the stimulus breaks through the infant's hypersomnolent state, he or she is difficult to console. Although irritable, these infants rarely become aroused enough to sustain a vigorous cry, the result of a depressed CNS.

The cocaine-exposed infant, like the narcotic-addicted infant, is hypertonic and tremulous, with jittery, uncoordinated patterns of movement. They provide little positive feedback to their caregivers as they are frequently poor feeders and have poor interactive abilities.

Babies exposed prenatally to drugs are at high risk for Human Immunodeficiency Virus (HIV), which can lead to the symptomatic stage of Acquired Immune Deficiency Syndrome (AIDS). It is predicted that by 1991 there will be over 10,000 HIV-infected children throughout the country, clustered in areas with populations of HIV-infected drug users. Many mothers of these children cannot handle the responsibility of a sick child, or are ill themselves. Often the babies languish in hospitals because few are adopted or placed in foster care due to the hysterical fear of contamination (Boland, 1988). Families who do take the babies in foster care are often ostracized by their neighbors and families who fear "catching" AIDS. But AIDS or HIV infection can only be transmitted sexually, through infected intravenous needles, or contaminated blood transfusions. In caring for infants, use of latex gloves, adequate hand washing and avoidance of contact with body fluids protects caregivers (Regan, 1989). The general public needs education to dispel myths and misconceptions about this disease.

It is estimated that 35–65 percent of infants born to HIV-positive mothers will be infected at birth. A woman exposed to HIV has a 50 percent chance of giving birth to an infected infant. Although some infants convert to seronegative status some time after birth as their own immune systems develop antibodies, most do not and they suffer debilitating illnesses. Their development is erratic, and most of them die before they become 5 years old. Although drug abuse crosses all socioeconomic levels, the highest percentage of infants at risk for AIDS comes from the inner cities, born of poor black or Hispanic women who use intravenous drugs or who engage in prostitution (Miller, 1988). Developmentally, babies infected or at risk for AIDS present all the typical behaviors of drug-exposed infants. However, their developmental progress is very chaotic, and they do not respond well to the medication used for detoxification; indeed, this symptom may be one of the first markers that the infant has AIDS. They show abnormal posturing, fluctuating tone, athetoid-like movement (undulating, uncontrolled movement pattern), and very flat affect (unanimated facial expression). They do not present much positive feedback for their caregivers, which impairs the bonding and attachment process necessary for optimal emotional growth between parent and child (Greenspan, 1985).

Increasingly we are dealing with the effects of AIDS in infants as the following case history shows.

Danny was born at 38 weeks gestational age to a drug-abusing mother. He was born addicted at birth to the heroin and cocaine his mother had taken intravenously during her pregnancy. He showed all the classic signs of addiction; irritability, poor sleeping, ravenous appetite, tremors, sweating, high tonicity (stiff limbs), and agitated motor activity with restricted range of motion (ability to move limbs smoothly away from his body and get his hands to his mouth). His nose, mouth, chin, knees and elbows, were all excoriated from his frantic motor activity.

Danny was treated medically for his addiction, and in approximately six weeks he was detoxified, although his rather slow response to treatment was worrisome. The average length of treatment in most cases is three weeks. Danny was tested and was found to be seropositive for HIV. Danny had been evaluated using the Brazelton scale from age 3 days and then on a weekly basis to determine his developmental progress. He had difficulty sustaining interaction with the examiner, showing gaze aversion and fussiness. He responded better to inanimate stimuli, the sound of a rattle and tracking a red ball. He also used abnormal posturing, holding his arms in a semi-flexed, extended posture. When held, he exhibited fluctuating tone, with writhing noted. His affect was flat and unemotional. These behaviors continued to be documented up to the second month of life. Also noted during assessments were paling, mottling, and nasal flaring. These are all signs of autonomic disorganization, unusual for an infant two months old.

At three months Danny was still developmentally delayed and was still seropositive for HIV, as a result of his mother's positive status and his sharing her antibodies. It was felt that this baby would continue to be positive and would not revert to seronegative status. His poor response to treatment, the abnormal posturing, tone and flat affect are common markers for HIV in high-risk infants. Danny is still hospitalized at

four months of age and is being monitored developmentally and treated with an experimental drug. Prognosis is poor, and chances are that Danny will develop AIDS. He may be discharged to his mother's care if she is well enough to care for him, or remain in the hospital in a special program for infants with AIDS. There is no cure at present for this disease.

The problems associated with prenatal drug exposure and AIDS in infants are relatively new in our society, and no definitive longitudinal studies are yet available to provide information about long-term developmental outcome. The first noticeable effect when HIV babies contract AIDS is that they lose their ability to play; then language is affected; and finally motor abilities are affected before they die (Ultmann, 1985). Some new drugs are being tested to see if they can reverse the effects of this dreaded disease, but as of now, there is no cure.

CONCLUSION

Prevention is, of course, the answer to all of these problems for high-risk infants. Prematurity can be prevented in many cases by education, good nutrition, and early prenatal care. Education needs to begin early for young people to learn how important it is to maintain their health and care for their bodies before they have babies. Education and publicity can help people understand the catastrophic effects drugs have on the developing fetus and the need to avoid drug taking, especially when pregnant.

There is an urgent need for more well-designed research studies to pinpoint the subtle and long-term effects of PDE and also for greater interagency collaboration. There is also a need to develop good early intervention programs aimed at helping high-risk infants and their families, as well as society, curb the cost of substance abuse—human, emotional, and financial. Other factors leading to the morbidity and mortality of high-risk infants need to be addressed, such as poverty, poor nutrition, and poor or absent prenatal care (LaRue-Jones, 1989). Only then will the incidence of high-risk infants be reduced and the maximal potential of all infants be realized.

Part Two

INFANTS AND TODDLERS

We have learned more about the development of infants and toddlers in the last two decades than in all the years preceding. The idea of very young children as "lumps of clay" to be molded or "blank slates" to be written on is far from the truth. From birth, infants can use all their senses — vision, touch, hearing, smell, taste — and have capabilities to organize incoming information. Although these small wonders don't process and interpret environmental data the same way adults do, the complexity and range of their actions are quite miraculous! Three productive areas of research on infants are the developmental progression of (1) infant abilities, such as language and emotions, (2) attachment behaviors, and (3) social interaction.

Playing an equally important role in our understanding of infant development is a rapidly changing worldview. The number of working families (one single parent or two parents) with infants under 1 year old has more than doubled since 1970. Economic and social factors are sending a majority of new mothers back to the labor force. Children are experiencing a variety of new environments and caregivers at an early age. Parents are playing roles different from those their parents played, and few new parents are familiar with these new models of working and parenting. How will changes in parental attitudes and child-rearing practices affect the behaviors of children? We need to take a closer look at which aspects of the environment influence (positively or negatively) normal development and how we provide and support those that benefit both child and family.

One of the child's most dramatic achievements during the first three years is the development of communication skills. How does this happen? In the first reading, Acredolo and Goodwyn trace the development of symbolic gesturing during a child's second year, illustrating one of the precursors to oral language. The combination of (1) growing cognitive ability that enables a child to symbolically represent a thought or activity and (2) opportunities for information-sharing interactions allow the young child to use and understand our greatest human tool — language. The interaction among cognitive, social, and physical domains is clear, and the role of the adult in modeling and imitating gestures is crucial. Unfortunately, when we attempt to teach young children language in school settings, we often neglect the sensorimotor origins of representation. "Acting out" ideas is crucial to internalizing a new concept and assigning words to it.

Language and thought always garner the attention of researchers, but during the past decade psychologists like Michael Lewis have placed more serious emphasis on studying the development of emotions. Emotions not only temper how we deal with objects or people in any given situation, but also mirror our feelings during interactions. Other people interpret our behaviors based on our emotional signals (sad face, grimace, and so on). A child's emotional responses play a crucial role in the attachment relationship as an indicator of the child's feelings regarding an action or event. Emotional responses also reflect the child's cognitive understanding of the world and his or her relationship to it. For example, anger arises once an infant understands that his or her attempt at overcoming an obstacle is being thwarted. The infant must see a relationship between the cause of frustration and the action needed to overcome it. Michael Lewis has researched the influence of emotional development on cognitive ability and social opportunities including attachment relationships, validating its standing as an important aspect of human development.

Attachment—an enduring emotional tie between two people—has been a key concept in human development for many years. The majority of studies have examined the attachment patterns of mothers and infants. More recently, attachment behaviors have been examined between fathers and infants, and in some cases infants and their supplementary caregivers. The progress and quality of the attachment relationship have been described with regard to interactions between parent and child, the child's responses to separation episodes, and a toddler's level of compliance with adult requests and demands. Ideally, these interactions are reciprocal (have a give-and-take quality), synchronous (each partner is in step with the needs of the other, although clearly the adult carries the burden of maintaining synchrony), and playful (relaxed, warm, and interesting). These seemingly simple behaviors build the foundation for the all-important attachment relationships and the child's ongoing ability to communicate with the outside world.

In the Honig reading and the McBride and DiCero reading, we see how the quality of the attachment relationship, as an ever-present variable, affects responses to separation and compliance demands. Both child and parent play important roles in this relationship. Researchers are challenged to discover who influences whom and when. Each partner brings a history of interactive behaviors with the other. For example, a parent may be continually inconsistent in her responses to her infant—playful at one moment and withdrawn or punitive the next. The infant in this relationship may respond with exaggerated behaviors, withdrawal, or chaotic attempts to read the mother's cues. In addition, the child's level of cognitive development and the mother's feelings about separation episodes may also contribute to the child's distress.

Compliance and control are issues that lie at the forefront of child-rearing theories. Some parents believe they must control their children from the outset, and do not create reciprocal interactions. These parents are often unresponsive to their child's demands and have difficulty interpreting the child's needs and/or distress signals. When the quality of the attachment relationship is controlling and often unaffectionate, the number of child compliance responses plummets. (It's unfortunate that controlling parents believe they are working toward the opposite effect!) Again, the progression of the attachment relationship over time is important. Early cooing and imitative conversations must give way to information sharing and compliance responses with the same reciprocal tone. The end goal is to help children in becoming self-disciplined by establishing inner controls, rather than maintaining constant adult control over a child's actions.

Child care situations introduce children to their peers at an early age. As our understanding of infant capabilities continues to grow, researchers explore new frontiers such as peer interaction between toddlers (see Lauter-Klatell article in this part of the book). Can children as young as 12 or 24 months actually communicate with each other and interact in a purposeful way? If so, what do they do together, and how did they learn to do it? With so many toddlers in group settings, researchers, parents, and professionals need to know what to expect and how this new context will influence development.

There is no question that a majority of the infants and toddlers who we are studying today will be part of "The Day-Care Generation" (Wingert and Kantrowitz, the sixth reading in this part of the book). The effects of having parents who work and of full-time child care on very young children are virtually unknown in the field of human development. What are the most salient changes in children's lives? How will these changes affect long-term outcomes for these children? What can we, as a society, do to mediate negative effects? We must address these questions quickly and completely.

The use and growth of innate and learned abilities of infants and toddlers depend on the quality of each child's interactions with the world. Most important is a child's interaction pattern with one or two significant others—usually his or her parents. Many questions remain about the contributions of nature and nurture and the long-term effects of early experiences. We need to understand which events are crucial to optimal functioning so we can compensate for less than ideal circumstances created by the child's response patterns or the environment. Using what we know about infant and toddler development, we must ensure a good start for every child.

Symbolic Gesturing in Language Development: A Case Study

Linda P. Acredolo and
Susan W. Goodwyn

Sometime between the first and second birthday, children begin to use symbols to communicate. A symbol, for purposes of communication, is a "standardized" graphic representation, a word, or a gesture that more than one person can understand. In the beginning, children explore symbolization in two arenas—pretend play and language. Cognitive shifts in children's thinking as described by Piaget allow children to extend their imitation of gestures and sounds (Stage 5, tertiary circular reactions) to lay the foundation for the use of functional symbols during Stage 6 (invention of new means).

At 12 months, many infants use a hand to wave "bye-bye." They are imitating an adult behavior that will eventually become a standardized symbol the child will use in many situations. By 18 months, many children have invented their own gestures, which become an endearing part of a family's communication system. For the child described in this essay, "sniff-sniff" became a recognizable symbol for flower. A child's spontaneous use of "symbolic signing" not only documents the cognitive ability to use and understand symbols, but also underlines the desire to communicate in a conventional way before the child is verbally proficient. How does a toddler figure out that a symbol, which often has nothing in common with the object it represents, can be used repeatedly to stand for one specific item, action, or feeling?

A fisherman at one end of the lake signals the impressive size of his latest catch to a friend at the other end of the lake by holding his hands out wide. Such behavior by adults is hardly surprising, exemplifying as it does the well-documented fact that gestures provide a way to communicate when vocal communication is difficult or impossible (Ekman and Freisen, 1969). But distance is not the only hindrance to vocal communication, and the use of gestures to compensate is not found only among adults. In their landmark studies of congenitally deaf children, Goldin-Meadow

and Feldman (1975, 1979) found evidence of the spontaneous development of symbolic gestures among six 1½- to 5½-year-old children never exposed to formal sign language training. These behaviors, labeled "characterizing gestures," were used to name and describe objects and to depict actions. For example, two hands flapping up and down was used by at least one child to refer to birds. What these data demonstrate is that, despite their disability, these children clearly had grasped perhaps the most basic principle of language—that a specific pattern within some modality can be used to represent a real-world referent, be it object, action, quality, or concept.

The achievement of symbolic representation is obviously a major milestone in the lives of all children,

L. P. Acredolo and S. W. Goodwyn. (1985). Symbolic gesturing in language development. *Human Development, 28,* 40–49.

hearing or deaf. As Piaget pointed out, the symbolic function lays the foundation for representational behavior in a wide variety of domains, of which language development is only one. The infant who intentionally performs a one-time reenactment of a behavior he or she witnessed in the past (i.e., deferred imitation) is relying on symbolic representation, as is the infant who pretends to be feeding a baby doll, the child who clumsily sketches a house, and the infant who learns to represent objects with verbal names. In all these cases the infant is intentionally allowing a symbolic vehicle to depict a referent. Of these four manifestations of symbolic representation, the one most relevant to language development is, of course, the last one: the process of naming. It was this specific use of the symbolic function that was finding expression in the spontaneous development of idiosyncratic signs in the deaf infants described by Goldin-Meadow and Feldman (1975, 1979). These infants were trying to communicate.

But what about the development of the naming function in normal infants? Is it strictly a vocal phenomenon, or might it be that, at least for some children, there is a time when the desire to communicate and the ability to understand the naming function exceed the capacity to adopt vocal patterns as symbolic vehicles? For such children the use of physical gestures would be a sensible alternative, growing as they would out of the infant's sensorimotor knowledge of the world: Actions *on* objects would be transformed, in the service of naming, into actions *to depict* objects.

The suggestion that this might be the case in the course of normal language development was made most convincingly by Werner and Kaplan (1963) in their now classic book entitled *Symbol Formation*. According to Werner and Kaplan, the use of gestures in this way would constitute an example of the often-quoted developmental dictum that old forms serve new functions. The old form, of course, would be the sensorimotor scheme, and the new function would be naming. What would make sensorimotor schemes seem particularly amenable to use as symbolic vehicles is the fact that an association would already exist between the action and the referent in the experience of the child. At the very least, therefore, memory would be aided. As development proceeds, the argument continues, one can expect a gradual distancing of vehicle from referent, a process Werner and Kaplan call "decontextualization." The end result is a tolerance, and even preference, for truly arbitrary symbols (i.e., words).

As outlined by Werner and Kaplan (1963) the theory certainly makes sense. But is there any evidence to support it? Do normal infants in fact exhibit spontaneous signing behavior in the early stages of language development? A phenomenon described by Bates et al. (1979, 1983) as "gestural naming" might at first glance seem to be a candidate. Yet despite the terminology, these researchers themselves admit that the behaviors they have catalogued might more accurately be labeled "symbolic play." Specific examples illustrate the point. Among the most commonly observed instances were pretending to drink out of an empty container, lifting a toy telephone to one's ear and/or pretending to talk, pretending to eat with a utensil, pretending to feed a baby doll, and hugging a doll or stuffed animal. The basis for referring to all these behaviors as "gestural names" was that (1) most of them reflect the symbolic function in some way (as all pretend behavior does), and (2) the use of an object-appropriate behavior indicates that the infant has recognized the object. But do such behaviors represent naming in the same sense that a word labels an object? Bates et al. (1983) themselves admit that the answer is "no," based on the fact that they never saw such behaviors used communicatively. But the lack of communicative intent is not the only drawback to describing these behaviors as gestural names. We would also suggest that they fail to qualify because (1) there is no consistency in their form from time to time, (2) they usually involve action *on* the object rather than action to *depict* the object, and (3) the motivation behind them often seems to be enjoyment without any intention to name.

The purpose of the present case study is to examine examples of gestural naming—or "symbolic signing," as we will call it—that do meet these criteria. Although admittedly limited to one child, the data are made valuable by the fact that the subject exhibited an impressive number of spontaneous signs, each of which was well documented in terms of its history and relation to vocal development. In this sense the present data take us well beyond the few anecdotal reports of such behavior that currently exist in the literature (e.g., Ferrier, 1978; Perez, 1911, cited by Werner and Kaplan, 1963; Stern and Stern, 1928, cited by Werner and Kaplan, 1963) and point us in some directions for future research.

OVERVIEW

The subject, Kate, was a first-born female of professional parents. Both parents and child had normal hearing. Relatively informal observations of her development were made up until 9 months, when her first word, "kitty," appeared. After that, recordings were made on a weekly basis and continued until her second birthday. The original goal was to document the arrival of each new vocal word. However, after the spontaneous advent of Kate's first gestural name at 12.5 months, information about the acquisition and use of such nonverbal communicative behaviors was also included.

The first sign, a sniff for "flower," occurred in response to a rose bush. While still about 3 feet away from the bush, Kate pointed at it and sniffed. From then on the sign occurred regularly in response to real flowers and pictures (always from a distance) and in answer to various verbal prompts (e.g., "What's that?"). Two weeks later she spontaneously generalized an arm raise gesture for "big" which she had learned in the game "How *big* are you? *So* big!" She continued from this time on to use the gesture to describe items, particularly animals, that impressed her as being especially large.

At this point it became clear to the adults around her that Kate was interested in communicating and capable of learning nonverbal as well as verbal labels. The result was the informal introduction of signs concocted on the spot without reference to any formal sign language system. Simple gestures that captured a relatively unique aspect of an item were used. At the same time she was being taught signs, Kate also continued to generate symbolic gestures on her own. For example, rocking of her torso represented "swings," a downward wave of her hand represented "slide," and alternating waves of both hands represented "ball." In all she accumulated twenty-nine signs between the ages 12.5 and 17.5 months, including 13 (43 percent) with some spontaneous component. Those representing objects were used flexibly to refer to real objects, pictures, and verbal prompts. They occurred frequently, were consistent in form over time, and usually accompanied by pointing and looking to an adult. In other words, they functioned the same way early *verbal* labels do. A complete list of Kate's signing vocabulary, in order of acquisition, is provided in Table 1.

By 17.5 months, Kate's verbal vocabulary had reached 109 words, she had begun to combine words (at 16.75 months), and parental interest in teaching her new signs waned. Many of the signs, however, continued in use for a long time and even entered into her two-word combinations. Both word plus sign and sign plus sign combinations were seen.

FORM OF THE SIGNS

By definition a sign is a fairly simple gesture which represents a real-world referent; it is not the referent itself. A question which naturally arises, therefore, is why a particular gesture is selected as the symbolic vehicle out of the myriad gestures presumably available for use. This question is particularly intriguing in the case of the types of signs under discussion here, because it seems reasonable to assume that the choice of a particular gesture over another by an infant may provide at least some insight into the nature of that child's earliest concepts and/or the strategies by which referents and symbols become paired.

Fundamental to any discussion of the form of signs is the distinction, first introduced by Peirce (1932) and recently applied to infant behavior by Bates (1979), between iconic and indexic signs. Unlike "symbols" which, in the scheme of Peirce (1932), bear no resemblance to their referent and are, therefore, truly arbitrary, both iconic and indexic gestures do mimic something about the real-world object or event being represented. In the case of iconic gestures, the resemblance is to the physical characteristics of the object itself—how the object looks. For example, cupping one's hands to represent "ball" would be an iconic gesture. In contrast, indexic signs are those which depict not the object itself, but another object, action, or quality that frequently co-occurs with the referent. In particular, actions in this case include those that one could do *with* the object. For example, a throwing motion for "ball" would be an indexic sign because throwing is an action frequently associated with a ball. This iconic-indexic distinction should remind those familiar with the existing literature on language development of a second distinction: form versus function as the basis for early concept formation during infancy. If, as some have hypothesized, the perceptual features of an object provide the basis for a child's earliest concept of it, then one might predict the choice of an iconic sign to represent it. On the other hand, if the function of an object, and in particular how the child interacts with it, is the "core" of the child's concept (e.g., Nelson, 1974), then indexic gestures portraying those interactions would be expected to predominate. Analysis of symbolic gestures like those in Kate's repertoire actually allows a particularly clear look into the nature of concept development. Unlike words, which themselves provide no hint about underlying semantics, the development of a sign forces the child to make some choices between form and function and between icons and indices. Let us now turn to Kate's signs and see what insights they provide.

One thing that becomes apparent almost immediately is that in the majority of cases one can predict the specific form of the gesture from knowing the context in which the sign evolved. All of the signs which were directly taught, as well as nine out of the thirteen signs

Table 1. SYMBOLIC SIGNS, IN ORDER OF ACQUISITION, PRODUCED BY CASE STUDY SUBJECT

Signs	Description	Age of Sign Acquisition Months	Source	Number of Words	Age of Word Acquisition Months
Flower	sniff, sniff	12.5	SI	3	20.0
Big	arms raised	13.0	DT/SG	8	17.25
Elephant	finger to nose, lifted	13.5	DT	8	19.75
Anteater	tongue in and out	14.0	DT	13	24.0
Bunny	torso up and down	14.0	DT	13	19.75
Cookie monster	palm to mouth plus smack	14.0	DT	13	20.75
Monkey	hands in armpits, up-down	14.25	DT	13	19.75
Skunk	wrinkled nose plus sniff	14.5	DT	19	24.00
Fish	blow through mouth	14.5	SI	19	20.0
Slide	hand waved downward	14.5	S	19	17.5
Swing	torso back and forth	14.5	S	19	18.25
Ball	both hands waved	14.5	S	19	15.75
Alligator	palms together, open-shut	14.75	DT	19	24.0
Bee	finger plus thumb waved	14.75	DT	19	20.0
Butterfly	hands crossed, fingers waved	14.75	DT	19	24.0
I dunno	shrugs shoulders, hands up	15.0	SI	22	17.25
Hot	waves hand at midline	15.0	SI	22	19.0
Hippo	head back, mouth wide	15.0	DT	22	24.0
Spider	index fingers rubbed	15.0	DT/SG	22	20.0
Bird	arms out, hands flapping	15.0	DT	22	18.5
Turtle	hand around wrist, fist in-out	15.0	DT	22	20.0
Fire	waving of hand	15.0	S	22	23.0
Night-night	head down on shoulder	15.0	S	22	20.0
X-mas tree	fists open-closed	16.0	DT	48	26.0
Mistletoe	kisses	16.0	DT	48	27.0
Scissors	two fingers open-closed	16.0	DT	48	20.0
Berry	"raspberry" motion	16.5	S	48	20.0
Kiss	kiss (at a distance)	16.5	SI	48	21.0
Caterpillar	index finger wiggled	17.5	DT	109	23.0

S = Spontaneous; DT = directly taught; SI = spontaneous imitation of adult action; SG = spontaneous generalization to new context.

with some spontaneous component, were learned or developed within the context of short, frequently repeated routines between parent and child. In each case one specific gesture was consistently modeled by the adult in the presence of the referent object and/or word, and it was inevitably this gesture which the child adopted as the symbolic vehicle. In other words, it was the adult who, consciously or unconsciously, chose the form of the sign. (See Table 2 for a description of how these nine spontaneous signs were acquired.)

That this should be the case for the directly taught signs is hardly surprising. However, the fact that adult modeling within predictable routines was also the basis for most of the spontaneous signs is quite instructive. One thing that it indicates is that, from Kate's perspective, these nine spontaneous signs were indexic rather than iconic in that they represented an action frequently experienced in association with the referent. Even though the adult may have been, con-

sciously or unconsciously, portraying iconic information (e.g., the finger movement for spider in "Eency Weency Spider"), for Kate the relationship was probably indexic.

Implicit in this assumption is also the possibility, indeed Bates (1979) would say *probability*, that for Kate the associations between gestures and referents in these cases were as arbitrary as is commonly held to be the case between words and their referents. In other words, Kate may have adopted these gestures because of the paired-associate relation, not because she understood why the gestures and object were paired in time. According to Bates (1979, p. 52), "Human children are apparently equipped with a tendency . . . to reproduce new acts that are quite arbitrary from their point of view, serving as signs purely by association with particular situations." Unfortunately, it is impossible to determine with certainty whether or not Kate understood the relationships being portrayed at the time a sign was adopted. Our best

Table 2. MANNER OF ACQUISITION OF NINE SIGNS CONTAINING SPONTANEOUS COMPONENTS WHICH WERE ACQUIRED WITHIN ROUTINES

Sign	Description	Manner of Acquisition
Flower	sniff, sniff	mother would routinely pick a flower, sniff it herself, then hand it to Kate to smell
Big	arms raised	learned in context of game, "How big are you? So big!" in which baby is taught to raise arms over head
Fish	blow	mother and child would routinely take turns blowing a fish mobile over Kate's bed
I dunno	palms out	parents routinely modeled it in combination with the question "Where's the —?"
Hot	hand wave	mother routinely waved hand to indicate food was hot
Spider	fingers rubbed	modeled by adults as part of "Eency Weency Spider" song; generalized by Kate to all spiders
Fire and fireplaces	hand wave	generalized from adult modeling for "hot"
Berry	"raspberry"	generalized from word "raspberry" applied to sound made when adults blew on her tummy
Kiss	kiss	routinely modeled in combination with phrase "Give me a kiss"

guess is that in some cases she did and in other cases she did not. It would seem likely, for example, that she did understand the relation between blowing and the movement of the fish mobile (see Table 2). She may also have understood the relation between the act of sniffing and "flower." On the other hand, it is quite unlikely that she understood the relation between the finger movement from "Eency Weency Spider" and real spiders, and we know she did not grasp any meaningful relation between the raspberry sound and real berries, because there was no meaningful relationship to be understood. What she did in this last case was note the association between the sound made by adults on her tummy and the word "raspberry" with which it was labeled. She next noted the association between the similar label "berries" and real berries. She simply cut out the middleman and linked the sound with the real-world object, an act of pure association.

The claim, then, is that nine out of the thirteen spontaneous signs were based upon adult gestures learned in the context of structured routines, and therefore, were indexic in nature. But what about the four remaining spontaneous signs? To our mind these are the most interesting of all, precisely because they did *not* arise out of specific routines and were *not* imitations of adult gestures. These four, "swing," "slide," "ball," and "night-night," were Kate's own inventions, and as such they provide clues to early concept development that the other signs do not. For one thing, they indicate quite clearly that infants are not entirely dependent upon the creation by adults of highly structured situations in which specific gestures are modeled. What they may be dependent upon, however, is the existence of some action which typifies their own interaction with, or experience of, a particular refer-

ent. Thus, for example, Kate chose to rock her torso for "swing" and to pantomime bouncing a ball for "ball." This latter is particularly instructive, given the fact that an iconic gesture portraying the roundness of balls might have been expected instead. Quite clearly the function of these objects and events was given priority over their form, a finding which is certainly consistent with the predictions about early concept development made by Nelson (1974). In fact, even Kate's readiness to pick up gestures observed in structured routines and adopt them as symbolic vehicles can be interpreted as support for the importance of function. After all, each of these routines (e.g., blowing the fish or sniffing a flower) represents the way in which Kate initially interacted with the referents. Thus, Kate's data provide striking evidence that actions on objects can provide building blocks for early naming behavior. This is clearly what Werner and Kaplan (1963) would predict. If one originally knows the world through one's actions on it, it makes sense to use those actions as one's gestural labels whenever possible rather than come up with new gestures to describe perceptual features.

RELATION TO VOCAL LANGUAGE

The relation of symbolic gesturing to vocal language is a multifaceted issue. One question which naturally arises is whether the use of a gestural system impedes or enhances development of the vocal system. In this regard Kate's data are consistent with at least some of the data available on hearing infants purposefully exposed to both ASL and spoken language (e.g., Holmes and Holmes, 1980). Like the infant in that study, Kate's rate of vocal development was faster than average, in fact, considerably faster. See Table 3 for a comparison of Kate's vocal development in comparison to norms provided by Nelson (1973).

Table 3.   MILESTONES OF VOCAL LANGUAGE: KATE VS. SAMPLE OF NELSON (1973)

Milestone	Kate	Nelson's Subjects
First 10 words at age, months	13.5	15.1
First 50 words at age, months	16.0	19.75
10 phrases at age, months	17.25	19.8
Vocabulary at 24 months[a]	752	185.9
MLU at 24 months	4.26	1.91

[a] Nelson's vocabulary figures were estimates based upon tape-recorded sessions; the figure for Kate's vocabulary is based upon an actual listing of all her words by her parents.

Of course, it is impossible to determine the reasons behind what is basically a correlational relationship. While it is possible that the signing behavior enhanced vocal development by promoting communication and/or by providing early opportunities to practice the naming function, it is equally possible that both signing and vocal behaviors in Kate were symptomatic of more rapid than normal development of the underlying symbolic function. These data, however, do argue against the theory that the development of a gestural system inevitably delays vocal language acquisition.

A second question pertaining to the relationship between gestural and vocal language is whether the signs complement or duplicate the vocal vocabulary items. Here again the answer is clear. In each case, a referent object was symbolized by either a sign or a word, not both. Moreover, with two exceptions, the signs disappeared almost immediately after the verbal label was conquered. The two exceptions were "big" and "hot." In these two cases the signs appeared first and were retained and used in conjunction with the words for a time. The predominance of complementary usage in Kate's data is consistent both with what has been noted in infants exposed to ASL and spoken language (Holmes and Holmes, 1980; Prinz and Prinz, 1979) and with the results of studies of bilingual children (Volterra and Taeschner, 1977). Related to this is the observation, apparent from Table 1, that all but one of the signs were acquired before Kate's verbal vocabulary reached 50 words. It would appear that symbolic signs, as Werner and Kaplan (1963) predicted, are definitely a phenomenon of *early* language development.

TWO-WORD STAGE

At 16.25 months of age, Kate uttered her first two-word phrase, "Door bye-bye," in answer to a question about her father's whereabouts. When at least three additional two-word utterances occurred that same day, it became clear that Kate had suddenly figured out something important about language. What makes this development even more striking is the fact that a fifth phrase also occurred that day, but in this case it was Kate's first sign plus sign combination (excluding point plus sign, which had occurred all along). The new rule by which items could be combined was apparently considered by Kate to be equally applicable to both her verbal and gestural vocabularies, a clue, perhaps, to their equivalence in her mind. The event which stimulated this particular phrase was the disappearance from the TV screen of a computer-generated graphics display of flower-like designs which changed form in time to music. Kate had been entranced by the entire segment, and when it was over, she turned in dismay to her mother and signed "flower" (sniff-sniff) plus "I don't know" (shrug). It was clear to the adults around her that she wanted to know where the flowers had gone.

From then on she frequently used signs within phrases, either in combination with words or in combination with each other. The two signs most frequently used in this way, "pivot" signs if you will, were "I don't know" and "big." This capacity for combining signs either with one another or with words is clearly reminiscent of the observation of Goldin-Meadow and Feldman (1975, 1979) of two- and three-sign combinations in their deaf children.

SIGN USAGE

Up to now the discussion of Kate's signs has necessarily been sketchy and analytic. As a consequence, little of the richness of her signing behavior has been conveyed. Simply saying, for example, that the signs were used flexibly to refer to real object and pictures does not communicate exactly how integral a part of her day-to-day life these signs really were. For example, one day Kate accompanied her father to the large lecture hall where he was administering an exam to his undergraduate class. All was fine until a particularly hairy male student entered. Kate immediately began looking to her father, then pointing to the student and making her monkey sign. She continued to do so in such an agitated fashion that she finally had to be removed from the classroom so that the students could concentrate. Episodes like this one have convinced us that Kate was definitely using her signs to communicate. On many occasions she pointed out spiders she wanted removed or scissors that she wanted to play with. A visit to the local zoo or even a toy department was always a fertile ground for signing behavior. Kate's signs enriched her interactions with the adults around her by allowing communication where otherwise none would have existed. Her signs literally doubled her vocabulary at 15 months, thereby doubling the number of items and events about which she could "talk." Thus, although one can certainly debate the theoretical implications of Kate's signing behavior for current theories of language acquisition, there can be no debating the fact that the signs were a positive force in her life and the lives of those around her. For this reason alone they are deserving of our attention.

Emotional Development in the Young Child

Michael Lewis

Is a newborn's smile an expression of joy or evidence of stomach troubles? Can an infant be angry? How can a young child's emotional expressions inform us about his or her needs and capabilities? Michael Lewis charts a progression of affective development from generalized, undifferentiated emotions that are present at birth (that is, interest, general upset, and disgust) to specific feelings such as empathy, envy, pride, and guilt. Clearly demonstrated emotional expressions are an excellent indicator of cognitive ability. For example, in order to experience feelings of shame and guilt a child must have the cognitive ability to understand self in relation to others and to be aware of a standard of behavior against which his or her own actions are evaluated. A child who expresses shame or pride as a result of his or her actions knows that he or she has fallen short of or exceeded a particular standard.

Emotions are a rich and complex dimension of our lives. All children need opportunities to express a full range of emotions in different contexts (sadness when parents leave, or rage when they lose a toy). Variables such as cognitive ability, temperament, and parent-child interactions play a role in the development of emotions and must be considered when assessing a child's functional competence.

This article explores children's emotional development in the first three years of life. The discussion is divided into three parts: (1) the role of emotion in children's lives; (2) the development of emotions over the first three years of life; and (3) individual differences in emotion or emotionality.

ROLE OF EMOTIONS

Darwin viewed emotion as part of the biological apparatus of humans.[1] He saw emotions as a set of action patterns that enable children to behave in specific

M. Lewis. (1989, May). Emotional development in the preschool child. *Pediatric Annals, 18*: 5, 317–326.

ways. For example, anger is not only a set of expressions but includes vocal growling and gross motor patterns, which enable the child to try to overcome a frustrating event. Darwin and those after him elaborated a system of scoring facial expression using the neuromusculature of the face.[2-4] This coding system allows developmental investigators to map out emotion.

Although clinicians recognize the importance of children's motor, sensory, and cognitive development, relatively little attention has been paid to children's emotional life. This is surprising because children's emotions play such a central role, both for the parent and the clinician. Consider, for example, a child who looks at an object, decreases his or her activity level, and smiles. On one hand we consider this an accurate

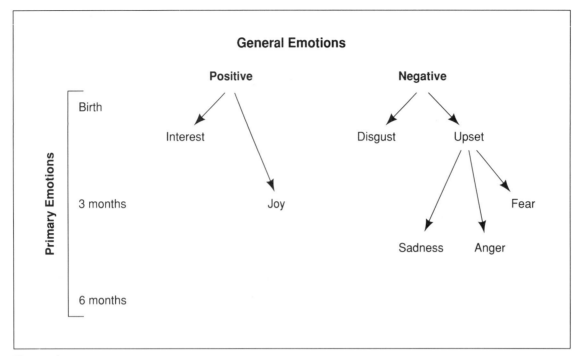

Figure 1.
Emotional Development in the Preschool Child.

marker for central nervous system integrity; that is, the child who is able to attend for long periods is not at risk for subsequent attentional disorders. The same behaviors that index attention also index the emotion of interest. Thus, from a clinical point of view, interest (an emotion) has important implications.

Many other examples of our use of emotions to mark children's ability can be found. Surprise is an emotion that has an important function in assessing development. A child who shows surprise when something unusual occurs has knowledge about the environment. In a series of studies, children as young as 6 months of age were placed in the company of different people.[5,6] We observed that when the infants were placed in the presence of children, the infants smiled and moved toward them. When the infants were placed in the presence of an adult, they showed some wariness (itself an emotion). When the children were placed in the presence of a midget (a small adult), they showed surprise.[6] This emotional response is used as a marker of cognitive ability, as surprise can be interpreted to mean that the infant understands that the midget is an unusual social stimuli. Thus, by 6 months of age the normal infant has already learned something about people.

Emotional behavior as a clinical tool is important. Testing for language acquisition begins with items related to hearing. When testing for hearing loss, children's emotional behavior is assessed. For example, one item in the test asks, "When the infant hears a human voice and sees a human face does it brighten?" This brightening response has to do with changes in emotional expression. The knowledge of children's emotional development aids in the assessment of children's abilities and provides a basis for understanding the normal and dysfunctional development of the young child.

From parents' point of view, the emotional behavior of the child is the first signal parents have to indicate that they are acting appropriately. It is important for the mother to know that the care of a crying child results in the child's smiling. She interprets this signal as an indication that she has solved her child's distress. Careful analysis reveals, therefore, that the emotional life of a child plays a significant role in the ability of adults to determine the child's internal state.

DEVELOPMENT OF EMOTIONS

Emotional differentiation moves from the general to the specific (Figure 1).[7] The first emotions that emerge are the most general; they are characterized as positive or negative emotions. This division between a positive and negative emotion soon undergoes differentiation. Joy and interest become differentiated within the positive side, and fear, sadness, anger, and disgust within the negative side. These emotions are called the *primary emotions*, and all emerge within the first 6 months of life.

In terms of the positive emotions, interest appears present at birth. Joy shows a developmental path. Smiling, at least in the first few months of life, is related to a reflex action, in particular the reduction of tension. Smiling as a reflex has less to do with environmental conditions than with simple physiologic changes. At approximately 2 to 3 months of life, smiling as an emotion emerges (joy appears). The smiling response now becomes tied to social events associated with happy situations. For example, at this time children start to smile at facial stimuli, the presence of soothing sounds, and human-like faces. The smiling response becomes further differentiated over the next 6 to 8 months. Smiling becomes increasingly related to external events of a social nature. By 8 months children no longer smile in response to just any social stimulus, the smiles are now restricted to familiar people and events.[8]

Interest is evident at the beginning of life. Children show interest in response to changes in stimulus intensity and complexity. The interest response grows over the first 6 to 8 months of life but, even in the earliest period, interest expressions are tied to autonomic nervous system responses associated with taking in and processing information.[9]

The early negative emotions are also undifferentiated at birth. General upset (characterized by crying and fretting behavior) is the most prevalent, although the disgust emotion appears soon after birth. Disgust is associated with the expelling of noxious tastes and smells and appears early in the child's life, certainly sometime during the first month. This response is quite different from the general upset or distress response, which is related to any uncomfortable or painful stimulus event.

The three negative emotions—sadness, fear, and anger—appear to differentiate themselves from the general upset emotion. Fear occurs early, although it may be seen as a reflex-like response to certain events, such as falling or loud noises.[10] By 6 months, loss of control evokes fear.[11] Sadness also does not appear to emerge before the third or fourth month of life. Sadness occurs to the loss of social interaction. Anger has still another pattern related to specific cognitive abilities. The anger response is evolutionarily programmed as an attempt to overcome an obstacle. Prior to 4 months, the child is unable to understand the relationship between the cause of a frustration and the response needed to overcome it. For this reason, prior to 4 months frustration does not produce anger, but general distress. At about 4 months and older, frustration produces anger. For example, a 2-month-old when physically restrained by an experimenter will show general distress. However, by 4 to 6 months when this constraint is applied the child shows anger.

In addition to anger, the infant is able to focus attention on the source of frustration. This integration of cognition with emotion to produce anger is only one of the examples of the interface between emotion and cognition.[12]

By the middle of the first year of life, the undifferentiated emotions that existed at birth have become differentiated. By this time *joy* is seen under two conditions: (1) when the child comes in contact with a significant social other, such as the caretaker, mother, father, or other family members; and when the child is able to demonstrate mastery over particular events. *Interest* is observed when the child is confronted with novel events or events that require elaborated attention to be understood. *Fear*, wariness, or suspicion is often observed in situations that involve violation of expectation or being introduced to strange and unusual people. *Sadness* is observed over the loss of the mother or significant other, either if the mother moves away from the child or terminates an interaction. *Anger* emerges in frustrating situations; for example, when the child is unable to reach for something it wishes to obtain. *Disgust* appears early, particularly around noxious tastes and smells.

Secondary emotions emerge after the primary emotions, typically after the first 18 months of life. These emotions are sometimes called *self-conscious emotions*, for their emergence is dependent on the development of a particular important cognitive capacity: self-awareness. Self-awareness or self-consciousness is the human capacity reflected in statements such as "I am," "I am hungry," or "I know you know I am hungry." At about this time the child develops personal pronouns such as "me" or "mine," and the child seems to know it has a specific location in time and space.[13] We often recognize this cognitive milestone as the "terrible twos." It is at this time that the child demonstrates a "will" of its own; parental directions are ignored and the child follows its own desires rather than parental direction.

This cognitive milestone allows for the development of the self-conscious emotions. This large class of emotions requires a self-system, in particular self-awareness.[14] Consider the emotions of embarrassment, empathy, guilt, shame, and pride. They all require a self-system. Exposure of the self, produced by public attention being drawn to the self, elicits embarrassment.[15] Empathy requires that the young child place itself in the role of the other.[16] However, for emotions such as shame, pride, and guilt to be felt the child must not only be self-aware, but a standard of behavior against which the self can evaluate its own action must be understood. Shame and guilt are elicited when the standard of behavior is not attained; the child evaluates its own behavior and finds it lacking.

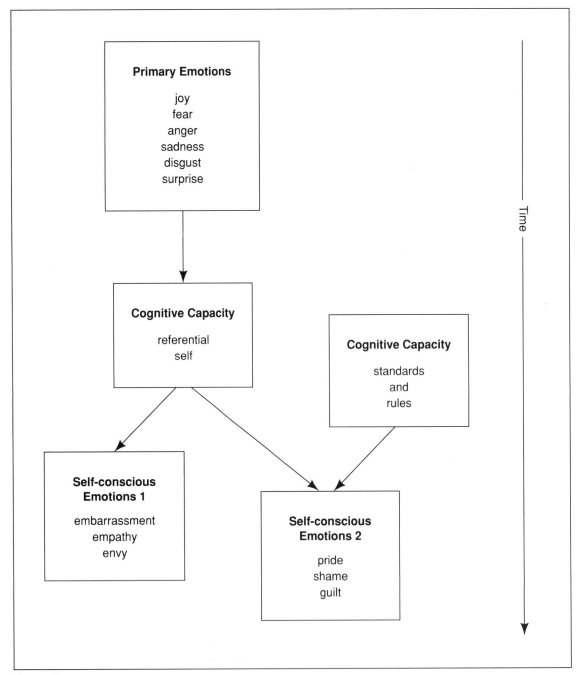

Figure 2.
Model for the Development of Emotions.

In the case of pride, the child evaluates itself against the standard and finds that its behavior exceeds the standard. All of these emotions require that the child has a self-system capable of referring to itself, a self-referential concept called *consciousness*.

Figure 2 describes the general developmental model this article presents.[17] In Stage 1 the primary emotional states appear. In Stage 2, self-consciousness appears. This is the last phase of the self-system, which has been developing during the first two years

of life.[18] The appearance and consolidation of this cognitive skill—consciousness—provides the underpinning of all the secondary emotions.

The first class of self-conscious or secondary emotions to appear includes embarrassment, empathy, and perhaps envy; these emerge during the last half of the second year of life. In addition to developing self-consciousness, the child is learning about other aspects of its social world, including how and when to express emotions as well as particular rules of conduct. The development of these standards is a lifelong process that begins as the child's cognitive representation of social reality emerges.

Because of this cognitive support, a second class of self-conscious emotions—self-conscious evaluative emotions—becomes possible: emotions such as guilt, shame, and pride. Whereas the first class of self-conscious emotions appears by 18 to 24 months, the self-conscious evaluative emotions appear later because more cognitive capacity is required. This second class of self-conscious emotions emerges sometime after the second half of the third year of life.

The development of these primary and secondary emotions takes place in the first three years of life. The process begins with the undifferentiated emotions of pleasure and pain. Reorganization and differentiation ultimately lead to the complex emotions that are species specific. Their emergence involves the socialization of standards and rules, the cognitive capacities to recognize the nature of environmental stimuli, and the development of self-consciousness. Failure in the emergence of any of these capacities results in distortion of the developmental process. Thus, failures of self-consciousness in autistic children result in their inability to develop the self-conscious evaluative emotions.

INDIVIDUAL DIFFERENCES

The progression of the normal sequence of emotional development is dependent on a complex set of variables. Individual differences in rate of development as well as in intensity of expression are observed by parents and clinicians. Differences in individual rates of emotional development are dependent on the child's cognitive capacities. In terms of anger for example (one of the primary emotions), children who are able to acquire an understanding of the means to achieve a particular goal are more likely to express this emotion earlier than children who have not obtained this cognitive milestone. Likewise children who have not attained a mental age of 15 or 18 months are unlikely to develop self-consciousness.[18]

The rate at which this cognitive capacity is ac-

quired affects all the emotions associated with it. Down's syndrome children who have not attained a mental age of 15 to 18 months do not show self-consciousness and therefore lack self-conscious emotions.[18] Autistic children also show a delay in self-consciousness and, therefore, a delay in secondary emotion development. Individual differences in the parent-child relationship may also affect emotional development.[19,20] How parents help regulate their child's expressive behavior can lead to differential emotions.

Individual differences in the intensity of emotional expression also have been studied under the general category of temperament, a topic first introduced and made popular by Thomas and Chess[21] and by Carey.[22] Individual differences in temperament appear to be stable over the first few months of life.[23] Temperament relates to three aspects of a child's emotional response to stimulation: (1) level of threshold, (2) ease of dampening the response once it occurs, and (3) patterns of habituation to repeated exposure.[24] Individual differences in temperament are important for both parents and clinicians. Temperament acts on the parent-child interaction.[25] A child with a difficult temperament is most likely to cause parent-child interactive problems, as the parent is unable to soothe the child. Parents of these children are more likely to appear at the pediatrician's office for help. In general, differences in children's emotionality are related to particular features of temperament and are best understood in that context.

CONCLUSION

Emotional development in the [young] child has received relatively little attention in both the psychological and pediatric literature; in part, because the focus has been on sensory, motor, and cognitive development. Nevertheless, the emotional life of a child is important. A child's emotions are an evolving developmental system progressing from an undifferentiated to a highly differentiated state. This system interacts with other domains of competence and bears upon the child's social life.

Compliance, Control, and Discipline

Alice Honig

"Why doesn't my child do what I say? Why won't he (or she) cooperate? How can I control my child's behavior?" Parents (and caregivers) ask these questions throughout the course of a child's development. But they are particularly poignant when the child is a toddler or preschooler and learning how to balance his or her newfound autonomy with the need to comply with adult wishes.

Ideally, the reciprocity between parent and child observed during infancy should continue through toddlerhood. Firm, consistent limits, as well as responsiveness to a child's distress signals, are also required. A parent's desire to set limits and model positive social behaviors often clashes with the child's need to experiment with the environment and resist external demands. Toddlerhood demands a lot of parents and children.

Some parents feel a strong need to "control" their child early. They often use command prohibitions ("Don't touch that!") or physical actions to do so. Research, however, documents that strategies such as positive suggestions (telling the children what to do, rather than what not to do), indirect controls ("Can you put the blocks on the shelf?"), a warm and affectionate tone of voice, action controls (physically guiding the child to the lunch table), and physical assistance by adults are most likely to elicit compliance in young children. Parenting strategies are powerful predictors of compliance and independent control of one's actions. The goal of discipline is the child's ability to exercise internal self-control—not forced compliance.

"Time for lunch," called Mama as she entered 20-month-old Jason's playroom. Jason clutched his ball and ran waddling and laughing to the other side of the room, repeating, "No, no, no, no, no!" Mama stood calmly and pretended to sniff the air. "Mmmm. Hamburger. Yum, yum. Mmmm carrots, yummy carrots!" she remarked with relish. Jason stopped, turned, and galloped past her and into the kitchen. Climbing into his high chair near the table, Jason eagerly called, "Meat, mama, meat!"

. . .

Mr. Sims was pouring milk into the dry cereal bowls set for each of the group of children ready for breakfast. "No milk for me," announced Shana, shaking her head vigorously to reinforce her request. "OK, Shana," agreed Mr. Sims, as he skipped her bowl and poured milk for the other children. Shana struggled with her dry cereal. Then she looked up, just as Mr. Sims was walking back toward the refrigerator,

and announced, "Milk, now, Mr. Sims." He walked back with a smile and poured the milk cheerfully.

Both Jason and Shana are cooperative children. They follow safety rules and play with others without interfering with their rights. But toddlers and young preschoolers often just *need* to say no. During the second and third years of life, children learn how to assert their own wishes and express their uniqueness. A certain amount of *no* saying will punctuate the con-

A. S. Honig. (1985, Jan.). Compliance, control, and discipline. *Young Children, 90* (2), 50–58. (Portions of the original article have been deleted.)

versations of fairly cooperative children. As adults, we can accept their assertions and appreciate the self that is struggling to express its own desires and coordinate those desires with others' wishes.

ORIGINS OF COMPLIANCE

One of the most perplexing problems for parents and teachers is how to help infants, toddlers, and preschoolers, who are already struggling to master locomotion and language skills, also to master compliance and cooperation in a variety of settings. *Choosing discipline techniques wisely depends on understanding the development of compliance.* All adults who care for young children, therefore, must understand how compliance, and ultimately self-control (internalized compliance), emerge.

What Is Compliance?

Compliance refers to an immediate and appropriate response by the child to an adult's request. A *control technique*, on the other hand, refers to all attempts to change the course of a child's activity (Schaffer and Crook, 1980).

How does compliance emerge? What adult actions promote compliance? How is compliance related to the situation? How can adults promote children's inner controls?

The earliest compliance that infants show is their self-comforting behavior in response to a loving adult's request to stop crying. A very young infant cuddled in an adult's arms hears a soothing voice and tries to focus on the adult's eyes—and quiets down. Infants may put their fists or thumbs into their mouths and thus find another way to comply with the request for self-soothing.

Babies are born with built-in biological skills for learning to comply. Then during the first year of life, effective adult-infant interactions build reciprocal, mutually satisfying chains of compliance in feeding, soothing, diapering, gazing, and play interactions (Honig, 1982a). These often wordless communication games enhance later patterns of mutual cooperation.

> Heather's mother was talking on the phone while her 9-month-old daughter was playing with scraps of paper on the coffee table 12 feet away. Heather crumpled one piece of paper into a small ball, looked at her mother, and offered the ball to her. Heather's mother continued to talk on the phone but glanced at her daughter's gift. Then she took the ball of paper from her daughter, held it a moment, and gave it back. Heather took the ball of paper, put it in her mouth for a few seconds, and then again handed it to her mother. During the next three

> minutes, Heather sustained contact with her mother, who remained talking on the telephone, through the exchange of a crumpled, and increasingly wet, ball of paper. (Ziajka, 1981, p. 67)

The development of social cooperation is necessarily, then, a joint enterprise of adult and child (Schaffer, 1984).

Piagetian theory implies that preschool children, at a preoperational level of thinking, cannot understand the rationale behind cooperative social skills. Yet research on prosocial behavior shows that young infants *are* capable of empathic responses to others (Honig, 1982b). Many 1-year-olds are quite cooperative in holding out an arm for dressing, or when asked, can stand *fairly* still to have their overalls snapped.

Between 9 and 12 months, infants comply with simple requests such as "Come" or "Show me the doggie in the book." Hay and Rheingold (1983) describe an 18-month-old boy who said, "Night, night, bear" as he put his bear in a cradle, covered it with a blanket, and kissed it. Babies learn to imitate kind, helpful adult behavior.

These researchers also observed 18-, 24-, and 30-month-old children either with their mothers or fathers in a laboratory suite of homey rooms. All of the children joined in to cooperate in some of the experimental tasks set by the parents, such as putting away groceries, sweeping up scraps, and folding laundry. "On the average, parents were assisted by the 18-month-olds on 63 percent, by the 24-month-olds on 78 percent and by the 30-month-olds on 89 percent of the tasks" (Hay and Rheingold, 1983, p. 83). And the children responded to parental requests for help with alacrity. They even helped an *unfamiliar* adult to shelve groceries! Their cooperative intentions were often expressed with statements such as "I gonna clean up mess."

Research on moral development reveals that a large majority of children understand the need for controls and discipline between the ages of 4 and 5½. When young children, regardless of age, sex, or social class, were presented with stories of non-cooperative children (who were throwing sand, refusing to give a toy back, or were rude to grandmother), they judged that the mother was "good" (rather than "not good") when she told the child to stop the misbehavior (Siegal and Rablin, 1982). Even very young children seem to realize that people must mutually get along with each other so that their needs are fairly considered.

ADULT LANGUAGE AND COMPLIANCE

Compliance thus is an early-appearing social skill. Young children are so primed to comply that they will comply if they understand the *verb* of a request—even though the words of the request are scrambled! Two- and 3-year-olds complied with their mother's request in 90 percent of normal word order requests ("Give the ball to Mommy"), 81.5 percent of misplaced word order requests ("Can the you throw ball?"), and 79.5 percent of scrambled word order requests ("You how jump me show") (Wetstone and Friedlander, 1973).

In another study, children complied with *implicit* verbal requests ("I can't wash your hands unless you put your Teddy down") as well as explicit requests (Holzman, 1974).

SECURE ATTACHMENT: PREDICTOR OF COMPLIANCE

Much research in the past decade confirms the critical importance of secure infant-mother attachment for the development of compliance. Secure attachment is fostered by a positively responsive parent who

- is aware of and accurately interprets infant distress signals

- responds to distress signals promptly and effectively to comfort the baby

- has tender and gentle holding and feeding patterns (Ainsworth, Bell, and Stayton, 1971).

Stayton, Hogan, and Ainsworth (1971) studied compliance in the last quarter of the first year of life through in-home naturalistic observations of 25 middle-class mothers and their babies every three weeks for four hours. Three scales were devised to assess the degree of harmony in the mother-infant interaction: sensitivity-insensitivity, acceptance-rejection, and cooperation-interference.

Insensitive mothers are geared almost exclusively to their own wishes, moods, and activities. They tend to their babies only when they so desire, so their actions are rarely contingent upon the baby's signals. The accepting mother resolves conflicting or negative feelings about temporary restrictions that the baby may put on her activities, and accepts the responsibility for care.

> The cooperative mother avoids imposing her will on the baby but, rather, arranges the environment and her schedule so as to minimize any need to interrupt or control him (or her).... The interfering mother... seems to assume that she has a perfect right to do with him what she wishes, imposing her will on his, shaping him to her standards, and interrupting him arbitrarily without regard to his moods, wishes, or activity-in-progress. (Stayton, Hogan, and Ainsworth, 1971, p. 1061)

Infant compliance to commands such as "No, no!" or "Come here" was strongly and positively related to all three indicators of the quality of the mother-infant relationship. Thus, the findings of this study suggest that children are more likely to obey parental signals if they have a positive harmonious affectional relationship with their parents. Additionally, those babies who showed a progression toward self-control such as creeping toward a forbidden object and then not touching it (20 percent), had accepting, cooperative mothers who permitted their babies more floor freedom.

CHILD-REARING STYLE AND COMPLIANCE

Parental child-rearing styles are related to the level and quality of child compliance in the early years. Bishop (1951) was one of the earliest investigators to show that when mothers were more nonaccepting and directive with their 3- to 6-year-old children, then the children were more noncooperative and negative in play with their mother.

· · ·

McLaughlin (1983) videotaped 1½-, 2½-, and 3½-year-olds at home with toys and with each parent. Parents told their children what to do far more often than what not to do. For mothers, 61 percent of all controls were action controls and 30 percent were attention controls. Fathers used 72 percent action controls, which is consistent with the idea that fathers are more action-oriented with young children than are mothers.

Compliance was greater for attention-controls. The 3½-year-olds showed the most compliance. They also were *more compliant in response to indirect controls* (in the form of questions or declaratives) than they were for direct controls in the imperative form. The 1½-year-olds showed a nonsignificant tendency to comply more to direct (52 percent) than indirect controls (45 percent). Compliance was present more when there were also nonverbal supports to help the children obey.

How did parents handle noncompliance? One strategy was to repeat the utterance, which fathers did more than mothers. Repeats were higher for the youngest group. For mothers and fathers, the mean eventual compliance rate in episodes of repeating controls were 43 percent and 41 percent respectively. The rate was highest for 3½-year-olds (53 percent).

McLaughlin feels that when parents say "Look at the bear" or "Open the book" they are trying to keep a child attentive to objects and keep an interaction going rather than to stay in command, and these positive techniques work.

· · ·

SECURE ATTACHMENT, COMPLIANCE, AND PROBLEM SOLVING: THE MAGIC TRIO

Mahler's and Erikson's theories of toddler development both predict that the second and third years of life will reflect a struggle to develop autonomy and independent initiatives. Both predict that a child with a secure attachment will later exhibit more competence, flexibility in problem solving, and resourceful ability to recruit adult help when needed.

Matas, Arend, and Sroufe (1978) provide powerful evidence that the quality of early attachment is related to later competence *and* toddler cooperation with parents. Initially, forty-eight female infants were classified with the Ainsworth strange situation* paradigm as securely, avoidantly, or ambivalently attached. Then, at 24 months, toddlers returned to the laboratory for a ten-minute free play period, a six-minute clean-up period, and problem-solving tasks, some of which were too hard for a toddler to solve alone.

When mothers asked them to clean up after play, securely attached toddlers showed as much typical opposition as their insecurely attached peers, but their behavior was radically different during the problem-solving tasks.

Compliance with mother's requests during problem-solving tasks was significantly higher (57 percent) for the securely attached toddlers than for the insecurely attached (39.5 percent). Securely attached toddlers ignored the mother less. They were significantly more enthusiastic about solving the problems, spent less time away from task, exhibited fewer frustration behaviors, and were lower on saying "no," crying, and whining. They tried to cooperate with their mothers' suggestions for solving the problems.

Temperament was not related to toddler compliance, nor was general intelligence. *Secure attachment allowed toddlers to use mother as a positive resource when help was needed and there were important problems to solve.* Helpful mothers had more competent toddlers.

The mother's quality of assistance relates more specifically to the cognitive aspect of second-year adaptation.

. . . This requires sensitivity to the child's cognitive, perceptual-motor and information-processing skills—aspects of more autonomous behavior. . . . Simply telling the child what to do, or overly controlling him, [or her] was not seen as good quality assistance. The mother of a 2-year-old demonstrates her sensitivity . . . by giving the minimal assistance needed to keep the child working and directed at the problem solution without solving it for him and by helping her child see the relationship between actions required to solve the problem. (Matas, Arend, and Sroufe, 1978, p. 555)

Thus, the quality of adult helpfulness can facilitate toddler compliance at developmentally difficult tasks.

In a subsequent study, Sroufe (1979) found that

securely attached infants showed a particular pattern of behavior across tasks. When they came to [a] more challenging . . . problem, they maintained their involvement but sought more help. They increased their compliance and decreased their opposition. Their mothers, in turn, maintained a high level of support and offered more directives. . . . The resistant, difficult-to-settle group, on the other hand, fell apart completely: They became increasingly oppositional, highly frustrated, angry, and distressed, even though they did increase their help seeking. Their mothers increased their directives, but the quality of their assistance decreased markedly. . . . [Avoidant infants] made little adjustment to the harder problem. (p. 840)

Ego resiliency refers to flexibility of controls. Overcontrolled children are rigid, not spontaneous; undercontrolled children have difficulty in controlling impulses and cannot delay gratification. At 5 years of age, the children who had earlier been classified as secure in Sroufe's study were described by their teachers as highly ego resilient, self-reliant, and moderate in self-control. Children who had been avoidant and resistant babies were at 5 years of age significantly less resilient, and were respectively more overcontrolled and undercontrolled. Thus, *self-control,* the ultimate goal of socialization for cooperation in homes and classrooms, *has been found to be significantly linked to early attachment patterns.*

. . .

---

*The strange situation consists of three 8-minute episodes where a baby is in a playroom with toys and mother. Two brief separations from and reunions with mother are staged. In one, the baby is left alone with the stranger. In the second, the baby is left alone. Secure attachment is scored when a baby actively greets mother and seeks and accepts physical contact and comfort on reunion, and can then settle down from distress and resume play with toys. Insecure babies are classified as either avoidant (showing less separation protest and behaving less positively to being held and more negatively to being put down) or ambivalent (very distressed by separation, resistant to comfort, anxious and unable to play well on mother's return).

COMPLIANCE AS A FUNCTION OF TIMING AND SETTING

Child compliance may well be related to the particular circumstances under which adults are trying to get children to obey. Asking a child to come in from a playground just before her long-awaited turn to ride the new tricycle will probably result in less compliance than if the request were made just after the ride.

In a Laboratory Playroom

Control techniques adopted by mothers of 15- and 24-month-olds in a laboratory play situation were timed in such a way that the probability of eliciting requested actions from toddlers was high (Schaffer and Crook, 1979). Generally, the mothers used controls in sequences. Thus, action controls were used at the optimal moment—*after* the mother had used attention controls and had ensured that the toddler's attention was properly focused. Each mother in the playroom had been instructed to make sure that her toddler played with each of eight suitable toys. The mothers of younger toddlers spent one-half their time on attention-focusing devices. Mothers of 2-year-olds spent one-quarter of their time this way. Mothers said, "Look," "See," or asked "Where is...?" to focus toddler attention. When the mothers asked for actions, they fully specified the behavior they wanted: "Can you spin the top?" "Now put on the orange ring."

Fewer than 6 percent of the mothers' utterances were prohibitions. These mothers were far more likely to propose a new activity rather than directly prohibit a current one. They used distractions frequently. These toddlers were quite compliant.

In the Supermarket

The supermarket is a setting in which child management techniques are sometimes inadequate to what Holden (1983) calls the "triple threat to a mother: there is food shopping to be done, a child to be managed who is afforded a diverse array of enticing objects, and all the while both mother and child are in the public eye" (p. 234).

Holden observed 24 mother-child dyads (mean child age 31.5 months) on two trips to a supermarket and also interviewed the mothers. Requests for objects (seen as undesirable interruptions to the mother) or gross motor behaviors (such as standing up in the shopping cart) were coded as *child elicitors*. The child was considered to have been compliant with maternal responses to these elicitors if the child terminated an elicitor within 20 seconds following the mother's response.

Mothers refused children's requests 86 percent of the time, usually by responding with reasons or with power assertions. Generally, children complied (69 percent). Power assertion and reasons were used to gain compliance more (about 70 percent) when children acted out motorically rather than made requests.

After a request, the probability of child compliance depended on the type of maternal response. If mothers gave reasons or distracted the child, compliance was 68 percent. Compliance after power asser-

tion was 54 percent. Ignoring or just acknowledging the child led to only 25 percent compliance. Mothers who consented to the elicitor received compliance 92 percent of the time.

All of these mothers employed proactive controls such as initiating conversations with the child or providing the child with a cracker or toy to keep her or him content. *Proactive controls avoided power battles by engaging the child's attention.*

Holden notes that with proactive controls

a child learns what is acceptable behavior in the supermarket under the mother's direction....The mother, through indicating what behavior is appropriate, facilitates the process of translating the child's view of the supermarket from a place where there are tempting items to play with to one where merchandise is purchased....Mothers often discuss which items to buy and why....[They] may be socializing their children into concordant relationships. (p. 239)

Thus, by using disciplinary techniques that reduce the frequency of conflicts in a shopping situation, parents may teach their young children a complying rather than a test-the-parent orientation.

These data are in strong agreement with Hoffman's (1975) position that *inductive discipline works best.*

Induction includes techniques in which the parent gives explanations or reasons for requiring the child to change...behavior. Examples are pointing out the physical requirements of the situation or the harmful consequences to the child's behavior for himself or others. (Hoffman, 1970, p. 286)

A much less effective discipline technique is *power assertion*, which includes physical punishment, deprivation of material objects or privileges, and use of force or love withdrawal, such as refusing to speak to the child. Hoffman notes that love withdrawal, even though it is not a physical threat to the child, is typically more prolonged and has a highly punitive quality. "It may be...devastating emotionally...because it poses the ultimate threat of abandonment or separation" (p. 285).

In reviewing research studies, Hoffman notes that the "frequent use of power assertion by the mother is associated with weak moral development" (p. 292) quite strongly, whereas induction discipline and affection are associated with advanced moral development.

In the Home

In an in-home study of the long-term effects of power assertion, the most positive predictors of child compliance were mother's consistent enforcement of rules, amount of play with the child, and use of psychological rewards and reasoning (Lytton, 1980). Maternal use of psychological punishment and father's physical punishment were negatively associated with compliance. These findings support Hoffman's prediction that inductive methods are more likely to achieve compliance than are power assertion techniques.

Eimer, Mancuso, and Lehrer (1981) point out that if the parent consistently makes demands that are too difficult or incongruous with the cognitive capacities of the child, then quite possibly the child will not want to be around the parent. This avoidance behavior is likely to be interpreted as noncompliance, sneakiness, or unresponsivity to adult controls. The authors suggest that teachers ask the noncompliant child to think about her or his conception of a rule-related situation in a new way. "I want you to tell me a story. Tell me the story of what I asked you to do. Then tell me what you did. And tell me why I asked you to do what I asked" (p. 10).

Separation: Maternal and Child Perspectives

Susan L. McBride and Kimbell DiCero

If you have ever worked in a child care center or provided home care for very young children, you have most likely witnessed a parent who had difficulty leaving his or her child, and a child who cried vigorously when the parent did leave. Parent and child were experiencing separation distress. With approximately 50 percent of our nation's youngest children (6 weeks to 3 years) in supplementary child care, this type of episode occurs many times each day. Why do some children become distressed when their parents leave them or return? How do parents feel when they must leave their crying child in the arms of another? Do the attitudes and feelings of parents affect how the child will respond to separation? These are new questions for human development researchers.

Researchers have traditionally studied separation distress as a characteristic of a child's attachment to his or her mother. They focused on the child's response (such as crying, going to door, continuing to play) at the time of separation. In the next article, McBride and DiCero broaden the context of the separation event to include both child and maternal perspectives. Response to a separation episode most likely includes several variables—child's temperament, parent's feelings and attitudes, quality of the attachment between parent and child, and the child's developmental level. Due to the realities of today's families, the most important question to ask is "How can we support both parents and children during difficult separations and reunions?"

Recent estimates are that over 50 percent of mothers of infants are participating in full or part-time employment outside of the home (Hayghe, 1986). If current trends continue, two-thirds of preschool children will have employed mothers by 1995 (Hofferth and Phillips, 1987). The daily separations that these mothers and young children experience often cause unhappy moments for both the mother and the child. When her child cries, at the time of departure or when she returns, a mother may question whether she is doing the best thing for herself or for her child. Why are these short-term separations so uncomfortable for some children at certain ages? Why do mothers feel sad or worry when they are away from their young children? How can parents and caregivers facilitate these parent-child separations?

Until recently, the focus of both research and practice regarding parent-child separations has been on how the *child* is adjusting to care by someone other than the parents and on the effect of separation on the child's development. For some reason, there has been little concern about the implications of mother-infant separations from the *mother's* perspective. Similarly, there has been little attention on the direct or indirect effect that mothers' feelings about separation may have on the child or the mother-infant relationship. This article will explore the separation experience from

S. L. McBride, and K. DiCero. (1990). Separation: Maternal and child perspectives. Original manuscript, Iowa State University, Ames, Iowa. Susan L. McBride, Ph.D. is an Associate Professor, Department of Human Development and Family Studies, Iowa State University, Ames, Iowa. Kimbell DiCero, M.S. is Director of the Adolescent Parents and Children's Center, Jamaica Plain, Massachusetts.

both the perspective of the child and the mother.* Suggestions for parents and caregivers for facilitating mother-infant separations will also be discussed.

CHILD'S PERSPECTIVE

Why do some young children find short-term separations from their parents and contact with strangers distressful? Actually, distress related to separation is part of a normal developmental process and related to the child's level of cognitive development. The following discussion outlines the developmental process of separation-related behavior in the first two years.

As children move through infancy and toddlerhood, their understanding of the world and their relationships with others change. The young baby's first relationship with the parent is characterized by dependence on the parent for attending to physical needs and responding sensitively to the baby's emotional states. Cognitively, the child is unable to understand him- or herself as separate from the parent before 3 months of age. This symbiotic relationship enables the baby to survive and grow (Mahler, Pine, and Bergman, 1975). As long as their needs are met by other caregivers, these young infants do not usually show overt signs of distress when separated from a parent.

Between 3 and 8 months of age, the child's undifferentiated response to strangers may change to one of wariness. The baby has developed cognitive skills that allow him or her to begin visually comparing familiar caregivers with strangers and to discriminate between them. If an unfamiliar adult approaches the child, the infant may wrinkle his or her brow and look back and forth between the mother and the stranger. After a few seconds, the baby may either bury his or her head in his mother's shoulder or begin to cry. This recognition is an early indication of the child's development of a separate sense of self (Kagan, 1984).

By 7 to 12 months of age, many children begin to show more obvious distress when separated from the parent. The child has now developed the cognitive ability to hold a concept (in this case, the parent) in his or her memory. When separated from the parent, the baby knows that the parent exists and that the caregiver does not match the representation of the parent held in the child's memory. The baby becomes uncertain and uncomfortable with this experience of

cognitive dissonance. As a result, he or she expresses distress and indicates a desire for the parent to return (Kagan, 1984).

As the child becomes more comfortable with his or her new cognitive awareness (12–15 months), the feelings of anxiety may fade back to wariness as the child begins to use the representation of the parent held in memory to soothe him- or herself. The child is also absorbed with practicing new motor skills and enjoying emerging autonomy (Mahler et al., 1975).

In later toddlerhood (18–24 months), however, stranger anxiety and separation distress may again appear. The child is developing skills to manage the environment independently through exploration and problem solving. These expanded cognitive abilities of the child open a new range of possibilities. The mobile toddler moves away from the parent to develop and practice new skills, yet often returns to the parent to refuel and to integrate new learning. Separation distress and stranger anxiety may occur when a child feels stressed by all the new information. At these times, he or she is now aware of and wants the safe, secure shelter of the one-to-one relationship with the parent. The toddler is also more aware of the relationship with the parent and begins to develop language concepts to name and describe it: "Where's Mommy?" or "I want to go with you" (Mahler et al., 1975).

It is important to note that although separation distress is age-dependent and occurs cross-culturally (Kotelchuck, 1972; Lester et al., 1974), not all children display overt negative signs of distress (crying, clinging) at separation from their parent. Spelke and associates (1973) note that the proportion of children 8–18 months of age who display distress at separation ranges between 20 and 60 percent. Children also display a range of individual differences in the type and intensity of responses to separation and strangers. These individual differences may be a result of the child's individual temperament (Kagan, 1984) or particular style of coping. A baby who is temperamentally easy may be able to cope more smoothly with the challenges and stress that separations and strangers provide, than a baby who is easily distressed and reacts intensely to every change in his or her environment. Parents' behavior and reactions during separations may also influence how safe the baby feels in the situation and how supported the baby feels when beginning to explore the environment in the presence of a "new" person. Field and associates (1984) found that a number of parent behaviors were related to the level of the child's distress at separation. Specifically, verbal explanation by the parent decreased the child's distress during separation, while distracting the child, latency to leave (delaying departure), and "sneaking

---

*We have limited this discussion to mothers, not because we believe that fathers do not experience separation anxiety with their infants, but because the origins for mothers and fathers may be different and separation may be a different experience for each.

out of the room" increased the level of the child's distress at separation.

In summary, a child's level of cognitive development dictates the attribution of meaning of separation from a parent and thus influences the child's display of distress. Responses of individual children are influenced by the nature of the child's personality and may be affected by parental behavior. Because the dyad experiences the separation, not just the child, it is reasonable to assume that mothers are also interpreting the separation situation and making adjustments. How do mothers feel about leaving their small infants? Do their reactions to these situations affect outcomes for their infants?

MOTHER'S PERSPECTIVE

When mothers are asked how they feel about leaving their young children for the purpose of employment or recreation, they report a wide range of responses. Although some women are not concerned about leaving their children in the care of others and do it matter-of-factly, others dread the thought of leaving the children and often change their plans to avoid having to do so. These various responses are evidence of a phenomenon described by Hock (1984) as maternal separation anxiety and is defined as an unpleasant emotional state tied to the separation experience. Levels of maternal separation anxiety are evidenced by mother's expressions of worry, sadness, and guilt as measured by a questionnaire, the Maternal Separation Anxiety Scale, or MSAS (Hock, McBride, and Gnezda, 1989).

The concern of mothers when separated from their young children is not, of course, related to a cognitive growth spurt in the parent! Both role-related aspects of the mother's culture, and specific characteristics of mothers and their children, help determine mothers' perceptions of separation events. The following discussion briefly highlights factors that may influence levels of maternal separation anxiety.

Sociocultural beliefs and practices about the role of the mother are major determinants of individual differences in maternal perspectives on separation. The degree to which mother-infant separation is considered acceptable is influenced by the ethnic and cultural context that sets the standards and provides guidelines for mother-infant separations (Frankel and Roer-Bornstein, 1982). In the United States, there is reason to believe that even though the majority of mothers of young children now hold paying jobs, many Americans are ambivalent, even critical, of employed mothers. In a recent survey of the attitudes of working men and women, 63 percent of the men and 52 percent of the women agreed that having a mother who works is

bad for children under 6 years of age (Public Agenda Foundation, 1983). Thus, despite the women's movement, our society has strong beliefs that families and young children suffer when mothers of young children work outside of the home. Given the high percentage (over 50 percent) of employed mothers with a child under 1 year, many women are working in a climate of criticism and doubt. The task of combining employment and motherhood is complex, and how well a family is able to do this may depend on a mother's feelings about balancing career and motherhood.

In a study of how older, well-educated mothers come to terms with balancing maternal and career roles over the first year of motherhood, DeMeis, Hock, and McBride (1986) found that maternal separation anxiety is related to both the mother's employment preference and actual employment status. Over the first year, the level of maternal separation anxiety expressed by employment preference mothers decreased, while the scores of mothers preferring to be home did not. By the end of the first year, those mothers who preferred to be at home, but were employed, expressed significantly less separation anxiety than mothers who preferred to be home and actually were at home. Thus work preference is a strong indicator of maternal separation anxiety, but after the first year levels of maternal separation anxiety may adjust to be consistent with actual work status. It is likely that those mothers preferring to be home became more convinced over time that separation for the purpose of employment is undesirable. For those who were employed, either the employment experience reduced levels of maternal anxiety or mothers repressed their anxiety to reduce dissonance between their preference and actual behavior. This study highlights the relationship between a psychologically salient factor such as maternal preference to work and the mother's actual work status.

Other characteristics of the mother and the child have also been found to influence maternal separation anxiety. McBride and Belsky (1988) found that mothers who were more interpersonally sensitive expressed greater levels of separation concerns. Most likely this is because they are more empathic to the feelings of their babies. In terms of characteristics of children, mothers of secondborns have expressed less anxiety with the second child than they did with the first (Pitzer, 1985). Mothers of children with colic (Humphry, 1985) and more difficult temperaments (McBride and Belsky, 1988) have expressed higher levels of maternal separation anxiety. Given that these studies confirm that mothers also have specific concerns related to separation, what is the effect of mothers' separation anxiety on their children or the mother-child relationship?

Several studies give us some information about this relationship between mothers' feelings and children's reactions to separation. In an early study, Hock and Clinger (1981) found maternal attitudes about separation (assessed in an interview when the infants were 8 months old) related to the infant's style of coping during a separation experience in a lab at 12 months. Infants of mothers who were most concerned about their babies' being distressed during the separation and believed that only they could meet their babies' needs, had infants who, indeed, were the most distressed at separation and were most likely not to be able to use the environment or a stranger as a source of comfort. McBride and Belsky (1988) studied the relationship between maternal separation anxiety (measured by the MSAS at 3 and 9 months) and the quality of infant-mother attachment at 12 months. Mothers of secure infant-mother relationships (compared to insecure relationships) had moderate amounts of general maternal separation anxiety related to being away from their infants, but higher levels of separation anxiety specifically related to separations due to employment. These researchers suggested that there may be optimal levels of separation anxiety that facilitate mothers' abilities to relate to their infants in particularly sensitive and security-promoting ways.

Finally, Hock, DeMeis, and McBride (1988) demonstrated that levels of maternal separation anxiety may influence the use and selection of type of child care for young children. Over a three-year period, they found that employed mothers who enrolled their infants in day-care centers rather than using babysitters or family day-care homes expressed lower levels of anxiety. In addition, of those who used day-care centers, mothers who expressed more separation anxiety about balancing employment and motherhood used day care fewer months over the three-year period. Although this study does not demonstrate the direct effect of maternal separation anxiety on child outcomes, it does provide evidence that the ecology of the child's experience is influenced by this maternal variable. These studies confirm maternal separation anxiety is a valid phenomenon and that maternal attitudes about separation do affect the child. Given this, how can caregivers support the separation experiences of both these mothers and their children?

ROLE OF CAREGIVERS

Caregivers in family and group day care are in an unique position to facilitate parent-child separations. Although they provide a service to the parent and child, they also can become caregiving partners with parents and trusted caregivers to the child. Since separation distress is a result of a normal developmental phenomenon, a time of dependency that is necessary for later growth and autonomy, the goal of the caregiver is to help the child through this important period of time. Infants and toddlers can be very adaptive, depending on how caregivers respond to the individual needs of the child and how they structure the environment. Thus, knowledgeable and caring caregivers can facilitate the processes of parent-child separation and reunions in a variety of ways.

Facilitating Separations for Young Children

Caregivers can help children during separation by providing a consistent, secure environment for the child to rely on both during and after separation from the parent. The following suggestions may make separations easier for some children:

- Preparing the child for separations is important. Even infants should be informed about when and why the parent is leaving and when he or she will return. This preparation should be brief, and helps reduce the anxiety of both the child and the parent. A parent should never be encouraged to sneak away without the child knowing that the parent is leaving.

- For young infants, having the same caregiver each day will help both the child and the parent establish a trusting relationship. This familiar person should greet the child each day and help in the transition. The caregiver might coach the parent and child through the process of separation, but should not take it over. A particular goodbye routine will help the child be able to anticipate and cope with the event.

- Familiar objects from home such as a favorite toy, blanket, or pillow or an object that belongs to the mother may be of comfort to the child during separation.

- The child's expression of emotion related to the separation should be validated by the caregiver and accepted. The child must be comforted and assured.

- The individual characteristics and needs of children should guide caregivers' approaches to facilitating separations. Some children prefer enthusiastic interactions with lots of laughing and excitement, while others need gentle coaxing to slowly start to participate in activities. Some children prefer to be left alone to sort out situations and to adapt, while others need and want more attention.

Overall, children will feel more comfortable during separations if they are given the message from all adults involved (particularly the parent) that the day-care situation is a safe and fun place to be.

Facilitating Separations for Parents

It is very important for caregivers to develop a relationship with the child and family that is supportive, *not* competitive. Equally important is to acknowledge that the emotions that parents feel when separating from their very young child are real and a natural part of the process. Caregivers can support parents in a number of ways:

- From the beginning, caregivers should verbally acknowledge the parents' primacy in their child's life and demonstrate this acknowledgement in their actions on a daily basis. Parents will feel more confident about leaving their child with a person who they feel will not take over their role. Recognize that potential problems of anger and jealousy may occur, and be ready to handle them without being defensive.

- Parents can also be encouraged to participate in the day-care environment. Communicating with the parent about the child's daily activities helps the parent feel a part of the child's day and informs the parent about how the child coped with the separation and other situations.

- Provide opportunities for parents to feel reassured about their child. One-way mirrors allow a parent to linger and be assured that their child is settling down before the parent actually leaves. It may be important to suggest that parents call during the day to check on the child. This can be especially supportive to parents if the child had a difficult separation, as the suggestion validates the parents' concerns.

- Access to information can also be supportive for parents. Caregivers can offer knowledge about the normal expectations for separation distress, why it occurs, and strategies for handling it. Knowing that at 7 months an infant will be distressed when the mother leaves, because of the infant's cognitive development, not because the mother is employed, can facilitate the parent's understanding of the situation and put in perspective any guilt about being away from the child.

- Acknowledging mothers' anxiety as natural, and as experienced by many women who are employed and have children, is often comforting. It is essential that caregivers not be judgmental of parents' work decisions!

Particular attention should be paid to parents who are in stressful life situations. Single parents may have a harder time separating from their children, and the caregiver may be in a position to be especially supportive of such parents. Families living in poverty or facing illness may bring more or less anxiety to the separation process. Teen parents may not understand the cognitive abilities of their young children or be able to recognize their emotional needs.

CONCLUSION

Separation is inherently a difficult process. Starting from the first hour of life, human beings grow, develop, and learn within the context of relationships. At the same time, in order to function in the world, people must develop a sense of self separate from others and must learn how to independently manage their environment. Anxiety is a part of the separation process and may even function to continue the attachment relationship as the parent and child learn how to become more separate. Caregivers have the opportunity to become part of the process and can facilitate both attachment and separation. Successful negotiation of separation experiences for the child and parent requires supporting children as they learn to manage challenging developmental processes and helping parents feel successful and comfortable with their dual roles as parents and workers.

How Do I Say, "Let's Play"?
Social Interaction Between Toddlers

Nancy Lauter-Klatell

Toddlers are the great explorers and innovators of childhood. They wander through the uncharted realms of new ideas, new objects, peer relations, and verbal communication with an overwhelming need to know. The rapid growth of child care settings has forced us to look at toddler behavior in new contexts. One question that demands attention is "How do toddlers interact with peers in group settings?" A related question is "What are our expectations for behavior when toddlers do interact?"

Toddlers are often drawn to their peers through object play or by sharing an interesting idea (for example, jumping off the step at the same time). Each child must discover how to communicate with a peer, how to invite the other toddler to interact, how to maintain the interaction, and how to solve problems when the interaction breaks down. Even though most toddlers are skillful in interacting with adults, toddler peers do not respond to social overtures as adults do. They must learn and practice a new range of skills.

What can adults do to support toddlers in their efforts to "discover" the delights of peer interaction? Should adults make the same demands on toddler interactions as they do with older children (such as sharing or taking turns)? Can adults provide an environment that fosters interactions and also keeps toddlers safe and active?

Ben (16 months), Sara (10 months), their caregiver Sue, and several other children are playing in the infant room of a day-care center. Sara is leaning on the back end of a small, floor-level rocking horse, slowly fingering the tail of the horse and watching another child who is using blocks close by. As Sara leans on the horse and pushes on the tail end, the horse rocks gently back and forth. The movements catch Ben's eye. He drops the beads he has been holding, and toddles over to the rocking horse. He picks up speed as he gets closer and has his hand outstretched toward the head of the horse.

Sue notices Ben approaching the horse. She swoops down, puts her hands on his waist, and gently pulls him away from the horse and onto her lap. "No! No! Ben! Sara is using the rocking horse now. You can't take the horse away from her. It is her turn." Sara momentarily looks up to see who is talking, and then she crawls over to the blocks. Ben, however, appears to be upset and confused. He is struggling to get free of Sue's hold and off her lap. The rocking horse is now available and goes unused.

Did Sue's actions interfere with the possibility of peer interaction between toddlers? Do toddlers need interactive experiences in order to discover the social properties of an age mate?

RESEARCH ON PEER INTERACTION

For almost fifty years, very little research has been done on social interaction among young peers. Piaget's extensive work is partially responsible: in his studies of young children's thinking, he promoted the notion

N. Lauter-Klatell. (1990). How do I say, "Let's play"?: Social interaction between toddlers. Original manuscript; Wheelock College, Boston, Massachusetts. Nancy Lauter-Klatell, Ed.D. is an Associate Professor, Professional Studies Department, Wheelock College, Boston, Massachusetts.

that young children are egocentric. He meant that children have a difficult time thinking about two viewpoints at the same time. For many years, this idea of egocentrism carried over into our concepts of social development. It was believed that young children could not successfully interact with each other because they had little sense of the "other" and would not be able to adapt their thinking or behaviors to those of other children.

With the advent of child care and the technology to record young children's social interactions, this view is changing rapidly. Anyone who has spent time with a group of infants and toddlers knows that toddlers do interact successfully with one another. Their level of social skill and self-and-other concepts may be different from those of adults, but are far from egocentric. Several studies have already documented that infants and toddlers do engage in social interaction (Becker, 1977; Brenner and Mueller, 1982). And—perhaps surprising some—the majority of these interactions are positive. One study of toddler pairs at home (Rubenstein and Howes, 1976) reported that negative behaviors occurred about only 1 percent of the time.

The same study also documented that the presence of a peer heightens a toddler's level of cognitive functioning. Peers make an environment more interesting because they manipulate objects and make those objects move, click-buzz-whizz, and change form. When in the company of a peer, a child is stimulated to explore the unique properties of the physical environment. Once toddlers come together over an object, they may begin to negotiate the possible social patterns that will allow them to jointly explore the object. Toddler learning would be sorely limited if joint exploration of a material were cut off because of an adult expectation that an aggressive struggle would erupt.

As caregivers know, and research validates (Eckerman, Whatley, and Kutz, 1975), a toy in the hand of another child is much more exciting than a duplicate of the same toy lying on the floor. It isn't the toy *per se* that attracts the toddler's attention, it is the toy being held and moved by a peer. For example, if Amy is pulling a string that activates a fire truck to roll and its bell to ring, then that is the fire truck with which Sara wants to play. She is not interested in the truck that merely sits inert on the shelf. Yet how many times does a caregiver say to a child involved in an object struggle: "Here, Sara, here's a truck just like Amy's." In Sara's mind, the truck is *not* just like Amy's, because she has not seen it functioning in the same way. Part of the interest in that object's movement and sound is that a peer, rather than an adult, a machine, or a natural force is "connected" to those movements. The peer has taken an object that was not initially appealing to the child and made it interesting. The combination of peer and object is more novel (and therefore more interesting) to a toddler than an adult manipulating an object in a conventional way. Consider this example:

> *Maria and Adam, 15 and 17 months, are in a small playroom with various materials available. Neither one is initially engaged. Maria approaches a table that displays two small cymbals, two sandpaper blocks, and two rhythmsticks. Maria picks up a cymbal, looks at it, and bangs it on the table. Adam turns at hearing the noise the cymbal made. He goes to the table. He reaches out to Maria's cymbal with an open palm. Maria pulls her hand with the cymbal away. Adam looks at Maria. Adam picks up the other cymbal and hits it on the table. Maria watches closely. Maria hits her cymbal on the table. Adam laughs. Maria laughs. Adam picks up the sandpaper block and hits his cymbal with it. Maria does the same and laughs. Both children repeat this action three times. Then Maria bends at the waist and hits her block, then her cymbal on the floor. Adam turns and hits his block and his cymbal on the wall, and moves to the radiator and does the same, and then to the bulletin board. Maria follows and listens each time Adam's instruments make a different sound.*

WHAT DO TODDLERS DO TOGETHER?

The more opportunities toddlers have to interact with each other, the better they are at interacting in positive and complex ways (Brenner and Mueller, 1982). After becoming familiar with each other through consistent and continual time together, toddlers begin to show some of their special social skills and to share ideas of "themes" for playing.

In order to interact with a peer, a toddler must be able to

1. Take a turn during a particular time frame (if a child waits more than a second or two to respond to a peer's action, the interaction opportunity may be lost)

2. Pay attention to the "speaker" (the toddler must focus on the message the partner is sending and not be distracted by superfluous gestures or other environmental distractions)

3. Coordinate his or her acts with those of the partner (if the partner has offered a toy, the receiving toddler must think of a response that "makes sense" or goes along with the initial gesture)

4. Use the basic structure of an interaction to share ideas (for example, agreeing to jump off a step together or play "Ring Around the Rosy")

Although the structural "rules" of interaction are the same for adult-child and peer interaction, the peer context poses an all-new situation for the toddler. After all, the peer context is unpredictable. At the start of an interaction, the child has no idea how his or her new friend will react to a particular gesture or vocalization. This situation is quite different from interactions with adults where standard patterns of behavior have already been learned (for example, peek-a-boo games, reading stories, being comforted). Adults are always ready to repair or restart an interaction; restate or repeat a response; and modify, simplify, or adjust an idea if necessary. But another toddler is not as dependable. Luckily, even though their skills are lacking, toddlers are driven to find out about their peers through interaction. They approach this new challenge with the same fervor and inventiveness that characterize their other learning encounters.

What toddlers do together is very different from what they do with adults or older siblings. Toddlers have their own special repertoire of play themes and social games. Because toddlers are not always competent in language, they communicate through actions, gestures, looks (eye contacts), and affect (positive, negative, and playful). In this way, they manage to agree on shared "themes" for play. The content of their exchanges is as varied and creative as each individual child. These themes may include copying each other's actions or sounds, struggles over objects or space, rough and tumble play, verbal play with words, run-chase sequences, goal-oriented exchanges, information sharing, and eventually pretend play (Brenner and Mueller, 1982; Lauter-Klatell, 1983).

SUPPORTING PEER INTERACTION: THE CAREGIVER'S ROLE

In order to foster social development among toddlers, caregivers must provide children with settings, materials, and modes that promote the full range of peer exchanges. Unfortunately, peer interaction is often given low priority. The physical space and activities encourage groups of four or more, when we know that early interaction occurs most often and most easily in groups of two. Caregivers, with the good intention of sticking to a prearranged schedule, often interrupt toddlers' interactions in order to start a new activity. Many adults presume that one toddler approaching or touching another calls for immediate action in order to forego a major battle. Obviously, there are some toddlers whose dominant mode is aggressive, but this number is relatively small. We must not hover over toddlers in anticipation of negative behaviors until they have given us clear and repeated indications that hovering is warranted. In other words, it is time to give up the "terrible two" expectation.

It is not necessary for caregivers to talk to and direct toddlers all the time. One study (Atwater and Morris, 1984) reports that high adult verbal involvement and proximity actually reduce toddler language and peer interactions. Although some people think it is lack of experience with peers that leads to struggle and aggression, it seems to me that constant adult presence, let alone interference, makes young children anxious. Therefore, their behaviors may become more impulsive and uncontrollable. We should examine our own behavior, as well as the physical space and materials we provide to toddlers, if we want to enhance the amount and quality of peer interaction.

The Day-Care Generation

Pat Wingert and Barbara Kantrowitz

In our country, more than half of the mothers of infants under 1 year old are in the labor force. A larger percentage of working mothers have preschool and school-age children. Child care is reality for the majority of children in the United States. Yet we do not know what long-term effects full-time day care may offer these children. Theory, research, and our present "worldview" are tumbling about in the cauldron of heated debate.

Theories of mother-child attachment have long relied on one research paradigm, the "strange situation," to collect data. Do day-care children respond to strangers and new situations the same way children raised at home do? And is this the only or best way to measure a child's relationship with a mother or father? When we ask, "Is day care good for

babies?" are we posing the right question? Has day care alone altered the lives of young children or are factors such as increased demands on working parents, changing attitudes toward family and work, and additional stress on families influencing children's behaviors?

No one would disagree that poor child care is bad for children. The effects of high staff-child ratios, inattention to health issues, and unresponsive caregivers put young children at risk. However, federal regulation, additional and equitable funding from government and industry, and training for child care professionals can diminish, if not eradicate, ill effects resulting from poor child care programs. Advocates for children and families have much work to do in the years ahead.

Meryl Frank is an expert on child care. For five years she ran a Yale University program that studied parental leave. But after she became a new mother two years ago, Frank discovered that even though she knew about such esoteric topics as staff-child ratios and turnover rates, she was a novice when it came to finding someone to watch her own child. Frank went back to work part time when her son, Isaac, was 5 months old, and in the two years since then she has changed child care arrangements *nine* times.

Her travails began with a well-regarded day-care center near her suburban New Jersey home. On the

surface, it was great. One staff member for every three babies, a sensitive administrator, clean facilities. "But when I went in," Frank recalls, "I saw this line of cribs and all these babies with their arms out crying, wanting to be picked up. I felt like crying myself." She walked out without signing Isaac up and went through a succession of other unsatisfactory situations—a babysitter who couldn't speak English, a woman who cared for ten children in her home at once—before settling on a neighborhood woman who took Isaac into her home. "She was fabulous," Frank recalls wistfully. Three weeks after that babysitter started, she got sick and had to quit. Frank advertised for help in the newspaper and got thirty inquiries but no qualified babysitter. (When Frank asked one prospective nanny about her philosophy of discipline, the woman re-

P. Wingert and B. Kantrowitz. (1989, Winter–Spring). The day care generation. *Newsweek, 114,* Special Issue on the Family, 86–87, 89, 92.

plied: "If he touched the stove, I'd punch him.") A few weeks later she finally hired her tenth babysitter. "She's a very nice young woman," Frank says. "Unfortunately, she has to leave in May. And I just found out I'm pregnant again and due in June."

That's what happens when a *pro* tries to get help. For other parents, the situation can be even worse. Child care tales of woe are a common bond for the current generation of parents. Given the haphazard state of day care in this country, finding the right situation is often just a matter of luck. There's no guarantee that a good thing will last. And always, there's the disturbing question that lurks in the back of every working parent's mind: *what is this doing to my kids?*

The simple and unsettling answer is, nobody really knows for sure. Experts say they're just beginning to understand the ramifications of raising a generation of youngsters outside the home while their parents work. Mothers in this country have always had jobs, but it is only in the past few years that a majority have gone back to the office while their children are still in diapers. In the past, most mothers worked out of necessity. That's still true for the majority today, but they have also been joined by mothers of all economic classes. Some researchers think we won't know all the answers until the twenty-first century, when the children of today's working mothers are parents themselves. In the meantime, results gathered so far are troubling.

Some of the first studies of day care in the 1970s indicated that there were no ill effects from high-quality child care. There was even evidence that children who were out of the home at an early age were more independent and made friends more easily. Those results received wide attention and reassured many parents. Unfortunately, they don't tell the whole story. "The problem is that much of the day care available in this country is not high quality," says Deborah Lowe Vandell, professor of educational psychology at the University of Wisconsin. The first research was often done in university-sponsored centers where the child care workers were frequently students preparing for careers as teachers. Most children in day care don't get such dedicated attention.

Since the days of these early studies, child care has burgeoned into a $15 billion-a-year industry in this country. Day-care centers get most of the attention because they are the fastest-growing segment, but they account for only a small percentage of child care arrangements. According to 1986 Census Bureau figures, more than half of the kids under 5 with working mothers were cared for by nonrelatives: 14.7 percent in day-care centers and 23.8 percent in family day care, usually a neighborhood home where one caretaker watches several youngsters. Most of the rest were in nursery school or preschool.

Despite years of lobbying by children's advocates, there are still no federal regulations covering the care of young children. The government offers consumers more guidance choosing breakfast cereal than child care. Each state makes its own rules, and they vary from virtually no governmental supervision to strict enforcement of complicated licensing procedures for day-care centers. Many child development experts recommend that each caregiver be responsible for no more than three infants under the age of 1. Yet only three states—Kansas, Maryland, and Massachusetts—require that ratio. Other states are far more lax. Idaho, for example, allows one caregiver to look after as many as 12 children of any age (including babies). And in 14 states there are absolutely no training requirements before starting a job as a child care worker.

Day-care centers are the easiest to supervise and inspect because they usually operate openly. Family day care, on the other hand, poses big problems for regulatory agencies. Many times, these are informal arrangements that are hard to track down. Some child care providers even say that regulation would make matters worse by imposing confusing rules that would keep some potential caregivers out of business and intensify the shortage of good day care.

No wonder working parents sometimes feel like pioneers wandering in the wilderness. The signposts point every which way. One set of researchers argues that babies who spend more than twenty hours a week in child care may grow up maladjusted. Other experts say the high turnover rate among poorly paid and undertrained child care workers has created an unstable environment for youngsters who need dependability and consistency. And still others are worried about health issues—the wisdom of putting a lot of small children with limited immunities in such close quarters. Here's a synopsis of the current debate in three major areas of concern.

There's no question that the care of the very youngest children is by far the most controversial area of research. The topic so divides the child development community that a scholarly journal, *Early Childhood Research Quarterly*, recently devoted two entire issues to the subject. Nobody is saying that mothers ought to stay home until their kids are ready for college. Besides that, it would be economically impossible; two-thirds of all working women are the sole support of their families or are married to men who earn less than $15,000 a year. But as the demographics have changed, psychologists are taking a second look at what happens to babies. In 1987, 52 percent of mothers of children under the age of 1 were working, compared with 32 percent ten years earlier. Many experts believe that day-care arrangements that might be fine for 3- and 4-year-olds may be damaging to infants.

Much of the dispute centers on the work of Pennsylvania State University psychologist Jay Belsky. He says mounting research indicates that babies less than 1 year old who receive nonmaternal care for more than twenty hours a week are at greater risk of developing insecure relationships with their mothers; they're also at increased risk of emotional and behavioral problems in later childhood. Youngsters who have weak emotional ties to their mothers are more likely to be aggressive and disobedient as they grow older, Belsky says. Of course, kids whose mothers are home all day can have these problems, too. But Belsky says that mothers who aren't with their kids all day long don't get to know their babies as well as mothers who work part time or not at all. Therefore, working mothers may not be as sensitive to a baby's first attempts at communication. In general, he says, mothers are more attentive to these crucial signals than babysitters. Placing a baby in outside care increases the chance that an infant's needs won't be met, Belsky says. He also argues that working parents have so much stress in their lives that they have little energy left over for their children. It's hard to find the strength for "quality time" with the kids after a 10- or 12-hour day at the office. (It is interesting to note that not many people are promoting the concept of quality time these days.)

Work by other researchers has added weight to Belsky's theories. Wisconsin's Vandell studied the day-care histories of 236 Texas third-graders and found that youngsters who had more than thirty hours a week of child care during infancy had poorer peer relationships, were harder to discipline and had poorer work habits than children who had been in part-time child care or exclusive maternal care. The children most at risk were from the lowest and highest socioeconomic classes, Vandell says, probably because poor youngsters usually get the worst child care and rich parents tend to have high-stress jobs that require long hours away from home. Vandell emphasizes that her results in the Texas study may be more negative than those for the country as a whole because Texas has minimal child care regulation. Nonetheless, she thinks there's a "serious problem" in infant care.

Other experts say there isn't enough information yet to form any definite conclusions about the long-term effects of infant care. "There is no clear evidence that day care places infants at risk," says Alison Clarke-Stewart, a professor of social ecology at the University of California, Irvine. Clarke-Stewart says that the difference between the emotional attachments of children of working and of nonworking mothers is not as large as Belsky's research indicates. She says parents should be concerned but shouldn't overreact.

Instead of pulling kids out of any form of day care, parents might consider choosing part-time work when their children are very young, she says.

For all the controversy over infant care, there's little dispute over the damaging effects of the high turnover rate among caregivers. In all forms of child care, consistency is essential to a child's healthy development. But only the lucky few get it. "Turnover among child care workers is second only to parking-lot and gas-station attendants," says Marcy Whitebook, director of the National Child Care Staffing Study. "To give you an idea of how bad it is, during our study, we had tiny children coming up to our researchers and asking them, 'Are you my teacher?'"

The just-released study, funded by a consortium of not-for-profit groups, included classroom observations, child assessments and interviews with staff at 227 child care centers in five cities. The researchers concluded that 41 percent of all child care workers quit each year, many to seek better-paying jobs. In the past decade, the average day-care center enrollment has nearly doubled, while the average salaries for child care workers have decreased 20 percent. Typical annual wages are very low: $9,931 for full-time, year-round employment ($600 less than the 1988 poverty threshold for a family of three). Few child care workers receive any benefits.

Parents who use other forms of day care should be concerned as well, warns UCLA psychologist Carollee Howes. Paying top dollar for au pairs, nannies, and other in-home caregivers doesn't guarantee that they'll stay. Howes conducted two studies of 18- to 24-month-old children who had been cared for in their own homes or in family day-care homes and found that most had already experienced two or three changes in caregivers and some had had as many as six. In her research, Howes found that the more changes children had, the more trouble they had adjusting to first grade.

The solution, most experts agree, is a drastic change in the status, pay, and training of child care workers. Major professional organizations, such as the National Association for the Education of Young Children, have recommended standard accreditation procedures to make child care more of an established profession, for everyone from workers in large for-profit centers to women who only look after youngsters in their neighborhood. But so far, only a small fraction of the country's child care providers are accredited. Until wide-scale changes take place, Whitebook predicts that "qualified teachers will continue to leave for jobs that offer a living wage." The victims are the millions of children left behind.

When their toddlers come home from day care with a bad case of the sniffles, parents often joke that it's "schoolitis"—the virus that seems to invade classrooms from September until June. But there's more and more evidence that child care may be hazardous to a youngster's health.

A recent report from the Centers for Disease Control found that children who are cared for outside their homes are at increased risk for both minor and major ailments because they are exposed to so many other kids at such a young age. Youngsters who spend their days in group settings are more likely to get colds and flu as well as strep throat, infectious hepatitis, and spinal meningitis, among other diseases.

Here again, the state and federal governments aren't doing much to help. A survey released this fall by the American Academy of Pediatrics and the American Public Health Association found that even such basic health standards as immunization and hand washing were not required in child care facilities in half the states. Inspection was another problem. Without adequate staff, states with health regulations often have difficulty enforcing them, especially in family day-care centers.

Some experts think that even with strict regulation, there would still be health problems in child care centers, especially among infants. "The problem is that caretakers are changing the diapers of several kids, and it's difficult for them to wash their hands frequently enough [after each diaper]," says Earline Kendall, associate dean of graduate studies in education at Belmont College in Nashville, Tennessee. Kendall, who has operated four day-care centers herself, says that very young babies have the most limited immunities and are the most vulnerable to the diseases that can be spread through such contact. The best solution, she thinks, would be more generous leave time, so that parents can stay home until their kids are a little older.

Despite the compelling evidence about the dark side of day care, many experts say there's a great reluctance to discuss these problems publicly. "People think if you say anything against day care, you're saying young parents shouldn't work, or if they do work, they're bad parents," says Meryl Frank, who is now a consultant on family and work issues. "For a lot of parents, that's just too scary to think about. But we have to be realistic. We have to acknowledge that good day care may be good for kids, but bad day care is bad for kids."

There is a political battle as well. Belsky, who has become a lightning rod for controversy among child development professionals, says "people don't want working mothers to feel guilty" because "they're afraid the right wing will use this to say that only mothers can care for babies, so women should stay home." But, he says, parents should use these problems as evidence to press for such changes as paid parental leave, more part-time jobs, and higher-quality child care. The guilt and anxiety that seem to be part of every working parent's psyche aren't necessarily bad, Belsky says. Parents who worry are also probably alert to potential problems—and likely to look for solutions.

Part Three

PRESCHOOL CHILDREN

In the preschool years, children are increasingly skillful, active, imaginative, and love to share ideas through language and play. Their new ability to use symbolic representations offers many vistas for exploration and mastery. Children create complex play episodes with several characters, combination plots, and a variety of real and imaginary props. Language and an understanding of the world around them afford preschoolers access to any adult willing to listen and opportunities to observe and model adults other than parents. Although young children often appear to think logically and "act grown-up," there are limitations on their abilities to link events in a consistently logical manner. Preschoolers have bits and pieces of lots of information, but they haven't yet woven this knowledge into a rational framework.

Bruner's article is a classic introduction to the interrelationship between play, thought, and language. Play is child's work, *not* because it is frivolous or simplistic, but because, given a young child's cognitive skills, it is the best medium for using symbols, modeling behaviors, solving problems, and engaging peers. Pretend play is a complex activity that reflects a child's cognitive and social development. Unfortunately, opportunities for child-initiated play have decreased in early childhood programs. Without these essential opportunities to think, experiment, and negotiate, a child's foundation for conceptualizing information may be insecure later on.

The article by Flavell emphasizes the preschooler's difficulty in distinguishing between reality and fantasy or appearance. Young children center on one aspect of the information given. Because they lack the concrete operation of reversibility, they cannot replay their earlier understanding of an object or process. If clay is presented as a large, round ball one minute and in a long snake shape the next, the preschooler may regard the clay as two separate entities because they "look different." In addition, a 3-year-old may focus on the scary noises a babysitter is making and forget that the sitter is only pretending to be a lion. The child may become truly frightened and remain unconvinced that the lion babysitter is "only pretending." Similarly, imagine a parent's frustration when he or she takes a preschooler to the biggest toy store in town to show the child the life-size stuffed animals and the child shrieks in fear. Preschoolers may focus on the animal's size, not the fact it is stuffed with straw.

By 4 or 5 most preschool children begin to think more rationally and their ability to organize ideas and "construct" applicable systems of thought grows rapidly. One good example is the child's awareness of print. Reading and writing are part of a larger "system" of developing and using literacy skills. Beginning with the infant's first story-reading experiences, young children begin to build knowledge of our communication system (verbal and written words). Developing the skills of reading and writing takes place over several years. They are not taught in any single six-month period by a teacher who uses tedious worksheets and repetitive drills. Young children construct a "theory" of reading and writing by integrating the experiences offered by the environment with their beginning understanding of language rules. The third article in this part of the book, "Young Children Can Learn Some Important Things When They Write," presents writing stages of one 4-year-old child. It is easy to see how significant changes, dictated by the child's accommodation of new information about print, occur over time.

Roedell discusses giftedness (a genetic variable), by illustrating the outcome for a gifted child whose development doesn't match the curriculum of the preschool program. DeYoung highlights the child's role in child sexual abuse (an environmental variable) cases that go to court. Each article underlines the need to view children holistically. A gifted preschool child cannot tell us that his or her advanced cognitive skills have resulted in frustration and boredom in a preschool classroom. Instead, she or he acts out those feelings through aggressive acts or withdrawal from the group. An abused preschool child cannot articulate (or understand) the intent, progress, or exact timing of sexual abuse episodes, but *can* describe what happened in his or her *own* words. An understanding of how preoperational children think and organize information can help adults get reliable information from the child. Too often we dismiss the words or thoughts of children as incorrect and their behaviors as inappropriate because we don't understand how they came to present those particular ideas.

The preschool years are full of adventure, humor, and earnest problem solving. New friendships are formed and dissolved, new skills are mastered, and children construct a sense of self that they use to compare themselves with others. Most children begin "formal" schooling during this time, but for too many children, especially minorities, school is not a positive experience. Many schools have pushed academic competencies into the early grades at the expense of responding appropriately to the developmental needs of young children. The tasks of the preschool years are to function autonomously and build a positive self-concept as a learner and contributor to "society." To be autonomous does not mean to be independent of others, but to use language, cognitive, physical, and social abilities to obtain the resources and information needed to make rational decisions.

Play, Thought, and Language

Jerome Bruner

How would you define the concept of play? Does it serve any meaningful functions in the development of young children? Play is a phenomenon that conjures up different images and purposes to different people. In this classic article, Jerome Bruner, renowned child psychologist, describes play as the very essence of childhood. He believes its functions are diverse, and crucial to successful development. Bruner characterizes play as "a hothouse for trying out ways of combining thought and language and fantasy." Others have defined play as "messing around with ideas." Under the right conditions, play allows children (and adults) to discover and take ownership of new ideas. What is a new idea, anyway, but the recombination and reorganization of familiar ones?

I am thoroughly convinced that there is a very special place for a constantly renewing dialogue between those who spend time asking questions about children and those who work more practically with them on a day-to-day basis in playgroups, nurseries, and the like. I think that there has been a remarkably rapid progress among biologists, psychologists, and linguists in establishing findings about human growth in children that is highly relevant to the way in which we conduct our education and our play activities before that. We are living in a period in which many practical and theoretical interests concerning childhood are converging. It is a privilege to be a participant in that convergence. We have a special opportunity, it seems to me, for exchanging our ideas back and forth between research and practice.

My subject is the interrelationship of play, language, and thought. I shall try to be brief about it. Not that there is a lack of research on the subject to be reported, because a great deal has been accomplished.

J. Bruner. (1983). Play, thought and language. *Peabody Journal of Education*, 60 (3), 60–69.

But rather, I want to leave room at the end to talk about the practical implications of this subject: how to organize the play activity of children in playgroups in order to help our children realize their potential and live more richly.

Let me begin by setting forth in outline what I think to be the fundamental functions of play in activity of children.

Let me note first that to play implies a reduction in the seriousness of the consequences of errors and of setbacks. In a profound way, play is an activity that is without frustrating consequences for the child even though it is a serious activity. It is, in a word, an activity that is for itself and not for others. It is, in consequence, a superb medium for exploration. Play provides a courage all its own.

Secondly, the activity of playing is characterized by a very loose linkage between means and ends. It is not that children don't pursue ends and employ means to get them in their play, but that they often change their goals en route to suit new means or change the means to suit new goals. Nor is it that they do so only because they have run into blocks, but out of the sheer jubilation of good spirits. It provides not only a medium for exploration, but also for invention.

Closely related to the previous point, it is characteristic of play that children are not excessively attached to results. They vary what they are up to and allow their fantasies to make substitutions for them. If this variation is not possible, the child very quickly becomes bored with his activity. Watch an infant piling wood bricks and you will be struck by the diversity and the combinatorial richness of how he plays. It is an unparalleled opportunity for ringing changes on the commonplace.

Thirdly, in spite of its richness, play is very rarely random or by chance. On the contrary, it seems to follow something like a scenario. Recall the famous example of Sully's little twin sisters, the one saying to the other "Let's play twin sisters." And then they proceed to play a game in which the general object is to share everything with absolute equality, quite contrary to the way in which things go in ordinary life. Yet in some interesting way, this scenario of total equality is a kind of idealized imitation of life. Sometimes these scenarios are harder to discern than at other times, but it is always worth looking carefully to see what in a formal sense play is about. It is often, in Joyce's words, an epiphany of the ordinary, an idealization, a pure dilemma.

Fourthly, it is said that play is a projection of interior life onto the world in opposition to learning through which we interiorize the external world and make it part of ourselves. In play we transform the world according to our desires, while in learning we transform ourselves better to conform to the structure of the world. This is an extremely important activity for growth, and we will come back to it later. It gives a special power to play that is heady and, sometimes, a little frightening.

Finally, and it can really go without saying, play gives pleasure—great pleasure. Even the obstacles that we set up in play in order to surmount them give us pleasure in doing so. Indeed, the obstacles seem necessary, for without them the child quickly becomes bored. In this sense, I think we would have to agree that play has about it something of the quality of problem solving, but in a most joyous fashion. But let me be clear. Unless we bear in mind that play is a source of pleasure, we are really missing the point of what it's about.

Let me now say a word about the uses to which play is *put*, though I have just said that play is free and seemingly for itself. For it is the case that (though it is self-prompted) we often use play to achieve other ends we may have in mind. We do this necessarily but at our own peril.

Take first the way in which play is structured in order to instruct our children, however subtly, in the values of our culture. Take competition and competitiveness as a case in point. We often encourage competition in play, indeed use play to instruct our children how to compete well, and from a very early age. Let us even grant that Waterloo was won on the playing fields of Eton. But the children of Tengu in New Guinea play games in their society that do not terminate in one party winning, but only when the two sides have achieved equality. This emphasis on equality, you will not be surprised to find out, is also very characteristic of the adult society. Does this differential emphasis on the element of competition in play serve to make our society and Tengu society as different as they are? No, that would be going a bit too far. But nevertheless, the way the competitive element is handled in childhood play is a big factor in predisposing children in particular societies to take the competitive stance that they do as adults. There is no question that the games of childhood reflect some of the ideals that exist in the adult society and that play is a kind of socialization in preparation for taking your place in that adult society. We would all agree that it is important to be conscious about how much competitiveness we encourage in the play of children, lest we create so much of it that something of the freedom of play is lost. It is one thing to *use* play as an agent of socialization in some spontaneous way. But exploiting it is somehow a different matter.

We also have it in the back of our minds, when we encourage various *kinds* of play in childhood, that the activity will serve some therapeutic function for the child. Perhaps that puts it too strongly, but it is better to overstate it than to sweep it aside. Plainly, play with other children does have an important therapeutic role or, in any case, an important role in helping children to take their place more easily in the stressful social activities of later life. We know from research on isolated monkeys raised in the laboratory, that if they have twenty minutes of play with other monkeys they will not (like total isolates) lose their capacity to interact with other animals nor will they, like those others, show a decrement in intelligence. Twenty minutes a day of free play is all that is needed to save the sanity of these poor animals.

But to organize play mainly with the view toward fostering mental health in children is also to risk losing something very important. Again there is a danger of "taking the action away from the child." We may thank God and evolution that it is difficult to exclusively take the action away from children in order to organize their play in the interest of their mental health. I do not think we know enough to play the role of great engineers to the young in their or any other domain.

And then there is play as a means of improving the intellect. Yes, of course, but...we will come back to this matter, but the same strictures about great engineering will be found to be true again. There is everything to be said, indeed, for letting the child loose in a decent setting with rich materials and some good cultural models to follow. I think I can even give a practical argument for this view—that we can be quite relaxed about not pushing children through play in order to squeeze some appropriate behavior out of them. Let me tell you about an experiment.

It is an experiment I conducted with two colleagues, Kathy Silva and Paul Genova. It can serve as a little moral for my point. We studied children between the ages of 3 and 5. They were given an interesting little task to do. A child had to get a pretty little piece of colored chalk out of a transparent box that was placed some distance out of reach of them. The rule of the game was that they had to get the colored chalk while they remained seated in their chair some distance off. They had all sorts of things to use: some sticks, some clamps, some string. The solution to the problem consisted of making a longer stick by joining together shorter sticks with the clamps or string. If a child didn't succeed right off the bat in solving the problem, we would give him hints, and if that didn't serve, we would then give further hints until he finally got to the end. The first hints were something like "Are you thinking of some way in which you can help yourself solve the problem?" And eventually we would say things like "Have you thought about the possibility of clamping together two sticks?" Finally, all of the children solved the problem, even if we had to guide them all the way home. I can tell you that it was the sort of play that delights the children very much.

We divided the children into three groups.

The first group of children were given a period of play before facing our task, and in the course of that play they had an opportunity to fool around with the sticks, with the clamp and a string, however they might desire. In the second group we gave each child a little pedagogical demonstration explaining how you could join together two strings with a clamp, etc. And in the third group, we simply familiarized the children with the kind of material they were going to be playing with and gave them some simple demonstrations of what the material was like. By a little clever manipulation we saw to it that all of the children had roughly the same amount of exposure to the material as far as time is concerned, although, obviously, the quality of the exposure differed according to which of the three groups they were in.

Now let me tell you what happened to the children in those three different groups.

The children in that first group who had a chance to play with the materials in advance solved the problem better than the children in the other two groups. Let me call these children in the first group the "true players." Not only did they solve the problem more often, but they seemed to make better use of the suggestive hints we gave them than the other children. Besides, the "true players" had far less tendency to abandon the task en route when they ran into trouble. They were more frustration proof. They seemed altogether better at the way in which they went about things, those "true players." They knew how to begin simply; they had far less tendency to try out complicated hypotheses; and so forth.

Why did our "true players" do so well? To begin with, they seemed far less frustrated in carrying out the task than did the other children. They neither seemed to resent their failed efforts, nor did they feel they were losing face. That was what made it possible for them to begin simply, and also what made it possible to accept hints and suggestions more readily than the other children. The "true players" saw the task as an invitation to play around with a problem. They did not have to cope with putting a good face on their efforts or of dealing perpetually with self-esteem. They could be free and inventive.

I know this experiment is too simple-minded. But for all that, it was a little microcosm of life. Think of the hypothesis of the great Dutch historian Huizinga: that human culture emerged out of man's capacity to play, to adopt the ludic attitude. Or of those great laboratories of physics at Cambridge under Lord Rutherford or at Copenhagen under Niels Bohr—places known for their good humor, practical jokes, and funny stories. Perhaps our "true players," like those happy physicists, could benefit from those huge benefits in spirit that play grants us.

Let us pass now from the little world of experiments with children or with playful physicists in the great laboratories. Consider now how it is that human beings accomplish the formidable task of learning how to speak their mother tongue. For I think that we will also find here that there is a considerable role for playfulness in the child's mastery of the miracle of language. Do not be confused by the aspect of language that is innate or inborn. But remember that there is a great deal of it that also has to be mastered through try-out and experience. We have to learn all sorts of subtle things like, for example, that when somebody says "Would you be so kind as to pass the salt?" that they are not asking us about the limits of our kindness, but are making a request for the salt in a fashion that honors our voluntary role in complying. I have spent a great deal of time in these past ten years studying how children acquire the uses of their language, and I want to give you a few of my conclusions as they bear on the issues we have been discussing.

One of the first and most important conclusions is that the mother tongue is most rapidly mastered when situated in playful activity. It is often the case that the most complicated grammatical and pragmatic forms of the language appear first in play activity. Take as an example one of the first uses of the conditional in a child of 3 years who says to another child: "If you give me your marbles I'll give you my revolver if you're nice." It is a long time before such complicated language is used in the more tense, practical situations of ordinary life. In general it has been my experience that playful situations are the ones where one finds the first complicated predicate structures, the first instances of ellipsis, of anaphora, and so forth. There is something about play that encourages combinatorial activity in general, including the intrinsic combinatorial activity of grammar involved in producing more complex expressions in a language. Aside from that, it matters deeply in a child's mastery of his own language that there not be too many consequences that stem from making errors. Confrontations with adults or older children who insist that the younger child say something correctly will very frequently lead to certain kinds of expressions going underground and not being tried out for some while afterward.

There is one aspect of the early acquisition of language that is extraordinarily important in nourishing language. It poses a dilemma. The kind of talk by mothers that encourages children to enter into conversation is in what is technically called the B.T. register; that is to say, Baby Talk, talk that is at the level of the child, talk that the child can *already* understand. How can the child learn his language from talk that he can already understand? That is the dilemma. The solution is simple. The importance of Baby Talk is that the child gets an opportunity to try out the different ways in which he can combine the elements of the language that he already knows in order to make more complex utterances and in order to get different things done with the language that he already has in hand. The child is not simply learning *language,* but learning to *use* language as an instrument of thought and action in a combinatorial fashion. In order to be able to talk about the world in a combinatorial fashion the infant seems to have to be able to play with the world in that flexible fashion that the playful attitude promotes.

There are some celebrated studies by linguists like Ruth Weir and Katherine Nelson that have recorded the "conversations" that young children have after they've been put to bed all alone and the lights turned out. These bedtime soliloquies provide pure little experiments, in which the child is pushing language to

the full limits of its combinability. In Weir's observations, her son Anthony goes through sequences like this: "Mommy hat," "Mommy blue hat," "Mommy hat blue, no, no, no." Anthony was the classic instance of a spontaneous grammatical apprentice. Or Katherine Nelson's Emmy, who would spend five minutes of talk pushing to the limits the meaning of her father's utterance before bedtime, that only little babies cry, that she is a big girl, and big girls don't cry. The number of changes that she rings on the theme are monuments to her effort, half seriously and half playfully, to arrive at some meaning of her father's imprecation.

So we are left with the interesting dilemma that it is not so much instruction either in language or in thinking that permits the child to develop his powerful combinatorial skills, but a decent opportunity to play around with language and to play around with his thinking that turns the trick.

Now I think we can turn to the practical question about whether and how we can be, and whether we should be, engineers of play in our playgroups and nursery schools. I want to use as my text a report we published on the organization and conduct of playgroups and nursery schools here in Britain during the closing years of the 1970s.

As you all very well know, there developed during the last generation a curious ideology about the nature of play and how play should be conducted in groups. This ideology was founded on the belief that various activities were *really* play. Anything that had any structure to it, or that in any way inhibited spontaneity was not *really* play. Moreover, *real* play had to be free of all constraints from adults and be completely autonomous of their influence. True play, in a word, came entirely from the inside out. Its typical vehicles were fingerpaints, clay, water, sand, etc. I rather suspect that the basis of this ideology of play was principally the therapeutic, in the sense that it was designed to take all pressure off the child, although it had a touch too of the romanticism of Jean Jacques Rousseau.

Early in our inquiry in ordinary playgroup settings we started studying what in fact really produced rich and elaborated play in children, without any particular attachment to prevailing ideology. We went about our observations with the high rigor that serious experiments deserve, in order to find out something about what children really like to do, what kinds of themes and materials they like to work with, and what it is that produced richness and elaboration in their play. As some of you will recall, we made thousands of observations using the most modern techniques, and naturally and eventually, like the modern investigators we were, we eventually committed our findings to a computer to which we directed some very sharp questions. For example, we asked the computer to figure out for us the kinds of activities and the kinds of circumstances that produced the longest episodes of play and the ones that had the biggest set of elaborations on a theme. It isn't that hard to find such things out by hand, but when you have thousands of observations to sort out, the computer helps. The results were more than a little interesting.

The sequences of play that were the longest and the richest and the most elaborated were produced by materials that had a structure that could be called *instrumental*—that is to say, episodes that had means that led to an end. Mostly, these were activities and materials that made it possible for the child to *construct* something. They were constructions, moreover, whose progress could be appreciated by the child without instructions from or recourse to an adult. I have to tell you that water, sand, clay, and fingerpaint were not up at the top of the list of materials that produced this form of constructive and elaborative play. Such materials, though they have much worth, do not lead to the kind of combinatorial push of which we have been talking. In order to get that push, you need some sort of back and forth between means and ends.

A second answer our computer gave us about what produced prolonged concentration and rich elaboration in play rather took us aback. It was the presence of an adult. I do not mean an adult "over the shoulder" of the child, trying to direct his activity, but one in the neighborhood who gave some assurance that the environment would be stable and continuous, but would also give the child reassurance and information as, if, and when the child needed it. Let the adult intervene brusquely and steal the initiative from the child, and the child's play, or the children's play would become duller. In some ways, I think, this sympathetic presence of an adult or partner is similar to the role that an adult plays in the development of language about which we have already talked.

I think you'll be glad to learn that the third secret our computer divulged we already knew pretty well, although it is sometimes denied in the official ideology of the last generation. It is that one is a wanderer, two is company, and three is a crowd. More seriously, two children playing together can exchange ideas, can negotiate their intentions, can elaborate as needs be, and can go on for as long as necessary. One alone has difficulty sustaining play activity. And three is indeed a distracting crowd with nobody able to hold the floor long enough to carry the day. Watch two little girls playing at a tea party under a blanket spread across the backs of two chairs. They generate a domestic scenario of astonishing subtlety and richness. Listen to them: "Would you like a cup of tea, my dear?" And the other responds, "Oh, yes, but wait just a second, the tele-

phone is ringing." And the first continues after a pause, "I hope it was a friend of yours," and the other, "No, it was the tailor calling back." And on it goes for five minutes. It is perhaps more difficult to know why it is that children operating on their own, solo, have such trouble in maintaining concentration. I think it relates to a point that has been made by virtually every student of child development in the last half century. Thought and imagination frequently begin in the form of dialogue with a partner, and without the support of another, it quickly collapses. At least early on. The development of thought may be in large measure determined by the opportunity for dialogue, with dialogue then becoming internal and capable of running off inside one's head on its own.

Let me tell you one last finding of our study on the sources of richness in play. I must confess I was rather surprised by it. If a child is in a class or group that during some period of the day requires its children to take part in some high-level intellectual activity, then the child will play in a richer and more elaborated way when he is on his own. It is as if the activity of the class playing *together* serves as a model for the spontaneous play activity of the children playing on their own.

We can ask now whether these analogous research findings about play can help the playgroup organizer become a better engineer of the young human soul. Well, the answer will not be as simple as one would hope. There is little question that one *can* certainly improve the materials and the atmosphere in playgroups in a way to improve the concentration of the children and the richness of their play. That does not take very much doing. It is the sort of thing that we do through the Preschool Playgroups Association encouraging the construction or purchase of better materials and the use of better approaches to play. But there is a more interesting matter than that. It has to do with playgroup leaders and nursery school teachers and how they improve the quality of play of children. It takes surprisingly little to bring about small miracles. We found, for example, if they simply listened to a recording of themselves interacting with children— indeed, listened to it alone—they would often recognize immediately what was right and what was wrong. They recognized, for example, the extent to which they were either underestimating or overestimating the ability of children to take and to hold the initiative in conversation, the extent to which they were dominating, holding back, etc. Playgroup leaders, having listened to a tape of themselves with their children, would often say things like "But I don't *listen* enough to find out what they're saying." Or "I seem to be spending all of my time as a kind of fire brigade, looking after troubles rather than helping children with their projects." They knew intuitively what they should have done, but circumstances often had got in their way. It does not take a massive psychoanalysis to get these teachers back on the track! For example, our computer told us, to our surprise, that on the average, infants in a playgroup spoke to an adult only once every nine minutes, and that in the main, these exchanges were rather superficial. Some little experiments in which leaders looked at themselves teaching were promising. Play leaders found they could divide the labor so that one could be freed up to interact more. This went a long way toward increasing the quality, the frequency, and the length of conversations that children had with them. Play leaders became interested in what could be done. Once interested, consciousness is raised and improvement almost inevitably follows.

I doubt very much whether in any of these interventions, we really become engineers of the human soul. What it amounts to is setting up situations that make rich play possible. I happen to believe that rich, elaborated, and prolonged play makes better human beings than impoverished, shallow, and shifting play. To that extent, I suppose, I am an engineer. Or perhaps, just a human being with some interesting biases.

Let me draw some very brief conclusions to all this.

To play is not just child's play. Play, for the child and for the adult alike, is a way of using mind, or better yet, an attitude toward the use of mind. It is a test frame, a hothouse for trying out ways of combining thought and language and fantasy. And by the same token, there is much that one can do to help the process of growth. But do not overheat the hothouse!

We must remember that children playing are not alone and are not best alone, however much they need their periods of solitude. But as much as they need their solitude, they need to combine their ideas from their own head with the ideas that their partners have in theirs. Call it negotiation or whatever you will, it is the stuff not only of play but of thought. Let not the school cultivate only the spontaneity of the individual. For human beings need negotiation in dialogue. It will furnish the child with models and with techniques for how to operate on his own.

Finally, play under the control of the player gives to the child his first and most crucial opportunity to have the courage to think, to talk, and perhaps even to be himself.

Really and Truly

John H. Flavell

Have you ever confused appearance and reality—stuck your hand in a shimmering pool of water to find it was made of plastic? Young children in the early phases of preoperational thought fail to distinguish between reality and appearance even when the evidence seems crystal clear to adults. Between 3 and 5 years of age, children work under the assumption that what you see is real even if an object is being altered by an obvious variable (such as a color filter). For example, a child may be shown a glass of milk and then the same glass of milk with a red filter around it. When asked if the milk is "really and truly" red, children will respond that it is. Why are young children unable to hold two representations of milk (the real one and the milk that only appears to be red) in their minds at the same time? And perhaps more interesting and elusive, how do children develop an understanding of the distinctions between appearance and reality?

It looks like a nice, solid piece of granite, but as soon as you squeeze it you know it's really a joke store sponge made to look like a rock. If I ask what it appears to be, you say, "It looks just like a rock." If I ask what it really is, you say, "It's a sponge, of course." A 3-year-old probably wouldn't be so sure. Children at this age often aren't quite able to grasp the idea that what you see is not always what you get.

By the time they are 6 or 7 years old, however, most children have a fair grasp of the appearance-reality distinction that assumes so many forms in our everyday lives. Misperceptions, misexpectations, misunderstandings, false beliefs, deception, play, and fantasy—these and other examples of that distinction are a preoccupation of philosophers, scientists, artists, politicians, and other public performers and of the rest of us who try to evaluate what they all say and do.

For the past half dozen years, my colleagues and I have been asking children questions about sponge rocks and using other methods to find out what children of different ages know about the difference between appearances and reality. First we give the children a brief lesson on the meaning of the appearance-reality distinction by showing them, for example, a Charlie Brown puppet inside a ghost costume. We explain and demonstrate that Charlie Brown "looks like a ghost to your eyes right now" but is "really and truly Charlie Brown," and that "sometimes things look like one thing to your eyes when they are really and truly something else."

We then show the children a variety of illusory objects, such as sponge rocks, in a straightforward fashion and ask questions, in random order, about the reality and appearance of the objects: "What is this really and truly; is it really and truly a sponge or is it really and truly a rock?" "When you look at this with your eyes right now, does it look like a rock or does it look like a sponge?"

Or we show a 3-year-old and a 6-year-old a red toy car covered by a green filter that makes the car look black, hand the car to the child to inspect, put it behind the filter again, and then ask, "What color is this car? Is it red or is it black?" The 3-year-old is likely to say "black"; the 6-year-old, "red." We use similar procedures to investigate the children's awareness of the distinction between real and apparent size, shape, events, and the presence or absence of a hidden object.

In all these tests, most 3-year-old children have difficulty making the distinction between appearance and reality. They often err by giving the same answer (appearance or reality) to both questions. However, they rarely answer both questions incorrectly, suggesting that the mistakes are not random; the children are simply having conceptual problems with the distinction. By the time they are 6 or 7, however, most children get almost all the questions right.

Among 3-year-olds, certain types of illusory objects tend to elicit appearance answers to both questions (what we call a *phenomenism error pattern*), while others usually produce reality answers to both (an *intellectual realism error pattern*). The latter is the more surprising pattern because it contradicts the widely held view that young children respond only to what is currently most noticeable to them.

When we ask children to distinguish between the real and apparent properties of color, size, and shape, they are most likely to make phenomenism (appearance) errors. If, for example, we use lenses or filters to make an object that is really red or small or straight look black or big or bent, most 3-year-olds will say the object really is black or big or bent.

But if we ask them what object or event is really present or has really occurred, most make intellectual realism errors. For example, children say the fake rock looks like a sponge. When they are shown a display consisting of a small object blocked from view by a large one, they say the display looks like it contains both objects rather than only the one they see. When they are shown someone who appears from the child's viewing position to be reading a large book but who the child knows is really drawing a picture inside the book, most children say it looks like the person is drawing rather than reading.

We also find that children make more phenomenism errors when we describe the same illusory stimuli in terms of their properties ("white" versus "orange" liquid) rather than in terms of their identities ("milk" versus "Kool-Aid"). Exactly why the appearance usually seems to be more important to young children in the first case and the reality more important in the second case remains a mystery.

Understanding of the appearance-reality distinction seems so necessary to everyday social life that it is hard to imagine a society in which normal people would not acquire it. To see if our findings applied in other cultures, we repeated one of our early experiments with 3- to 5-year-olds from Stanford University's laboratory preschool with Chinese children of the same age at Beijing Normal University's laboratory preschool. Error patterns, age changes, and even absolute levels of performance at each age level proved to be remarkably similar, suggesting that our results were not due to a simple misunderstanding of the English expressions "really and truly" and "looks like to your eyes right now." Instead, it seems that 3 or 4 years of age is the time when children of both cultures begin to acquire some understanding of the appearance-reality distinction.

We have not yet found effective ways to test for possible precursors of the appearance-reality distinction in children younger than 3, but we have tried to find out whether 3-year-olds really and truly lack competence in this area or only appear to. If there is one lesson to be learned from the recent history of developmental psychology, it is that the mental abilities of young children are often seriously underestimated simply because researchers at first fail to come up with accurate ways to measure those abilities.

To avoid this mistake, we devised a number of what we thought were easy appearance-reality tasks to be administered to groups of 3-year-olds. We used the same object-identity (fake objects) and color (objects placed behind colored filters) tasks as in our previous investigations, but we tried to make them easier for very young children. The tasks still demanded some genuine, if minimal, knowledge of the appearance-reality distinction but came closer than the standard tasks to demanding only that knowledge.

In one easy color task, for example, we left a small part of an object uncovered by the filter so its real color was still visible to the children when the appearance and reality questions were asked. In another one, we took milk, whose real color is well known to young children, and used a filter to change it to a different color that they never see it have in reality. We thought this might help the children both keep the real color in mind and recognize the bizarre apparent color as mere appearance.

And since the repeated linking of questions about appearance and reality might confuse 3-year-olds, we further simplified matters by avoiding appearance and reality questions on some tasks. For example, at the beginning of the testing session, prior to any talk about appearances and realities, we asked the single "is" question about the toy car's color. Is it red, or is it black?

Similar strategies were used to create what seemed to be easier object-identity tasks: After a brief conversation about dressing up for Halloween in masks and costumes, the children were questioned about the real and apparent identity of one of the experimenters, who had conspicuously put on a mask. We assumed that young children would be more knowledgeable about this sort of appearance-reality discrepancy through Halloween and play experiences than with those created by the fake objects and filters we had used in previous experiments.

Our use of easier-looking, less demanding tasks to study appearance-reality competence was surprisingly unsuccessful. Some of the children did perform slightly better on the easy tasks, but as a group their level of performance was almost the same as on the standard tasks. The results suggest that the typical young preschooler cannot think effectively about appearances and realities even when the tasks are deliberately made "child-friendly."

In a final test for hidden competence on appearance-reality tasks, we selected sixteen 3-year-olds who performed very poorly on such tasks and trained them intensively for five to seven minutes on the meaning of real versus apparent color.

We demonstrated, defined terms, and repeatedly explained that the real, true color of an object remains the same despite repeated, temporary changes in its apparent color due to the use of a filter. We fully expected that this training would help the children, but when we retested them, only one showed any improvement, and that was slight. The difficulties 3-year-olds have with the appearance-reality distinction are apparently very real indeed.

Things soon begin to change, however. In both the United States and the People's Republic of China, we found that performance on our appearance-reality tasks improves greatly between 3 and 5 years of age. This is consistent with the reported increase, at around 4 years of age, in the ability (probably related) to talk with playmates about pretend play.

While 6- and 7-year-olds are almost consistently error-free on these simple appearance-reality tasks, their development of knowledge about the distinction is not yet complete. We found, for example, that even though 6- and 7-year-olds answer the questions correctly, they continue to have trouble with the concept and find it difficult to talk about appearances, realities, and appearance-reality distinctions.

Most don't show a well-developed, abstract understanding of the appearance-reality distinction until about the age of 11 or 12. In fact, it may not be until the time they reach adulthood that most people have a sufficiently rich and creative understanding of the concept that they can not only identify appearance-reality discrepancies but also reproduce them, change them, or create new ones.

Our studies of how the appearance-reality distinction develops may shed light on a larger development—the child's understanding that mental representations of objects and events can differ both within the same person and between persons. I can be simultaneously aware, for example, that something appears to be a rock and that it really is a sponge. I can also be aware that it might appear to be something different under special viewing conditions, or that yesterday I pretended or fantasized that it was something else. I know that these are all possible ways that I can "represent" the same thing. In addition, I may be aware that you might represent the same thing differently than I do, because our perspectives on it might differ.

Knowledge about the appearance-reality distinction is but one instance of our more general knowledge that an object or event can be represented in different ways by the same person and by different people. The development of our understanding of the appearance-reality distinction, therefore, is worth studying because it is part of the larger development of our conscious knowledge about our own and other minds. And that's an area of development worth investigating—really and truly.

Young Children Can Learn Some Important Things When They Write

Judith A. Schickedanz

How do young children learn to read and write? In the United States, where the illiteracy rate continues to rise, we are eager to answer this question. Do successful readers and writers merely accumulate discrete decoding skills (for example, what sound does the letter B make?) through rote memorization? Or are reading and writing, like language development, processes that take place over time according to each child's developmental pattern and prior experiences?

Until recently we used a term, "reading readiness," to denote a set of skills a child needs to acquire before she or he could begin the act of "real" reading. We also assumed that children needed to read first and write later. Thinking has changed on both issues. The term "emergent literacy" better describes how children become readers and writers over time. This process begins the first time a parent reads to an infant and extends through the child's interaction with hundreds of literacy experiences at home and in school.

In this article, Judith Schickedanz defines stages of writing as they emerge for one 4-year-old girl. The writing development of this child is determined by her changing understanding of how print works in the context of her daily life. Opportunities to observe and discuss reading and writing at home, access to materials, and acceptance of her writing attempts at school are some of the experiences that support and promote her literacy development. An important question is "How do we ensure rich literacy experiences for all children before and during their school years?"

Four-year-old Monica had attended her preschool for seven months. She had seen the names of her classmates daily, on the pockets of the attendance chart, on the jobs chart, and on the name cards she sometimes used at the classroom writing-drawing center. She also saw them when her classmates wrote their names on their paintings or drawings.

Monica's mother and father were surprised at

J. A. Schickedanz. (1990). Young children can learn some important things when they write. Original manuscript, Boston University, Boston, Massachusetts. Judith A. Schickedanz, Ph.D. is an Associate Professor and Coordinator of the Early Childhood Program, Boston University, Boston, Massachusetts.

Monica's ability to read many of these names. For example, when putting her own name card into a pocket of the attendance chart, Monica sometimes pointed to several other names and said, "That's Rachel's name," or "That's Adam's name," or "That's Jennifer's name." She did the same thing with the jobs chart: "Susan, Matthew, and Patrick are snack helpers today," she'd announce, after glancing at the jobs chart.

When Monica's parents had their spring conference with Monica's preschool teacher, they expressed their delight and pride in Monica's reading ability. "We're going to order a set of beginning reading books," they said, "because she seems to be ready to read. We saw an advertisement for a reading program

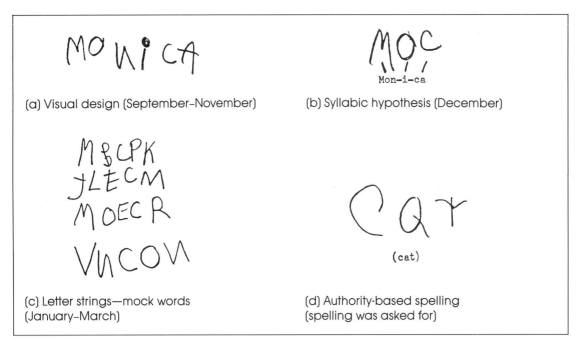

(a) Visual design (September–November)

(b) Syllabic hypothesis (December)

(c) Letter strings—mock words
(January–March)

(d) Authority-based spelling
(spelling was asked for)

Figure 1.
Monica's Writing Samples.

in a magazine. You teach letter sounds with worksheets they send to you, and then you use the reading books too."

The preschool teacher also expressed delight in Monica's interest in written words and in her ability to read words she saw often. And she commended Monica's parents for showing so much interest in their daughter's learning. She thanked them for taking some responsibility for teaching her: "Educating children is an enormous job," she told them, "too big for one teacher and for school. Parents must help."

But the teacher also had some reservations about the approach Monica's parents intended to use. Although they had pinpointed Monica's lack of awareness of the sound-based nature of written language, she said she felt that training on letter-sound associations, using worksheets, was a bit premature. She also wondered about the quality of the books that would be included in the reading program. In addition, she knew that the family's financial resources were limited, and she didn't like to see the parents spend money for a program that wouldn't be necessary, or even useful, especially at this point in Monica's development.

"You might want to wait awhile before ordering a program like that," she told the parents. "Often a special program, with special reading books, isn't necessary at all. Let me tell you what Monica is doing when she writes. This will help explain what I mean." She pulled out some samples of Monica's writing she had collected over the past few months (Figure 1) and explained to Monica's parents what the samples meant

in terms of Monica's assumptions about how the English writing system works. She gave Monica's parents a page summarizing the strategies children often use to create words (Table 1), thus making it possible for them to see where Monica was with respect to this area of development, and where she would likely move over the next year or so.

Before the conference ended, the teacher helped Monica's parents list materials and experiences they might offer her at home. They were excited about creating a space where Monica would have access to paper and markers, about putting magnetic alphabet letters on the front of the refrigerator door, and about asking Monica to add her own items to the family's weekly grocery list. They looked forward to answering her questions about words and spelling, as she played with these materials and engaged in these activities.

Monica's parents also planned to get a library card for her, and they now knew that books with considerable rhyme and repetition would be especially easy for her to read, after she'd heard them read several times over. The books they had thought about ordering probably used some of the same features, but now they knew that good picture books for young children also had these features.

They felt pleased as they left the conference. Not only did they now know that Monica was progressing well, but they also knew how to help her continue to learn in this area. It was good to know there was something they could do, and that they didn't need to spend $11.95 a month for the next two years on the

Table 1. WORD CREATION STRATEGIES

Strategy	Examples	
Physical Relationship	*/ / /*	for "Lisa," "because I three years old."
Visual Design	*Lisa* (scribble)	for "Lisa," "because this is how other people make my name."
Syllabic Hypothesis	*LS*	for "Li-sa"
Letter Strings (visual rules)	LSSI, LIISL	"These are words because they look like words."
Authority-Based (asking for or copying spellings)	MOM, DAD, JEREMY	"I know these are words because you told me what letters to use."
Early Phonemic (invented spellings)	MNSTR (monster) NBR (number)	"I know these are words because they sound like words."
Transitional Phonemic	Monster	"I know this word is spelled right because I asked for help."

Source: Adapted from J. A. Schickedanz (1989). The place of specific skills in preschool. In D. S. Strickland and L. M. Morrow (eds.), *Emerging Literacy: Young Children Learn to Read and Write.* Newark, DE: I.R.A.

reading program they had thought they should buy to support their daughter's learning. They couldn't wait to get started and to begin to collect writing samples like those they had been given by Monica's teacher.

WHAT'S THERE TO LEARN?

Written languages differ in the way they relate to the oral language they represent. Some written languages are not sound-based. In Chinese, for example, characters represent whole words or ideas, not sound segments within words. Other written languages are sound-based. But sound-based orthographies—written languages—can code at different levels. Some, like Japanese and Korean, code at the syllable level. Others, like English, French, and Spanish, code at the smaller, phoneme level. When children are learning to write and to read, they must figure out at what level the written language codes oral language.

Alphabetic orthographies—those in which sound is coded at the individual, phoneme level—present a conceptual difficulty for the very young child. Although a written language such as Chinese is burdensome in the long run, because it requires a learner to memorize 70,000 characters, it doesn't present a conceptual hurdle at the beginning. Children can understand that they need to associate specific characters with specific meanings. There is no code to break. Syllabic orthographies also apparently are simple to comprehend, because syllables are large, and obvious, units of words (Liberman et al., 1974; Mann, 1986). But phonemes—the individual units of sound within words—are difficult to detect and, in fact, humans don't naturally learn to detect them. The development of this

skill comes only with special experiences—interaction with an alphabetic language (Ehri and Wilce, 1980).

HOW DO CHILDREN LEARN THE ACTUAL FUNCTION OF ALPHABET LETTERS?

As we can see in Figure 1c and 1d, 4-year-old Monica still doesn't understand how alphabet letters work. Until very recently, she created letter strings that looked like actual words (Figure 1c), but they were not real words. She didn't know that letters must be selected, in terms of sounds they represent, and ordered, with respect to the sounds heard as a word is spoken. At first, Monica thought that every letter string was some word, but she didn't know which one. To find out, she asked adults, "What word is this?" More often than not, the adult would pronounce the word and say, "It looks like a word, but it isn't a real word. Sometimes, when you put letters together, it makes a real word. But, sometimes, it doesn't." After getting feedback like this for awhile, Monica decided that this approach wasn't very productive. "I might as well ask a teacher how to spell the words I want to make," she may have thought to herself. "I'm not having much luck with the way I'm doing it."

Just a few weeks before Monica's teacher met with her parents, Monica had begun to ask teachers for spellings, or to copy words she knew from the environment (Figure 1d). She was very attentive to spellings her teachers gave her and sometimes she even double-checked to see if she'd heard correctly: "B or P?" she asked in one case, when she wasn't quite sure what a teacher had said. But Monica still thought the essential task in making words was one of remembering the order of their letters—of knowing how each word was supposed to look. She didn't know there was a way to generate spellings, without literally memorizing them, word by word.

When Monica's teachers had time, they tried to make the relationship between written and spoken language explicit to Monica. They knew that this conceptual barrier was one Monica had to get past. To do this, the teachers often thought out loud, when Monica asked them for spellings, as if they had to think through just how to spell a word. After isolating each sound, teachers named the letter they had chosen to code it. When words contained silent letters, teachers simply announced that they were there, even though they couldn't be heard.

Monica's teacher explained that it's difficult to explain this process to a child. "You can't say, 'Letters represent sounds in words. You must think about the sounds you hear in words and then select letters that can represent these sounds.' A young child who doesn't yet think about words in terms of individual sounds wouldn't know what you meant, even if you said all this. And it doesn't help simply to teach children letter-sound associations. Children can learn these and still not know what to do with them. What teachers must do is demonstrate the process of phonemic segmentation, while children observe it.

"As demonstrations continue, over a period of weeks, or even months," Monica's teacher explained, "teachers begin to involve the child more and more by pausing longer after isolating a sound, as if puzzled about what letter to select. These pauses create opportunities for children to help with the spelling, which they often do. Soon after, children can be told to "sound it out" when they ask a teacher for a spelling. This request nudges them toward a period of independent spelling, one in which they create their own words, even though these aren't spelled conventionally. Their invented spellings differ from conventional spellings, because children at first code only sounds they actually hear and code some sounds in ways that differ from how adults code them" (Read, 1975). "The advantage to invented spelling is that children can write words by themselves and can practice their phonemic segmentation skills."

Monica's teacher did not go on to explain that children often become disillusioned with invented spelling, when they encounter words in books or the environment that are spelled differently from their own (Bissex, 1980; Schickedanz, 1990), and that this is an opportune time to acquaint them with some of the "rules of the game"—phonics rules and word analysis skills. Children are glad to know about "silent e," about double vowels, and about the need for a vowel in every syllable. These are the tricks children need if they are to spell conventionally. Children often are relieved and fascinated to know that spelling isn't as simple as sounding words out and coding what is heard (Schickedanz, in press). Monica's teacher might not have been familiar with these later developments, because they don't occur in most children until first grade, typically after a child has begun to read. Only then does a child encounter conventional spellings frequently and inspect them closely enough to begin, systematically, to compare them with his or her own. Only then is a child likely to begin to put two and two together and ask, "Hey! What's the problem here?"

WHY ISN'T THIS METHOD WIDELY USED?

On the way home, Monica's parents continued to discuss what they'd learned at the conference. "I wonder why people create special reading books and worksheets to teach children to read and to write when they can learn it in more interesting ways?" Monica's mother said to her husband. "Seems like such a waste of time and money."

"It sells," said Monica's father.

"You're too cynical," Monica's mother replied. "It seems so logical, really. It seems to make sense that first you'd teach children letters and sounds and that this would enable them to read. And you'd think that special books, with only certain words used to make reading simple, would be very helpful. I think people invent these things because they think they'll work. They're not out just to make a buck."

"You'd think the experts would know better. Some expert's name was on that reading program we saw advertised."

"John, we have Monica and we didn't know. I was just thinking about the pictures and other papers Monica has brought home this year. I think some of them had writing on them, and you know, John, we never really noticed. I mean, we didn't really know that it meant anything, that it could tell us something about what Monica understood about written language. I think you could live with this going on right under your nose and not necessarily see it. Know what I mean?"

"Uh-huh. It's there, but you don't see it. If you don't know about it beforehand, it passes you by."

"I think so. I think that's really quite possible. If her teacher hadn't told us, I don't think we'd ever have noticed what Monica is doing. We wouldn't have known what she knows or thinks, or how to help her to learn more without ordering that special program. John, we would have ordered it; we *would* have. And later we would have thought it was the program that had done it. We wouldn't have realized that other experiences had played a role, maybe even had been the crucial factor. We wouldn't have seen it that way."

"I think you're right."

Developing Social Competence in Gifted Preschool Children

Wendy C. Roedell

It is difficult for a 10-year-old to socially interact with a 5-year-old because each has a different cognitive view of the world. Similarly, an intellectually gifted child's social cognition (how he or she interprets social events) is beyond the abilities of agemates. Cognitively advanced children need adult support to initiate and maintain social relationships with peers. Often these children need to learn specific strategies for interacting with children (age mates) who do not possess the same cognitive abilities.

What happens to a gifted child—or any child with special needs—when the educational environment does not match his or her level of development? The outcomes are almost always detrimental to the child. Some children become social isolates, others try to hide their true abilities, and some become increasingly disruptive as a result of boredom. This article highlights the dilemma faced by some intellectually gifted children who find it difficult to interact with their agemates. Gifted children, like all children, demonstrate needs in each developmental domain—cognitive, social, emotional, and physical.

Effective educational programs for young children include a focus on the systematic development of social skills. Gifted preschool children may require special guidance to help them understand and cope with their unusual abilities. A sensitive understanding of gifted preschool children's social and emotional development provides the foundation for successful efforts to improve their social competence.

DEFINITIONS OF GIFTEDNESS

While the definition of giftedness differs from program to program, in most instances children are identified whose development is progressing faster than the average rate in designated areas of functioning. The University of Illinois Program for the Gifted, for example, has selected children who "are functioning

W. C. Roedell. (1985). Developing social competence in gifted preschool children. *Remedial and Special Education,* 6(4), 6–10.

considerably above their age mates in intellectual, creative, or cognitive fine motor" areas (Schwedel and Stoneburner, 1983, p. 34). The Child Development Preschool at the University of Washington has identified children with advanced development in the intellectual skill areas of verbal reasoning, spatial reasoning, memory, reading, and mathematical understanding (Roedell, Jackson, and Robinson, 1980). Thus, gifted children will be defined here as those who demonstrate advanced intellectual abilities.

INTELLECTUAL GIFTEDNESS AND SOCIAL COGNITION

It might be expected that children with advanced intellectual skills would also demonstrate an advanced understanding of the social world. Intellectual skills develop in a predictable way as children grow older. Similarly, children's understanding of what other people think, feel, and intend, and their ability to theorize about social relationships, friendship, and other social events change in predictable ways with increasing age. Moderate relationships have been found between children's intelligence as measured by intelligence tests and various aspects of social cognition. These relationships vary with the type of task, the type of intelligence test used, and the age, gender, and background of the children (Abroms, 1983; Roedell, Jackson, and Robinson, 1980). Few investigators have examined the development of social cognition in populations of gifted children, and very little information exists about gifted preschoolers. There is some evidence, however, that gifted preschool children may be advanced in some areas of social cognition.

Abroms and Gollin (1980), for example, found moderate relationships between mental age and performance on measures of perceptual, cognitive, and affective perspective taking in a sample of gifted 3-year-olds. The relationship between these tasks and IQ was low and nonsignificant, possibly due to a restricted range in IQ scores. The perspective-taking tasks were designed to indicate a child's ability to take the point of view of another person, an ability hypothesized to form the foundation for the development of positive social behavior. In this study, however, role-taking ability was not predictive of prosocial behavior as observed in the classroom.

In a study of social problem-solving ability in gifted preschool children, Roedell (1978) found that children with higher IQs had more ideas about ways to solve theoretical social conflicts and more ideas about ways for children to interact cooperatively. As in the Abroms and Gollin study, advanced social cognition was not related to increased prosocial behavior in the classroom.

In summary, it is clear that more research is needed to clarify the relationships between advanced intellectual ability, social cognition, and social behavior in young children. While some studies indicate that intellectually gifted preschool children may be advanced in some areas of social understanding, the effects are by no means clear-cut, and the research base is slim. Teachers should be aware, though, that a gifted child may be ready to explore issues and ideas about social relationships at a more complex level than the average child. Since advanced social understanding does not translate directly into mature social behavior, teacher guidance will be needed to help intellectually gifted children apply their powerful cognitive skills to the arena of social interaction.

INTELLECTUAL GIFTEDNESS AND SOCIAL ADJUSTMENT

In general, children with moderately advanced intellectual abilities tend to experience good social adjust-

ment, stable emotional development, and healthy self-concepts (Gallagher, 1958; Terman, 1925). On the other hand, good social adjustment is not automatic, but depends to a great extent on a supportive environment. When children's intellectual abilities are unusually advanced, difficulties in adjustment increase. The more different a child's intellectual functioning is from that of same-age peers, the more difficult it becomes for that child to find a comfortable niche in the social world (Hollingworth, 1942; Roedell, 1984; Tannenbaum, 1983). A 3-year-old, for example, who knows the Latin names of many dinosaurs and can converse articulately about their habitats and behaviors may have difficulty communicating with children who have less knowledge and less verbal skill. When children are obviously different from others of the same age, the chance that they will develop maladaptive behavior patterns increases.

Effects of Uneven Development

When one area of a child's development is unusually advanced, the result may be extreme unevenness in social, physical, and cognitive competencies. Adults and children alike can be misled by advanced abilities in one area to expect equally advanced performance in other areas.

While some intellectually advanced children may demonstrate comparably advanced social sensitivity, many display an intellectual-social gap. Although the reasoning ability of a gifted 4-year-old may be similar to that of a 7-year-old child, social-emotional behavior will most likely be similar to that of age mates. Many gifted preschool children still need help toileting and dressing, may hit other children when frustrated, have trouble communicating needs and feelings to other children, lack the skill to initiate cooperative play or to join a group, and have not learned to share and take turns. Although these children think and reason like much older children, socially they are similar to 3- and 4-year-olds of average intelligence (Roedell, Jackson, and Robinson, 1980).

Adults, expecting social maturity to match high-level intellectual development, may label a highly articulate, logical child as a behavior problem when he or she exhibits an age-appropriate tantrum. Adults may say to a child, "You know better than to behave that way." The child in fact may "know better," but may not have learned how to translate that knowledge into mature social behavior.

Equally damaging is the tendency to view a child's misbehavior as evidence of a lack of intellectual ability. The stereotype of the mature, self-directed gifted child sometimes prevents teachers from appreciating the extraordinary intellectual skills of a gifted but wiggly

3-year-old. Such children need the emotional nurturance and social guidance appropriate for their chronological age, but in addition require challenge for their intellectual strengths to develop a positive self-image with acceptance of their own abilities.

While some gifted preschool children are physically as well as intellectually advanced, others display the physical awkwardness and lack of coordination typical of their age mates (Roedell, Jackson, and Robinson, 1980). Young gifted children can become frustrated when their limited physical capabilities prevent the completion of the complex projects created in their extremely capable imaginations. They need sensitive guidance to direct their frustration into constructive problem-solving efforts. Otherwise, they may quickly give up on projects or even avoid starting them.

One technique for helping a child cope with frustration is to teach deep breathing for relaxation. At the moment of frustration a teacher can suggest to the child that he or she begin deep breathing before continuing with the project and attempting to carry it out in a different way.

Problems of Isolation

Children with unusually high levels of intellectual ability sometimes have a difficult time finding compatible peers. Hollingworth (1942) and O'Shea (1960) have suggested that problems of communication, starting in the preschool years, may be one root cause of the highly gifted child's involuntary isolation. A 3-year-old who uses the vocabulary of the average 6-year-old to express abstract ideas may not be understood by same-age peers. Four-year-olds who enjoy playing Monopoly and checkers with older children in the neighborhood have difficulty finding same-age playmates with similar skills and interests. One gifted 4-year-old boy was repeatedly frustrated when his neighborhood friends failed to keep appointments he had made with them; it was difficult for him to accept that they had not yet learned to tell time (Roedell, Jackson, and Robinson, 1980).

With their advanced conceptions of group organization and complex ideas for play activities, gifted children may develop an adult-like manner with others, and be labeled as bossy. When efforts to be accepted fail, a highly able child may withdraw from social interaction. One 4-year-old boy was diagnosed as emotionally disturbed by his preschool teachers because of his tendency to withdraw from social interaction. His worried parents enrolled him in a program for highly gifted children, where his friendly, outgoing manner demonstrated that his withdrawn behavior

had been the result of having no intellectual peers with whom to interact.

Rigid grouping of children into chronological age groups exacerbates the social isolation of the gifted. The assumption that children of the same age constitute a true peer group only holds true for children of average development. The term *peer* does not, in essence, mean people of the same age, but rather refers to individuals who can interact at an equal level around issues of common interest. Michael Lewis and his colleagues define the concept of a peer in the following manner: "We maintain that 'peer' should have a meaning related to *function* rather than *age*. That is, a peer would be on one occasion all the children who could climb a tree, while on another occasion it would be those able to sing songs" (Lewis, Young, Brooks, and Michalson, 1975, p. 58). The more highly gifted a child, the less likely that child is to find developmentally defined, true peers among age mates. Many gifted children prefer older companions. Given a choice, gifted children tend to form friendships with others of similar mental age (O'Shea, 1960; Silverman, in preparation).

For children whose development is highly uneven, true peers may vary depending on the activity. A child with extraordinary intellectual but average physical skills might have one set of peers for reading and discussing books and another set for riding tricycles and playing tag.

Special efforts are needed to help gifted children find companions with similar interests and abilities. Without such efforts, gifted children run the risk of being labeled different and strange by their age mates. They may internalize these labels and become socially alienated at an early age (Whitmore, 1980).

Of course, gifted children are capable of modifying their behavior to fit in with other children. One mother reported that her 4-year-old son wrote a note to hang on the front door, telling his friends that he did not want to play. He then crumpled the note and sadly explained to his mother, "I can't hang this note up, Mom. They can't read!" Gifted children can learn the skills necessary to interact successfully with many different types of children.

There is no substitute, however, for the social and cognitive growth that occurs through the interaction of peers at similar developmental stages. There is some evidence, for example, that gifted preschool children in self-contained groups engage in associative and cooperative play earlier than their average age mates (Abroms, 1983). Ronald, a 5-year-old in a program for intellectually gifted children, explained the situation well when he commented, "Do you know why Bill is my best friend? Because he's the only one who understands the kind of guy I really am."

Effects of Inappropriate Educational Environments

Although this article focuses on issues of social competence, it is important to consider the direct relationship between the development of social skills and the educational environment's acceptance of a child's intellectual needs. Even a warm, nurturant preschool environment can present the gifted child with intellectual stagnation and boredom that will preclude the development of positive social behaviors.

Most gifted preschool children arrive in the classroom already capable of recognizing and naming numerous colors and shapes, able to count and in some cases to perform arithmetical operations, and extremely knowledgeable about letters and letter sounds. Many read as well as second- or third-grade children. Some are only challenged by puzzles with 50, 60, or even 100 pieces. Extensive questioning, in-depth exploration of topics, and a passionate thirst for knowledge characterize their learning style. In short, they have mastered the cognitive content of the traditional preschool curriculum by the time they are 2 years old, and enter preschool ready and eager to learn concepts usually presented to older children.

If opportunities for complex play and advanced conceptual learning are not present in the classroom, the gifted child's energy and excitement about learning may be diverted to nonconstructive behavior. One 3-year-old boy was asked to leave three different preschools before he was enrolled in a program for gifted children. Teachers told his mother that his disruptive behavior could not be contained within their classrooms. Evaluation of his abilities indicated that he was a highly gifted child with extraordinary intellectual abilities. A program which offered many different options for intellectual engagement alleviated much of his disruptive behavior. Reduction of boredom and consequent frustration allowed for the development of more positive social skills, such as self-directed learning and prosocial interaction.

When teachers do not understand and accept the gifted child's unusual skills and interests, severe damage to the child's developing self-concept can result (Whitmore, 1980). Early readers may be told to put away their books and join a group lesson on letter identification; a highly verbal questioner may be told to be quiet and stop bothering the class; a child with a passionate desire to find out about space travel may find no one to share his or her interest.

Often gifted children learn at an early age to disguise their abilities. If no one else in the class is reading, and there is no sensitive adult to foster the idea that reading is a valued skill, then an early reader may pretend not to understand the written word. Such a child may even begin to feel ashamed of his or her ability. Gifted children need guidance in developing realistic understanding of their own strengths and weaknesses. They need to know that it's all right to know things that other children don't understand, and that it's equally fine to make mistakes and not know everything.

HELPING GIFTED YOUNG CHILDREN IMPROVE SOCIAL COMPETENCE

A comprehensive conception of social development should form the foundation of a social skills development program. The following outline presents major goals to be considered in planning to meet the social and affective needs of gifted preschool children. Of course, a program's goals will be determined by the characteristics and values of the community to be served, but the goals presented here offer a starting point.

1. *Self-understanding* — Children develop realistic understanding of their own strengths and weaknesses. They learn to accept themselves as individuals, and they develop positive self-images.

2. *Independence* — Children learn to assume responsibility for their own activities. They learn to make decisions and follow through on their plans, and they learn to focus their attention and continue their own activities when others are near.

3. *Assertiveness* — Children learn to stand up for their rights in nonviolent, assertive ways. They learn to express needs and emotions effectively without resorting to crying or whining.

4. *Social sensitivity* — Children learn to interpret and understand the needs and feelings of other people. They learn to help, share, and cooperate with others.

5. *Friendship-making skills* — Children learn to interact with other children and with adults. They learn how to ask others to join group activities and to respond appropriately to overtures from other children. They learn to mesh their own interests with those of others while participating in group activities, and learn what it means to be a good friend.

6. *Social problem-solving skills* — Children learn to negotiate differences and solve conflicts without resorting to physical violence.

These social skills can be fostered both informally, through classroom interactions, and formally, through structured group lessons.

Informal Approaches to Teaching Social Skills

Many of the strategies used to help average preschool children develop an effective repertoire of social skills can be adapted for working with gifted preschool children. The modifications should be based on an understanding of the intellectual strengths of gifted children, and of the particular vulnerabilities described in the preceding sections.

For example, reinforcement techniques work well with gifted preschool children if appropriate reinforcers can be identified. The most potent reinforcer for one 4-year-old boy with highly developed reasoning skills was the opportunity to take things apart. In working with this child to improve his ability to stay with a group during field trips, teachers tried many different types of contingencies. The most effective procedure was to provide time and tools to take apart and reassemble old appliances brought by teachers from home.

Working with a child's strengths to help improve weaknesses can be an effective approach. One 4-year-old boy, who had the reading skill of a third-grader, became disruptive during transition times between outdoor play and indoor group lessons. His behavior improved remarkably when teachers handed him a card listing the tasks to be performed during transition, and offered checkmarks or stickers as tasks were completed. By using his strength in reading, teachers built additional structure into the program for this child, without impinging on the independence of others in the group.

Attending to gifted children's needs for developmentally defined peers and for complex play and learning options can also foster improved social behavior. If the preschool program is not a program for gifted students, flexibility in student grouping is essential. A gifted 3-year-old may well work better both socially and intellectually with the 4-year-old group. Of course, careful observation of the individual child's play and friend preferences can help to guide grouping decisions.

Providing opportunities for complex activities can also be helpful. Adding more difficult puzzles to the puzzle center, providing opportunities for reading, setting up a tape recorder to record children's dictated stories, and offering unusual props for complex fantasy play can all enhance the gifted child's school experience and pave the way for development of positive social skills.

Structured Group Lessons

Several studies have demonstrated the effectiveness of small group instruction in teaching prosocial behavior and social problem-solving techniques (Slaby and Roedell, 1982). In designing group lessons for gifted children, it is important to remember their advanced reasoning ability, highly developed verbal skill, and ability to learn quickly.

Spivack and Shure (1974) devised a ten-week program using stories and puppets to encourage preschoolers to invent and evaluate their own alternative solutions to interpersonal conflicts. The program was designed for children from disadvantaged families, and was shown to improve children's social behavior. This social problem-solving curriculum can provide a context for discussing social skill issues with gifted preschool children. As teachers work with children in the classroom, they can refer to previous group lessons as children engage in everyday conflicts, and can encourage children to apply their advanced intellectual skills to real-life social situations. In adapting this program for use with gifted preschool children, adjustments should be made in the level and pacing of the lessons. For example, lessons in the sequence can be skipped or compacted as the children move quickly through the material.

Another program designed to enhance social problem-solving skills is AWARE (Elardo and Cooper, 1977). Although the program was designed for older children, the content and activities may be appropriate for gifted preschool children with advanced social cognitive skills (Abroms, 1983).

Teachers do not need to rely on a previously developed social skills curriculum to begin planning structured lessons, but can invent their own. Existing programs tend to follow a sequence of concepts:

1. Identifying feelings in self and others

2. Understanding differences between individuals

3. Identifying social problems

4. Generating problem solutions

5. Understanding the consequences of different solutions

6. Generating and practicing solutions and consequences through discussion, puppetry, or role playing

In conducting a lesson, the teacher first presents a stimulus for discussion—a story, picture, or puppet presentation. The discussion is followed by a chance for the children to role play or to use puppets or dolls to act out the feelings, problems, and solutions presented. Role playing and the use of dolls have been shown to be effective in helping young children learn new social skills (Combs and Slaby, 1977) and are an effective technique for use with gifted children who love to extend the open-ended possibilities of role-playing situations.

Although these approaches have been shown to be effective with average children, as yet there are no clear evaluation data indicating that any of these programs is particularly effective in teaching social skills to gifted preschool children. However, the fact that these techniques rely on a cognitive approach with open-ended activities to allow for complex reasoning shows promise for their use with the gifted. Since gifted children's intellectual skills are well developed, the goal of such approaches should not be to improve social cognition, but rather to help children translate social understanding into social behavior. The role-playing and puppetry aspects of these lessons would seem to be the key link. More research is needed to demonstrate which aspects of social skill programs are most effective with gifted preschool children.

CONCLUSION

Social skills development is an important component of a young child's educational program. Training in effective social skills may be particularly crucial for intellectually advanced children, who often find themselves in peer groups where they do not easily fit in. Communication with same-age peers may be quite difficult, particularly if a gifted child has acquired a vocabulary beyond the understanding of age mates. It may be equally difficult for gifted young children to overcome the physical and social differences between themselves and older children who are their peers in intellectual ability. Young children who are noticeably different from others may develop maladaptive patterns of social behavior that can make forming friendships difficult.

Many programs for gifted preschool children accept only children who demonstrate social maturity. It makes more sense to focus on the development of social skills as a critical element in the preschool curriculum rather than as a criterion for admission. The optimum environment for gifted preschool children is one which combines sensitively guided social experience with opportunities for enhancement of their advanced intellectual abilities. Without such an environment, gifted children are at risk for damaged self-concepts and social alienation, problems which can prevent them from developing and utilizing their outstanding potential.

Disclosing Sexual Abuse: The Impact of Developmental Variables

Mary deYoung

In today's complex society, children are often thrust into "adult" roles, and their behavior is subsequently judged as that of an adult rather than a child. One of these mismatched roles is a child who testifies in a court of law during a child sexual abuse case. Few adults understand that child testimony will not "sound" the same as an adult description of the same event. Although child development specialists know enough about how children think to interpret the information given, a child's testimony is rarely viewed from a developmental perspective.

This next article examines how children disclose sexual abuse and discusses how developmental variables influence a child's ability to share and describe relevant events. DeYoung notes that children may describe events in a disjointed or confused manner, because of cognitive constraints rather than because they fabricated information. Children in the preoperational stage of development often focus on unimportant facts, use "incorrect" vocabulary, have a poor sense of time (when events occurred and how often), and rely on transductive reasoning (pair two particular events that have no logical connection).

Sexual abuse is a serious problem. Fairness dictates that we learn to listen to young children with a full understanding of the cognitive and social constraints early development imposes.

"**W**hen are we going to give up, in all civilized nations, listening to children in courts of law?" (Varendonck, 1911, p. 133). The Belgian psychologist's lament has been echoing in courtrooms across the country for decades, and has resounded to a louder pitch in recent years as a steady parade of children, many of whom allegedly were sexually abused, has been brought into court as witnesses.

The myth of the young child as "the most dangerous of all witnesses" (Whipple, 1911, p. 307) has enjoyed a long and lively tenure in the legal community, despite sound scientific evidence to the contrary. Research has demonstrated, for example, that the common-law tradition that a child under the age of 7 is incompetent to testify (Wigmore, 1975) can be challenged by studies in child development that show that competency is more a function of cognitive and communicative skills than it is of age (Bernstein et al., 1982; Melton, 1981). Similarly, persistent complaints about the unreliability of a young child's memory have been debunked by a wealth of research demonstrating that when asked specific, direct questions about an event, a young child's memory is nearly as accurate, and for some types of events, as accurate, as that of an adult (Chance and Goldstein, 1984; Marin et al., 1979; Nelson, 1971). Even the issue of suggestibility, so long believed to be a hallmark of childhood, has been seriously questioned. Despite another of Varendonck's complaints: "Create, if you will, an idea of what the child is to hear or see, and the child is likely to hear or see what you desire" (1911, p. 133), research has shown that a young child is only slightly more sug-

M. deYoung. (1987, May/June). Disclosing sexual abuse: The impact of developmental variables. *Child Welfare, 66* (3), 217–223.

gestible to the influences and questions of adults than are other adults (Cohen and Harnick, 1980), and that in situations requiring careful judgment, a young child may be even less vulnerable to suggestion than an older child or an adult (Marin et al., 1979).

The increasing scientific evidence that even a very young child can be a credible witness (Melton, 1985), coupled with the allowance in some states for the videotaped testimony of the child witness (Bernstein and Claman, 1986), has created a considerably more congenial and supportive atmosphere for children in court than that existing a decade ago. In the case of sexual abuse, a crime that is continuing to bring a significant number of children into court every year, a review of cases shows that victimized children are emerging as reliable and believable witnesses, and that even in the absence of corroborating evidence, they can offer testimony that is compelling enough for a jury or judge to render a verdict (Melton, 1985).

Yet a persistent if somewhat narrow issue occurs in many sexual abuse cases that often is used to impeach the credibility of the child witness—the nature of the child's disclosure of the alleged sexual abuse. Frequently delayed, confused, and inconsistent, it often lacks the immediacy and confidence the law ideally would like to see in such an allegation, and perhaps may need to see before the credibility of the child as a witness can be evaluated. That this same issue has caused some researchers to assume a skeptical attitude about a child's account of sexual abuse (Ferenczi, 1949; Kaplan and Kaplan, 1981; Rosenfeld et al., 1979) shows how unsettling this problem is.

This paper examines the nature of the child's disclosure of sexual abuse and assesses the developmental variables that impact on that disclosure. Since the greatest skepticism seems to center on young children, the paper focuses on children between the ages of 2 and 7, and considers both intrafamilial and non-familial sexual abuse. For that purpose, the Brant and Tisza definition of child sexual abuse is used: "the exposure of a child to sexual stimulation inappropriate for the child's age, level of psychosexual development, or role in the family" (1977, p. 81).

DISCLOSURE OF SEXUAL ABUSE

If an accusation of sexual abuse typically were made with clarity, celerity, certainty, and consistency, few doubts as to the credibility of the complaining child would ever arise. The literature, however, shows that these qualities are rarely characteristic of a young child's allegation, and it is theorized in this paper that developmental factors interfere with these components of disclosure.

Clarity

A child between the ages of 2 and 7 is in the preoperational stage of development (Phillips, 1981) characterized by a cognitive style that would significantly obscure the clarity of a disclosure of sexual abuse. Centering in the thinking of a child in that age range, for example, causes the child to perceive and define an object in relation to its particular function (Phillips, 1981); therefore, a child may refer to ejaculation as urination since that is the perceived function of the penis. Similarly, the lack of conservation characteristic of the preoperational stage prevents the child from understanding that objects remain the same despite a change in physical appearance (Singer and Reveson, 1978), so that in the child's perception an erect penis, as an example, may no longer be perceived as a penis because of its change in shape and size.

A preoperational child is also very concrete in thinking and does not yet have the mental structures needed for logical or abstract thought (Singer and Reveson, 1978). The act of sexual abuse is a complex behavior that involves not only the act, per se, but an intricate network of corresponding motives, feelings, attitudes, perceptions, and assumptions that adults must understand in order to define and assess the act, but which the young child is largely unable to comprehend or communicate. Consequently, some essential elements of the act are likely to be missing from the child's disclosure, creating from the adults' perspective an unclear accusation. An additional and complicating factor of the cognitive style of the preoperational child is transductive reasoning which causes the child to reason from one particular to another without logically connecting them (Phillips, 1981), producing a vague, free-associative style of communication that precludes real clarity when a disclosure is made.

These developmental issues common to all young children, then, diminish the likelihood that an allegation of sexual abuse will have sufficient clarity to be credible in and of itself.

Celerity

An additional issue that must be considered is what both the literature and individual cases show is a lack of swiftness in a child's reporting of an alleged incidence of sexual abuse. Conte and Berliner (1981) found that only 16 percent of the 583 sexually abused children they studied reported the victimization to anyone within 48 hours of its occurrence. Delays in disclosure lasting anywhere from days to months to years are frequently mentioned in the literature (Farrell et al., 1981; Fritz et al., 1981), and in cases of incest, secrecy is such a powerful dynamic that many years are likely to separate the act from its disclosure (de-Young, 1982a; Meiselman, 1978).

What developmental variables contribute to these delays? Certainly a major factor is the young child's tendency to accommodate the demands of adults (de-Young, 1981; Summit, 1983). In the world of a young child, adults control all of the resources, so when those resources are manipulated, or when the adult threatens to withdraw them as a way of coercing or inveigling the child into keeping the sexual behavior secret, a delay in disclosure is inevitable.

An additional developmental variable contributes to this delay—the preoperational child's lack of attribution skills. As yet unable to use stable, dispositional constructs in predicting or judging the character of another person (Peevers and Secord, 1973; Rholes and Ruble, 1984), the child may be unable to determine that the offending adult is dangerous, or even likely to repeat the sexual abuse. Forced into that naive optimism by a developmental variable, the child may not swiftly disclose the sexual abuse simply because he or she does not have a full understanding of the immediacy of the problem.

Certainty

The same cognitive processes and lack of sophistication with the language that cloud the clarity of a disclosure of sexual abuse will also hinder its certainty. Further, to assure the secrecy of the behavior, the offending adult may tell the child that the sexual behavior is normal, desirable, or the fault of the child (deYoung, 1981; deYoung, 1982b), and that attribution of blame and reinterpretation of reality may create enough cognitive dissonance to leave the child confused and uncertain.

There is considerable speculation as to whether a young child's uncertain disclosure of sexual abuse is actually a product of the child's having fantasized about the act, and therefore of having difficulty in distinguishing fantasy from reality. Both sexual and aggressive themes are common in the imagination of a young child (Arieti, 1976; Freud, 1965) but there are several developmentally related features that restrain and shape those motifs. First, a preoperational child does not have the capacity for logical or abstract thought (Singer and Reveson, 1978)—hence the term "preoperational." That deficit leaves the child dependent on actual experiences for producing the images of fantasy. Second, the fantasies of a preoperational child reflect the pleasure principle and wishful thinking, so they inevitably have a positive tone. In fantasies the child gets what he or she does not have, goes places he or she has not gone, and figures out problems and resolves conflicts, all with positive, rewarding results. Third, mastery is a consistent theme, so that in fantasies the young child emerges as a hero, problem solver, and victor (Jersild, 1968)—not as a victim. Finally, the secondary process that is responsive to the environment allows the child to test reality and to distinguish it from fantasy (Arieti, 1976; Freud, 1965). These developmental features, then, would argue against the child's fantasizing about being sexually abused in the first place, and additionally would argue against the child's reporting fantasy as if it were reality.

Consistency

A lack of consistency in the disclosure of sexual abuse is another commonly reported issue. Amendments and even retractions of accusations occur with some frequency (De Jong, 1985; Summit, 1983) and are certainly most largely due to the pressure for secrecy placed on the child by the offending adult—often so compelling that it creates a traumatic reaction to disclosure (Finkelhor and Browne, 1985). Yet another variable that affects consistency is the intervention skill of the person(s) to whom the child is disclosing; what a child tells one person may be inconsistent with what he or she tells another because of the differences in the communication styles of adults, as well as the different degrees of trust the child, for whatever reason, will invest in various persons.

CONCLUSION

With the increase in knowledge about sexual abuse and child development, a more supportive and positive environment has greeted child witnesses in courts of law. The one factor that continues to be problematic and often is used to impeach the child as a witness—the nature of the disclosure—can be explained by carefully assessing the impact of developmental variables.

In response to the echoes of Varendonck's question, "When are we going to give up, in all civilized nations, listening to children in a court of law?" the answer must be that we do not have to give up—even young children can be competent witnesses, and their credibility increases when we make allowances for the impact of developmental variables on them and on their testimony as witnesses.

Part Four

MIDDLE CHILDHOOD

How do children between 6 and 12 see themselves as compared to the expectations of school, family, community, and peers? Because children have shifted to a new level of cognitive development (concrete operations) and are more socially and politically aware of themselves, they interpret sources of information differently—peers, television, video games, sport coaches, teachers, and so forth. School-age children begin to understand how they fit into the larger society, and how the views and mores of that society impact what they do. Events such as personal failure, prejudice, injustice, and rejection will probably enter their lives.

School-age children grow rapidly in all areas during the middle years. Physically, new coordination skills, stamina, and strength allow them to play and enjoy both individual sports (tennis, gymnastics, swimming) and team sports (soccer, baseball, hockey). Children are more interested in competition because they can understand game rules and can focus on developing new skills. It is extremely important for school-age children to be and remain active throughout their lives. Physical activity is one key to a sense of health and general well-being.

In middle childhood, children move from the preoperational to concrete stage of thought. Children can think logically and apply rules systematically to obtain new information. Children consistently use a subject and a verb when creating a sentence and combine numbers when they are asked to add. But there are still some limitations on the child's ability to fully understand abstract concepts. Kamii argues that although most schoolchildren can complete addition and subtraction problems, they do not conceptually understand what they are doing or how it relates to real numbers. Once children can apply the mechanics of math problems, schools present the materials in an isolated, sterile fashion. Math often becomes irrelevant to children's lives because at a logical level they don't understand how answers are acquired and every concept seems new because it appears unrelated to the one that came before. A look at the true level and limitations of the school-age child's cognitive abilities might lead to a productive overhaul of many math programs.

The articles by Schwartzberg, Postman, Norwood, and Grant focus on the social ecology of school-age children. How do the social contexts of peer group, media influences, and school impact development? Why do some children adapt easily to different social contexts and others appear unable to interact successfully? Which children have developed adequate self-discipline and problem-solving skills to cope with the barrage of information and temptation that assaults them daily (television, commercials, video games, drugs, and so on)? How do gender, race, and class influence development?

School-age children need skills that allow them to participate as group members. As Schwartzberg points out, acceptance is crucial during childhood, because a child rejected by peers during elementary school shows a high risk of being rejected five years later. Social rejection may lead to other, more harmful acts, such as aggressive acts, poor schoolwork, or even suicide. Helping these children to develop social skills is possible and should be pursued. In today's society, some school-age children spend time at home alone, while many others spend large amounts of time in after-school programs of every variety. Children are often forced by circumstances to a daily diet of "groupness" or "aloneness." A child's need for and success at both group and individual activity should be monitored. Different children have different social and emotional needs. Ideally, arrangements for individual children and programs serving large groups of children should be flexible and accommodating.

Media influences on school-age children may also affect self-image and behavior patterns. Postman argues that television brings about the demise of childhood. We no longer separate standards for children and adults because television homogenizes them. Television "sells" adult images and ideas to children who cannot yet play those roles. Does television undermine childhood by setting unreachable adult standards, thus negating children's developing self-

concepts? Norwood considers an additional threat to successful development during middle childhood: the media's message that taking drugs is a reasonable answer to problems. We know little about how a 6-, 8-, or 10-year-old processes all the subtle messages in the public media. Children don't have the same cognitive screening devices as adults. They often believe what they hear, and can't formulate arguments to negate or override the information given.

During these years, society's institutionalized responses to a person's race, gender, and class grow in influence. A child's sense of self, sense of group, and sense of belonging are clearly related to these environmental factors. Major inequities and barriers continue to confront children who are not white, male, and middle class. Can institutions such as schools address these issues and create better access to education and opportunity for all children? Grant suggests that we have much work to do before "Education for all" is a reality in our society.

Middle childhood is a time of steady growth in all developmental areas. Children who have confidence in themselves and in their interactions at home usually perform well in school and community activities. However, outside influences such as television, drugs, and violence worry both parents and children. Children's goals in middle childhood are to bolster their self-concept; to confront the social issues of acceptance and rejection, fairness, and self-discipline; and to meet academic and physical challenges. With these goals reached, school-age children are well prepared for the demands of adolescence.

Why Big Bird Can't Teach Calculus: The Case of Place Value and Cognitive Development in the Middle Years

Mieko Kamii

When you write the number 25, you know that the 2 "stands for" two tens and the 5 represents five ones. You "own" that information because you understand the nature of our base-ten numerical system. More specifically, you know a number's position affects its value. You realize you must multiply 2 times 10 to get 20, and that in order to get the total of the number represented, 25, you need to add 20 plus 5. When you use two-, three-, and four-digit numbers, you don't think about performing any of these operations, but conceptually they make sense to you. How and when did you come to understand these ideas?

Many children in the lower elementary grades spend hours completing worksheets of addition and subtraction problems. They know what to do to get the answer (the mechanics), but they don't know why they get the answers they do. Their level of cognitive functioning limits their conceptual knowledge of abstract features of our numerical system. Are we wasting our time teaching children operations they cannot understand? What do we need to know about how children process information in order to facilitate children's mathematical understanding?

A major challenge that children encounter in the first several years of formal schooling is two- and three-digit arithmetic, a task that requires an understanding of place value. The concept of place value seems quite natural to those who have learned it, and adults may have a hard time imagining what it is like not to know that, for instance, the 2 in 24 stands for two tens and the 4 for four ones. But children have a great deal of difficulty with the concept. Indeed, even by the fourth or fifth grade, as many as half of all children still lack a well-grounded understanding of what they are doing when they "carry" in addition or "borrow" in subtraction, despite the fact that they seem able to get proper answers when doing paper-and-pencil arithmetic problems (Ross, 1989; C. Kamii, 1986; M. Kamii, 1982).

Children's cognitive development in the realm of quantitative thinking is neither straightforward nor simple. It is characterized by successive levels of "confusion" or inadequate understanding, at least in relation to what adults think and know. A vast research literature inspired by the work of such theorists as Jean Piaget provides one example after another of the limits of children's thinking. Children do not arrive at erroneous conclusions or seemingly unreasonable judgments merely because they are inattentive or poorly instructed by adults. Rather, children's "wrong answers" and immature ideas reflect the fact that they are thinking and making the best sense they can of the problems and issues put before them. The dilemma is

M. Kamii. (1990). Why Big Bird can't teach calculus: The case of place value and cognitive development in the middle years. Original manuscript, Wheelock College, Boston, Massachusetts. Mieko Kamii, Ed.D. is an Associate Professor, Liberal Arts Department, Wheelock College, Boston, Massachusetts.

that children use their own, and not adults', knowledge or conceptual frameworks to construct meaning, draw relationships, make inferences, and gain understanding. A proper understanding of children's "structures of knowing" can help adults make sense of the "errors" children make on their way to developing more adequate concepts and critical, flexible thinking.*

CHILDREN'S LEARNING AND PLACE VALUE

When children are introduced to double-digit addition and subtraction in school, the conventional approach is to teach them that the value of a digit depends on its location (that is, whether it is in the "ones place," the "tens place," and so on) and that numerical quantities can be regrouped (for instance, thirty-two can be thought of as two tens and twelve ones). The presumption is that when children are armed with these ideas, they will perform the steps of double-digit arithmetic "with understanding," rather than performing "carrying" and "borrowing" in a purely mechanical way. However, a series of interviews conducted with children, many of whom use the procedural rules (algorithms) of arithmetic with success, cast a long shadow of doubt over this presumption.

Consider the responses of children in tasks such as the following (Ross, 1989; C. Kamii, 1986; M. Kamii, 1982). An interviewer gives a child a collection of twenty-five poker chips and asks the child to count them and then to write down how many there are. The interviewer then encircles the 5 of the child's written 25

and asks, "Does this part of your twenty-five have anything to do with how many (objects) there are?" Next the interviewer encircles the 2 of 25 and repeats the question. Finally the interviewer draws a circle around the whole numeral and asks whether it has anything to do with the quantity of poker chips on the table. The following is a sampling of the responses that first- through fifth-graders gave.

Jenny, a young first-grader, can count the chips and write down 25, but she resists the idea that a two-digit numeral such as 25 can be taken apart at all. Jenny shakes her head, no, to the interviewer's questions about the 5 and the 2 of 25 having anything to do with the amount of poker chips she had just counted, indicating that the digits bear no relationship to the quantity before her. When asked about the 25, however, she says it represents all the chips. For Jenny, splitting the whole numeral into 2 and 5 makes the number different and irrelevant to the quantity of objects she has just counted. Her classmate Steven has a different but equally "wrong" idea: he thinks that 25 refers to the last chip he has counted, and when separated, that the 5 means the fifth chip and 2 the second chip he has counted.

By the second grade, almost all children think that 25 represents the entirety of the collection. Adam, who is a second-grader, is quite certain that the whole numeral 25 represents the quantity of poker chips before him. When asked about the 5 of the 25, he counts out five chips and says the 5 stands for those chips. However, when asked what the 2 stands for, he is confused for a moment and then answers that the 2 of 25 stands for the two piles that he sees before him (the heap of twenty and the smaller collection of five chips). Diane, another second-grader, has a different idea and one that is predominant among second- and third-graders: she thinks that the 5 represents five chips; the 2, two chips; and the whole numeral 25 all twenty-five objects.

Third-graders are more likely to talk about "tens and ones" than are second-graders ("2 means two tens," they frequently say), but in their minds this knowledge or naming of the digit bears no relationship to the underlying numerical concept of two tens being the same as twenty. In a word, third-graders may *talk* about hundreds, tens, and ones, but most of them *think* about any and all digits as representing only their face value and not their place value as groupings of ten, one hundred, or larger amounts. So for example, when asked to count out the number of chips represented when the "1" is "carried" in a problem such as $17 + 15$, second- and third-graders count out one chip, not ten.

Not until the fourth and fifth grades do as many as half of the children identify the 2 of 25 as representing

---

*The focus of discussion here is children's development of mathematical understanding, but similar issues arise in other realms of cognitive development. For instance, children's acquisition of language also provides examples of "errors" that signify real progress. When children say "I goed with Mommy" or "She camed with me," they are demonstrating that they learn in a manner that is more complicated than just imitating what they are told, since no adult talks to them in such a way. At the same time, this "wrong" use shows that the child has grasped the idea of rule in verb formation and can apply the rule in innovative ways—the past tense in English is formed by adding the sound of "-ed." Armed with this rule of thumb, the child is probably better able to understand and use new verbs when they are encountered, and perhaps the child will even recognize and learn irregular verbs much faster, precisely because the irregular forms will stand out in contrast to the rule. In this sense, by constructing a "wrong" rule, the child has learned how to learn. If we focus too much on the fact that the child's rule is "wrong," we miss the significant cognitive development that has taken place. Moreover, since these "errors" in language often appear suddenly after the child has been using irregular verbs properly for some time, if we failed to understand that cognitive development takes place in circuitous ways, we might suppose that the child was regressing rather than advancing in language development.

twenty chips, showing that they understand the relationship between "2 in the tens place," "two tens" and the quantity twenty. The inescapable conclusion is that in the early grades many children are spending a considerable amount of time on their arithmetic exercises pushing around digits that in their minds lack the proper numerical meaning. Why are children having such difficulty, and what does the problem tell us about cognitive development?

CONCEPTUAL HURDLES

To begin with, the numeration system we are asking young children to grasp is one that took adults many centuries to figure out. Historians of mathematics tell us it was not completed until somewhere between the sixth and twelfth centuries A.D., and our modern algorithms for simple tasks such as division were not fully developed until the sixteenth century. Historians surmise that it took something like forty centuries to devise the elegant system that we use today (Kline, 1972; Wilder, 1968; Dantzig, 1967). But the elegance of the numeration system belies the complicated notions embedded in it. Among these, of course, is the place value feature of the system.

More formally, our numeration system is characterized by several properties. First, the system uses only the digits 1 through 9 and 0 (zero) to signify quantities both large and small. This is made possible by using written position as a vehicle for assigning a value to the digits. Second, ours is a base-ten system, with all numbers organized around ten and multiples of ten. Each position, beginning with the ones and going to the left, increases in value by powers of ten (ones $= 10^0$, tens $= 10^1$, hundreds $= 10^2$, thousands $= 10^3$, and so forth). Third, the value of a digit is determined by multiplying its face value by the value assigned to its position. The numerical values of the digits with face values of 1, 2, and 3 in the whole numeral 123 are 100 (1×10^2), 20 (2×10^1), and 3 (3×10^0). Finally, the value of the whole numeral is the sum of the values represented by its digits. To summarize, our numeration system has four important properties: the positional property, the base-ten property, the multiplicative property, and the additive property. To understand place value is to grasp each of these properties at least at an intuitive level.

These properties are neither self-evident nor easy for children to comprehend. Many first-graders are still struggling to understand quantities larger than ten or twenty in a manner that is more specific than just *beaucoup* ("many"). Rather few second-graders have more than a vague notion of the quantitative difference between eighty-nine and ninety-eight (for

example, is the difference between eighty-nine and ninety-eight really the same as between nine and eighteen?). And even fewer children at the third- and fourth-grade levels comprehend the magnitude of the difference between one hundred and one thousand. For these children, the base-ten property and the multiplicative property of the numeration system could not possibly have real meaning, no matter how intensively they were taught.

That leaves the positional and additive properties of the system as candidates for early instruction. Recall Jenny, the first-grader who refused to accept the idea that the whole numeral 25 could be taken apart at all. Jenny may have learned the *names* for the numbers, from "Sesame Street," long before she started school. Nevertheless, by the first grade she is still learning how to think about quantities as large as twenty-five, and writing the two-digit numerals corresponding to the counting words up to 100 is a challenge for her. For Jenny, the quantity as well as the numeral 25 are too fragile and uncertain to be further analyzed and made into an object of reflection. She is not yet ready to think about the positional property.

Adam, the second-grader, is much more confident about the quantity twenty-five. In contrast to Jenny, he is able to think about the digits that make up the whole numeral. For Adam, the 2 and the 5 can stand for "two and five of something." He is willing to partition the whole and to search for what those "somethings" could possibly be. He settles on five poker chips and two heaps of chips as reasonable possibilities. His behavior shows that he does not yet understand that 2 must refer to two groups of equal size. Furthermore he cannot yet think in terms of the relationship between the whole amount (25) and the parts (5+20), which must be equivalent to the whole. The additive property of the system seems still beyond his reach.

Diane's interpretation of the digits is more consistent than is Adam's. She singles out five and then two of the twenty-five chips for the digits 5 and 2, thus relying on their face values and treating the digits as if both represented ones. While Diane's idea is no more correct than Adam's, the fact that she applies the same interpretation to both digits gives her thinking a flavor of greater coherence. Similarly, Steven, the first-grader who insisted that the numbers in 25 stood for the second, fifth, and twenty-fifth chip, also shows the capacity to apply systematically a numerical concept that makes sense to him. But for both Diane and Steven, the coherence is ill founded from the standpoint of place value and numerical part-whole relations. They have better "wrong" ideas than Adam, but they are still wrong.

Jenny, Adam, Diane, and Steven's behaviors show no traces of awareness of either the positional or the additive properties of the numeration system. None of them truly understands place value.

COGNITIVE DEVELOPMENT AND LEARNING

Within the theoretical framework of Piaget, much of children's "confusion" makes sense. Piaget drew a distinction between the idea of number, which he argued had to be constructed by each individual child, and the acquisition of the culture's symbol systems for writing and talking about numbers, which had to be learned from others. To really understand the relationships between number and numeration, children have to construct (think through or reinvent for themselves) the numerical relationships undergirding the system itself.

In an effort to sort through how children acquire knowledge, Piaget categorized knowledge into three types—physical knowledge, social knowledge, and logico-mathematical knowledge—that are distinguished by their different sources for feedback or verification. In this scheme, physical knowledge is knowledge of the properties of objects in external reality, and is acquired by acting on objects and observing the results of those actions (for example, throwing different kinds of objects and observing that the round ones roll; dropping objects into a tub of water and observing that the light ones float). The source of feedback is largely empirical in nature.

Social knowledge includes knowledge of cultural objects and social conventions, and is acquired through interacting with people (for example, learning the vocabulary of one's native tongue and knowing appropriate dress for church, school, and beach). The source of feedback is other people.

The third category is the one most critical for this discussion, logico-mathematical knowledge. The content of logico-mathematical knowledge is logical and numerical relationships that are constructed by each individual child. Feedback comes neither from external reality nor from other people, but rather from the individual's own mental activity (thought), and it is experienced by the individual as "a feeling of logical necessity," a feeling that "this does or does not make good sense."

Piaget argued that number and numerical relationships are not "out there in the world to be observed," and that concepts such as these cannot be directly taught. Instead, the concept of number emerges from the child's mental activity, as he or she puts into relationship the results of all sorts of activities (for example, counting, ordering, and reordering objects, or dividing up objects among playmates). It is out of these mental activities that the child gradu-

ally structures (abstracts) a specific kind of equivalence, numerical equivalence, as a distinct idea (Piaget, 1965). Similarly, the child structures numerical part-whole relationships, numerical groupings, and other concepts as he or she thinks about objects numerically.

This analysis of how children acquire the ability to think quantitatively has implications for formal and informal education. If the counting words and the numerals that correspond to them are social objects, then knowledge of them must and can be acquired from others. It makes sense to teach these quite directly—Big Bird *can* teach children the digits and the words. Yet if number concepts and other quantitative relationships grow out of the child's ability to make relationships in his or her head, then direct instruction is not pertinent. In the view of Piaget and other developmentalists, children are not "little adult thinkers" who merely lack information. Children are different thinkers, and as such they do not and cannot absorb information in the same way as adults. For this reason, their level and pace of cognitive growth are not simply a function of having more information pushed before them sooner and faster. Big Bird *cannot* teach calculus to kindergartners. What adults can do is to structure activities that give children the opportunities and incentive to think about number. This means involving them in problems that interest them, problems that they are motivated to discuss and to solve at their own cognitive pace.

This is the rationale for a "constructivist" approach to math education: using math games rather than worksheets, and group discussions rather than individual seatwork in primary classrooms (C. Kamii, 1985). It is the reason why many teachers prefer to discuss quantitative problems arising in and from the immediate classroom environment rather than problems plucked out of a workbook. It is the justification for accepting children's invented procedures (such as solving $54 + 27$ by adding 30 to 54 and deducting 3) rather than stressing ready-made algorithms that are difficult for children to understand, although perhaps easy for them to use in a rote manner. An implication of Piaget's theory is that children who are exposed to a variety of thought-inducing activities will have rich and varied stores of data to mull over, and lots of practice putting ideas into relationship with each other. And they will come to understand math as a way of thinking about reality rather than as a body of procedures dreamed up by someone else and stuffed into their heads.

However, serious questions remain concerning the actual processes by which quantitative relationships are constructed. Piaget did not provide a detailed explanation of how the child's earliest ability to count objects or to make one-to-one correspondences becomes transformed into a real concept of number or, more relevant to place value, how the child's understanding of groupings of ten develops out of his or her understanding of ones. What are the steps, processes, or routes of construction? What happens from one moment to the next, rather than from one month or year to the next in the mind of the child? Although children may learn math quite readily in a constructivist setting, in the absence of a deeper theoretical explanation of the cognitive processes at work, we have no assurance that other educational methods are not superior.

Other theoretical perspectives in the cognitive sciences have focused more directly on thought as a process. Information-processing psychology, for example, uses the workings of the digital computer as its root metaphor for the workings of the human mind (Flavell, 1985). Just as computers process information in a variety of ways, store information in different types of memory, and perform a wide range of tasks, so does the human cognitive system. Information-processing psychologists are concerned with describing in detail how children perceive problems, such as the digit correspondence tasks described earlier: which aspects of the problem children attend to (encoding data or representing the problem), and which facts, procedures, or other knowledge they recall (strategies for accessing prior knowledge and retrieving information from long-term memory). Perhaps most important is information-processing psychology's effort to describe how children detect relationships by manipulating new information and prior knowledge in working memory, and how the results of those manipulations, including modified concepts, altered strategies, and new facts, are stored in long-term memory. Information processing raises questions about the development of the cognitive system, including children's attentional capacities, the organization of information in memory, and the acquisition of problem-solving strategies (Resnick and Ford, 1981).

Because information-processing psychology aims at describing and explaining cognitive processes and cognitive development at a much more specific level than did Piaget, it may in the future provide us with a far more detailed description of the constructive processes by which children advance from less to more adequate understandings in the quantitative domain. Armed with such insights, educators could revise the arithmetic curriculum in the middle years appropriately. However, the metaphor of the machine—in contrast to Piaget's metaphors of the mind drawn from biology and embryology—may presume greater order in children's learning than in fact exists. While both frameworks share an ultimate concern with understanding conceptual development, each poses questions, formulates research agendas, and explains its findings in a different way.

What about the implications of those findings—will a better description result in constructing new math workbooks, reshuffling topics in the math curriculum, developing a different set of prescriptions for classroom practices? It is hard to say. For example, the choice to focus classroom time on written arithmetic has a long and honored place in U.S. classrooms. It is not easy for the constructivist to explain to Johnny's parents, "No, he still hasn't learned long division in the fifth grade, but cognitively he's better off—wait until you see how well he does algebra in ninth grade!"

CONCLUSION

Written arithmetic places a burden on teachers to help children make sense of the *symbols* of mathematics (social knowledge), often at the expense of activities that encourage children to construct the ideas for which the symbols stand. Written arithmetic also lends itself to teaching children the algorithms, which has two potential pitfalls. First, it makes it possible for children to not think about actual quantities until the end, when they (hopefully) use the metacognitive strategy of asking themselves whether their answers make sense. Second, once children learn the algorithms, they are tempted to adhere to them as the only way of calculating. This stands in the way of developing other procedures that may ultimately enable the development of a better number sense and a more flexible way of thinking. In other words, an emphasis on written arithmetic alone seduces children and teachers into thinking that correct written answers reflect good thinking and understanding. They may, but they also may not.

From one perspective, the difficulties that children have with place value can be viewed as simply a troublesome obstacle for the designers of math curricula. From another perspective, however, they offer a window on the complexities of children's thinking and present puzzles about cognitive development. It is sobering to consider that if indeed adults' thinking is profoundly different from the way in which children think, then we may confront natural obstacles to fully reconstructing what it is like to think as a child. Nevertheless, although neither of the theoretical frameworks presented here, nor others that were not discussed, is as yet sufficiently rich, rigorous, or complete to put to rest all questions arising from what we observe in children's cognitive development, they do offer fruitful lines of inquiry for solving the puzzles that remain.

The Popularity Factor

Neala Schwartzberg

A child's social life—interactions with and perceptions of peers—is as important as the child's cognitive and physical success. But we often accept social success or failure as a given: some children "have what it takes," and others just don't. Research demonstrates that children who are unpopular or "invisible" lack specific social skills. They taunt and tease or stand on the sidelines while others know how to cooperate, share, and easily enter existing groups of peers. Fortunately, skills can be taught and behaviors can change. "Coaching" unpopular children in how to use appropriate social skills may be a good strategy for fostering self-esteem, enhancing school achievement, and lowering the school dropout rate.

The recurring themes of nature versus nurture and continuity versus discontinuity crop up here too. Do inborn factors such as temperament and cognitive ability limit a child's social skills? If a child experiences social problems at age 10, will he or she continue to be an outcast as an adolescent or an adult? The answer to each question is a qualified no. If the environment is supportive and responsive to the child's needs (and need to change), positive social interactions can replace unsuccessful ones.

Observers of children can't help but notice that some youngsters find playing with friends as important as food to eat and air to breathe, while other youngsters watch from the sidelines. Some children make friends wherever they go, and others can't even be with another child for five minutes before voices are raised and an adult must intervene. Why are some children popular and others not?

Some researchers place the origins of social behavior and social status within the family. When children feel secure in their relationships with their parents and feel good about their own abilities, according to Martha Putallaz, Ph.D., professor of psychology at Duke University, "they are able to explore new relationships with more confidence." They are more likely to be successful in those relationships because they can respond to other people without being preoccupied with their own needs.

Dr. Putallaz has been investigating the pattern of interaction between mother and child and how it relates to the child's social status. She has found that mothers of more popular children interact with their youngsters in a more positive manner. They are less likely to make power demands ("Do it because I told you to do it"), and they are concerned with feelings, both their own and those of their children. They listen carefully and ask their youngsters their opinions. One interpretation of these findings is that these mothers present a model to their children of how to treat others, a model that the youngsters apply when interacting with their peers.

As we might expect, the youngsters who are higher in social status engage in less squabbling and disagreement with their mothers, but the children also make more attempts to influence their parents. The

N. S. Schwartzberg. (1988, November). The popularity factor. *Parents*, 63 (11), 144–148.

105

way these youngsters exert their influence is intriguing. They do not use power plays. They are not strident or demanding. They use reasoning and even jokes to get their point across, demonstrating a fair degree of social facility and finesse, skills that probably carry over well to the playground and the classroom.

PEER OPINION COUNTS

Psychologists John Coie, Ph.D., of Duke University and Kenneth Dodge, Ph.D., of Vanderbilt University have been studying the characteristics that make a child popular or unpopular by going into the classroom and asking children to tell them the names of the youngsters they like the most and like the least. They use this information to form different groups of youngsters.

Popular children were those whose names appeared on the "liked most" lists and rarely on the "liked least" lists. Rejected children, like Melissa, rarely appeared on the "liked most" list but were frequently named on the "liked least" list. "Invisible" children, neglected by their peers, were rarely mentioned on anyone's list. Drs. Coie and Dodge have also found a group of children they labeled controversial whose names appear frequently on the lists of children liked most and liked least. Most classrooms seem to have at least one or two children in each category, with boys more likely than girls to be among those actively rejected.

The explanation for the children's differing social status seems to be found in their behavior. Rejected youngsters taunt and threaten other children more and are more likely to push and shove. They also wander through the classroom, annoying and antagonizing their classmates while they are supposed to be working.

Popular youngsters are seen by their peers as the leaders. They are the ones chosen to be in charge; they know how to cooperate, and they readily pitch in and take turns. Although the popular kids are often in control, they rarely alienate others by being bossy or demanding, and they ask for help only when they need it, rather than use it as a ploy to gain attention.

Controversial youngsters embody the characteristics of both popular and unpopular children. When they want to, they know how to organize and get things done, but they can also be disruptive and combative. In short, they are active and assertive, some children's best friends, others' worst enemies. Invisible children are the exact opposite of the controversial youngsters, making almost no impact on anyone. Furthermore, they abhor conflict of any kind. This lack of involvement makes it difficult for their classmates even to describe their personality.

WHY SOME KIDS ARE UNPOPULAR

Parents will tell you, however, that children's opinions of each other change frequently. To determine how much a child's social status was determined by circumstance as opposed to behavior, Dr. Coie and Janis Kuperschmidt, Ph.D., assistant professor of psychology at the University of North Carolina at Chapel Hill, examined the differences in the behavior of popular and unpopular boys as they played either in a group of children they all knew or in a group of youngsters who were unknown to each other.

If their social status was not based on personal attributes, the psychologists theorized, this fresh start should enable rejected boys to become more popular. But it didn't. By the end of the third week of being with new playmates, the unpopular boys' status in the group began to resemble their status in the classroom. They were again perceived as the most unpopular, and the reasons lay in their behavior. In both familiar and unfamiliar groups, the boys were intolerable, bossing the other youngsters, insulting and threatening them. They seem to create the conditions for their own rejection.

Surprisingly, this was not true for invisible children. In the new setting, with new playmates, the neglected boys were able to break from their usual social patterns. According to Drs. Coie and Kuperschmidt, these boys became "more talkative, engaged in more prosocial behavior and were as much involved in rough-and-tumble play as other boys."

What accounts for the change in this group of boys? "Children who are somewhat timid and avoid rough-and-tumble play tend to be less visible," observes Dr. Coie, "and they get lost in larger groups. When the groups become smaller, it becomes easier for them to get to know children and to make friends."

Irene is trying to join a group of children jumping rope. She watches for a while from the sidelines.

"I'm the best at jumping rope," she announces. The other children look at her briefly, then turn back to their game. Irene tries again.

"I can jump better than that," she says, hoping the others will invite her to show them. But they don't.

After a while, Irene leaves, calling out a final "Jump rope is a stupid game" over her shoulder.

At the other end of the playground, Jamie watches two of his classmates climbing on the play equipment. It looks like fun and he wants to join them, so he begins to climb up near them.

"You guys climb fast," he says as they reach the top together.

"Yeah," they agree, they are good climbers.

"Want to see who can get down the fastest?" Jamie asks.

"Sure," one of the boys answers as all three race down.

Making new friends and joining a group of youngsters already at play are typical social situations that can pose a difficulty for youngsters. Dr. Dodge and his colleagues found that youngsters judged to be socially competent in the early grades thought about and solved these child-size social dilemmas differently. When faced with the task of joining children already at play, some children behaved more skillfully than others. Socially competent children were more likely to place themselves physically close to the other children and imitate their behavior. Whether playing with blocks the same way or dancing around the room, they *merged* their behavior with that of the other children.

Children judged to be less socially competent tended to go off into another area of the room, making it impossible for others to include them, and to produce strange kinds of behavior that seemed nonsensical to the observers. When they did attempt to join the other children, they used what these investigators called a "weak demand," a polite, almost hesitant request that was easy for the other children to turn down. Host children's attempts to create a friendly atmosphere ("I have a red shirt and so do you") were met with disagreement ("No, mine is purple"). It was as if these less competent children were having difficulty entering the flow of the social exchange.

Even their pattern of social interaction was different. The conversations of competent children made sense; they gave information to a youngster who asked for it. Moreover, these youngsters were able to move from a more formal interchange ("Who's your teacher?") to one that was friendlier ("Do you want to build a house with these blocks?"), and they refrained from being irritable and disagreeable.

In short, popular kids have better social skills than unpopular kids. They adopt the group's frame of reference, for instance, by making statements about the play activity, but unlike Irene, they don't focus all the attention on themselves. Children who are successful at joining in the play of other youngsters, like Jamie, are rarely disruptive.

THE COSTS OF REJECTION

Studies in which youngsters are followed over time have shown that just about a third of rejected children will be rejected five years later. Another third end up relatively invisible. The rest do master enough social skills to be of average popularity, but almost none become social stars.

Invisible children, on the other hand, will probably fare better. According to Drs. Coie and Dodge, of the children studied who were invisible in elementary grades, about one-fourth stayed invisible. About half, though, went on to become more well-known and almost one-fourth of those children even became popular. Most became more popular because they are basically nice kids, who eventually found a social niche, a place for themselves. "They find interests that they can share and friends they can relate to," explains Dr. Coie. Often these formerly neglected youngsters find friends in special situations, such as the science club, the band, or the newspaper, and they blossom.

Researchers believe those youngsters who stay unpopular, either openly disliked or simply unacknowledged, are at risk for greater problems. For instance, says Kenneth Rubin, Ph.D., professor of psychology at the University of Waterloo in Ontario, who has been conducting extensive research among socially withdrawn youngsters, the self-perceptions of unpopular children are less positive than those of more popular youngsters.

Unpopular youngsters are lonelier and less satisfied. They perceive themselves to be less able generally, in their schoolwork and in their sports skills. By the middle years, the costs of social withdrawal include the experience of social failure and an emerging sense of personal incompetence. Not surprisingly, adds Dr. Rubin, these children are more likely to say that they have nobody to talk to in class, that it is harder to make friends, that they do not get along with their classmates, and that they generally feel left out of things at school.

TEACHING SOCIAL SKILLS

Psychologists are now addressing the problem of how to get these unpopular children back into the swing of things with their classmates: how to make these youngsters feel better about themselves and how to help them gain wider social acceptance.

One thought-provoking study found that tutoring a group of boys, who showed academic as well as social skill deficits, in math and reading eventually increased the children's popularity. Feeling more confident with their classroom work, the boys became less disruptive and less annoying to the other children as they worked harder on their own assignments. The academic intervention even proved more effective than the researchers' attempts to tutor the unpopular boys in social skills.

Tutoring for social skills, however, is not without merit, as some child psychologists are finding that certain children benefit from friendly intervention and assistance. For instance, many times when youngsters attempt to play with other children, their efforts are not immediately successful. Other children may react with something less than enthusiasm, or there may be a short period of play, followed by a lack of interest in continuing. When children interpret this as a personal rejection they are less likely to try again, jeopardizing their chance for future success. A self-fulfilling prophecy has been created. Training youngsters to cope with these difficult situations can break that cycle.

"Children without friends are often victims of their own social behavior," reports Steven R. Asher, Ph.D., professor of educational psychology at the University of Illinois at Urbana-Champaign. Dr. Asher has been developing and evaluating programs to teach social skills to these unpopular youngsters. Social skills training programs generally attempt to teach youngsters how to become involved in playing with other children and how to play constructively. There are important skills involved in resolving conflicts that arise when two youngsters disagree about what program to watch on television or what game to play outside. A youngster who can't handle these situations comfortably may learn how to assert himself without being aggressive, to offer to take turns and cooperate ("You choose first, and then I'll decide what to play"), or to play constructively with another child without constant squabbles.

HOW TO BE A GOOD FRIEND

Children need to understand how their behavior affects the other child—that what they do can cause another to like them or dislike them. This comes as a revelation to some youngsters. Most children aren't purposely obnoxious, but it may not occur to an unpopular child that demanding that other children play a game because *he* wants to might make him less fun to play with. Or that casually noting a classmate's shirt was "ugly" might hurt her feelings and make her pull away.

Other times youngsters may be rejected as play partners because they have different goals. Socially inept youngsters tend to play a game simply to win, not as a chance to play with another youngster and have a good time. Asher's programs aim to expand the unpopular child's point of view. "In coaching children," Dr. Asher notes, "we emphasize the idea that both players should have fun."

Finally, Dr. Asher emphasizes the importance of teaching these youngsters how to be supportive of another child, to make a friend feel good about herself. Yelling "Ha, ha, you lost" is a far less supportive statement than, "You played a good game." A comment like "Anyone could have made that mistake" shows a concern for the feelings of others that socially unskilled youngsters often lack. Although the results of coaching are not guaranteed, Dr. Asher says that about 50 to 60 percent of unpopular youngsters benefit from such social skills training.

As children grow, the criteria for being a good friend do change, from being someone who is fun to play with and share toys with, to someone whom you can trust and confide in. But at any age a child needs to have certain basic social skills. These skills are no luxury; they are the skills required for success and happiness throughout life.

The Disappearance of Childhood

Neil Postman

The invention of the printing press changed the world and the course of human development. Will our age of electronic media—constantly bombarding us with visual images—do the same? Our dependence on the oral and written word has shifted to a reliance on television, computer, and film-video languages. Our systems of communication have changed from words to instant, informative images.

Postman argues that the visual media have erased the dividing line between adulthood and childhood. Television-video-film is accessible to all and presents itself at a common level of understanding. (Children cannot read War and Peace *because the language and the plot are too complex. But anyone can watch "Hawaii Five-O.") Adults no longer keep "adult" issues—such as sex, illness, death, and war—*

from children. The media makes these issues daily fare. David Elkind, in his book The Hurried Child, *agrees that children are exposed to too much, too soon. We are reverting to the medieval practice of perceiving children as miniature adults.*

If children are besieged with fixed visual images on a daily basis and interact in a "watching" rather than an active mode, will certain developmental domains be affected? Do we, as adults, need to ensure clear distinctions between childhood and adulthood? The visual age is a far-reaching, multifaceted context. Children need creative strategies for using images as productively as we have learned to use the written word.

I am going to argue that a new media environment, with television at its center, is leading to the rapid disappearance of childhood in North America; that childhood will probably not survive to the end of this century; and that such a state of affairs represents a social disaster of the first order. When I have made my argument, I will stop. This isn't to say that there is no solution to the problem, only that my own imaginative reach for solutions goes no further than my grasp of the problem. . . .

Let me begin my argument with the observation that childhood is a social artifact, not a biological category. Our genes contain no clear instructions about who is and who is not a child, and the laws of survival do not require that a distinction be made between the

world of the adult and the world of the child. In fact, if we take the word "children" to mean a special class of people somewhere between, say, the ages of 7 and 17, who require special forms of nurturing and protection and who are believed to be qualitatively different from adults, then there is ample evidence that children have existed for less than 400 years. Indeed, if we use the word "children" in the fullest sense in which the average North American understands the word, childhood is not much more than 150 years old.

To take one small example, the custom of celebrating a child's birthday did not exist in North America throughout most of the eighteenth century. In fact, the precise marking of a child's age in any way is a relatively recent cultural tradition, no more than 200 years old. To take a more important example, as late as 1890, high schools in the United States enrolled only 7 percent of the 12- to 17-year-old population. Along with many much younger children, the other 93 percent

N. Postman. (1985, Mar.–Apr.). The disappearance of childhood. *Childhood Education, 61* (4),286–293.

worked at adult labor, some to them from sunup to sunset, in all of the great cities.

THE IDEA OF CHILDHOOD

But it would be a mistake at the outset to confuse social facts with social ideas. I want to discuss here the *idea* of childhood. The idea of childhood is one of the great inventions of the Renaissance, perhaps its most humane one. Along with science, the nation, state and religious freedom, childhood as both a social principle and a psychological condition emerged around the sixteenth century.

Up until that time, children as young as 6 and 7 were not regarded as fundamentally different from adults. The language of children, their way of dressing, their games, their labor and their legal rights were exactly the same as adults'. It was recognized, of course, that children tended to be smaller than adults, but this fact did not confer on them any special status. No special institutions existed for the nurturing of children. Prior to the sixteenth century, for instance, there were no books on child rearing, or indeed any books about women in their role as mothers. Children were always included in funeral processions, there being no reason anyone could think of to shield them from death. There are no references to children's speech or jargon prior to the sixteenth century, after which they are found in abundance.

If you've ever seen thirteenth- or fourteenth-century paintings of children, you may have noticed they are always depicted as small adults. Except for size, they are devoid of any of the physical characteristics we associate with childhood, and they are never shown on canvas alone (that is, isolated from other adults). Such paintings are entirely accurate representations of the psychological and social perceptions of children prior to the sixteenth century.

Here is how the great Cambridge historian J. H. Plumb described the situation:

> There was no separate world of childhood. Children shared the same games with adults, the same toys, the same fairy stories. They lived their lives together, never apart. The coarse village festivals depicted by Breughel, showing men and women besotted with drink, groping for each other with unbridled lust, show children eating and drinking along with the adults. Even in the soberer pictures of wedding feasts and dances, the children are enjoying themselves alongside the adults, doing exactly the same things. (Plumb, 1971, p. 7)

Barbara Tuchman, in her marvelous book about the fourteenth century called *A Distant Mirror*, summed it up this way:

> If children survived to age 7, their recognized life began more or less as miniature adults. Childhood was already over. (Tuchman, 1978, p. 50)

Why this was the case is pretty complicated to say. For one thing, as Ms. Tuchman suggests, most children did not survive; their mortality rate was extraordinarily high. It is not until the late fourteenth century that children are even mentioned in wills and testaments, an indication that adults did not expect them to be around very long. Certainly adults did not have the emotional commitment to children that people like us accept as normal. Then, too, children were regarded primarily as economic utilities, adults being less interested in children's character and intelligence than in their capacity for work.

But beyond question, the most powerful reason for the absence of the idea of childhood, the concept of a child, is to be found in what I call the communication environment of the medieval world. Since most people did not know how to read or did not need to know how to read, a child became an adult, a fully participating adult, at the point when he or she learned how to speak. Since all important social transactions involved face-to-face oral communication, full competence to speak and hear, usually achieved by age 7, served as the dividing line between infancy and adulthood. That is why the Catholic Church designated age 7 as the age at which a person can know the difference between right and wrong, the age of reason. That is why 7-year-olds were hanged along with adults for stealing or murder. And that is why there was no such thing as elementary education in the Middle Ages, because where biology determines your communication competence there is no need for elementary education. In other words, there was no intervening stage in the medieval world between infancy and adulthood; there was no concept of a child because none was needed.

THE PRINTING PRESS

That is, until the middle of the fifteenth century. At that point an extraordinary event occurred which not only changed the religious, economic, and political face of Europe, but also created our modern idea of childhood.... I'm referring, of course, to the invention of the printing press. No one had the slightest idea in the year 1450 that the printing press would have such powerful effects on our society as it did. When Gutenberg announced that he could manufacture books, as he put it, "Without help of reed, stylus or pen but by wondrous agreement, proportion and harmony of punches and types," he didn't imagine that his invention would undermine the authority of the Catholic Church. Yet, less than eighty years later, Martin Luther was in effect claiming that, with the word of God on every family's kitchen table, Christians did not require the papacy to interpret it for them. Neither did Gutenberg have any idea that his invention would create a new class of people; namely, children.

To get some idea of what reading meant in the two centuries following Gutenberg's invention, consider the case of two men, one by the name of William, the other by the name of Paul. In the year 1605, they attempted to burglarize the house of the Earl of Sussex. They were caught and convicted. Here are the exact words of their sentence, as given by the presiding magistrate:

> The said William does not read. To be hanged. The said Paul does read. To be scarred.

Now, Paul's punishment wasn't exactly merciful. It meant he would have to endure the scarring of his thumbs. But unlike William, he survived because he had pleaded what was called "benefit to clergy," which meant that he could meet the challenge of reading at least one sentence from an English version of the Bible. That ability alone, according to English law in the seventeenth century, was sufficient grounds to exempt him from the gallows. I suspect you'll agree with me when I say that, of all the suggestions I have ever heard about how to motivate people to learn to read, none matches the method of seventeenth-century England. As a matter of fact, of 203 men convicted of hangable crimes in Norwich in the year 1644, about half of them pleaded benefit of clergy, which suggests that the English, at the very least, were able to produce the most literate population of felons in history.

But, of course, that was not the only thing produced. As I implied, childhood was an outgrowth of literacy. It happened because in less than 100 years after the printing press, European culture became a reading culture; that is to say, adulthood was redefined. One could not become an adult unless he or she knew how to read. In order to experience God, one had to be able, obviously, to read the Bible. In order to experience literature, one had to be able to read novels and personal essays—forms of literature, by the way, that were wholly created by the printing press. Of course, in order to learn science, one not only had to know how to read but, by the beginning of the seventeenth century, to read science in the vernacular; that is, in one's own language.

Alongside all of this, the Europeans rediscovered what Plato had known all along about learning to read; namely, that it is best done at an early age. Since reading is, among other things, an unconscious reflex as well as an act of recognition, the habit of reading is best formed in that period when the brain is still engaged in the task of acquiring oral language. The adult who learns to read after his or her oral vocabulary is completed rarely becomes a fluent reader.

What this came to mean in the sixteenth century is that the young had to be separated from the rest of the community in order to be taught how to read; that is, in order to be taught how to function as an adult. Before the printing press, children became adults by learning to speak, for which all people are biologically programmed. After the printing press, children had to earn adulthood by achieving literacy, for which people are not biologically programmed. This meant that schools had to be created. In the medieval world, there was no such thing as primary education. In England, for example, there were 34 schools in the entire country in the year 1480, none of them what we would call an elementary school. By the year 1660, there were over 450, one school for every 12 miles—almost all of them what we would call elementary schools.

With the establishment of school, it was inevitable that the young would become viewed as a special class of people whose minds and character were qualitatively different from adults'. Because the school was designed for the preparation of a literate adult, the young came to be perceived not as miniature adults but as something quite different altogether: unformed adults. School learning became identified with the special nature of childhood. Childhood in turn became defined by school attendance and the word "schoolboy" became synonymous with the word "child."

We began, in short, to see human development as a series of stages, of which childhood is a bridge between infancy and adulthood. For the past 350 years, we've been developing and refining this conception of childhood. We have developed institutions for the nurturing of children and we have conferred upon children a special status, reflected in the ways we expect them to think, to talk, to dress, to play, and to learn.

THE ELECTRONIC MEDIA

All of this, I believe, is now coming to an end, at least very rapidly in America. It's coming to an end because our communication environment has been radically altered once again, this time by electronic media, especially television. Television has a transforming power at least equal to that of the printing press. It is my contention that with the assistance of other media, such as radio, film, and records, television has the power to lead us to childhood's end.

Here is how the transformation is happening. To begin with, television is essentially nonlinguistic. It presents information mostly in visual images. Although human speech is heard on TV and sometimes assumes importance, people mostly *watch* television; and what they watch are rapidly changing visual images, as many as 1,200 different shots every hour. The average length of a shot on a network television show is 3.5 seconds; the average length of a shot on a commercial is 2.1 seconds.

All of this requires very little analytic decoding. In America, TV-watching is almost wholly a matter of instant pattern recognition. Television's symbolic form, its visual form, does not require any special instruction or learning. In America, TV-viewing begins at about the age of 18 months, and by 36 months, according to studies by Dan Anderson of Harvard, children begin to understand and respond to TV's imagery. They have favorite characters, they sing jingles they hear, and they ask for products they see advertised. Thus there is no need for any preparation or prerequisite training for watching television. Television needs no analogue to the McGuffey reader. Watching TV requires no skills and develops no skills, and that is why there is no such thing as remedial television viewing. That is why you are no better today at watching TV than you were five years ago, or ten.

And that is also why there is no such thing, in reality, as children's programming on TV. Everything on TV is for everybody. So far as symbolic form is concerned, "Charlie's Angels" is as sophisticated or as simple to grasp as "Sesame Street." Unlike books, which vary greatly in syntactical and lexical complexity and which may be scaled according to the ability of the reader, TV presents information in a form that is undifferentiated in its accessibility. That is why adults and children tend to watch the same programs. I might add, in case anyone thinks that children and adults at least watch at different times, that according to Mankewicz and Swerdlow's book on television, called *Remote Control* (1979), and recently confirmed by the Nielsen organization, approximately two million children watch television in America every day of the year between 11:30 P.M. and 2:00 A.M.

Television, then, erases the dividing line between childhood and adulthood in two ways. First, because it requires no instruction to grasp its form, you do not have to invent an institution like the school to teach children how to do this. Second, because television cannot segregate its audiences, it has to communicate the same information to everyone, regardless of age.

TV erases the dividing line in other ways as well. You might say that the main difference between an adult and a child is that the adult knows about certain facets of life (its mysteries, its contradictions, its violence, its tragedies) not considered suitable for children to know. As children move toward adulthood, we reveal these secrets to them in what we believe to be a psychologically assimilable way. That is why there is such a thing as children's literature, for example. But television makes this arrangement impossible. Because TV operates virtually around the clock, it requires a constant supply of novel and interesting information. This means that all adult secrets (social, sexual, medical, physical, political, and the like) must be and will be revealed. Television forces the entire culture to come out of the closet. In its quest for new and sensational information to hold its audience, TV must tap every existing taboo in the culture: incest, divorce, promiscuity, corruption, adultery, sadism. Each is now merely a theme for one or another television show and in the process—and this is the point— each loses its role as an exclusively adult secret. . . .

You see, television is relentless in both revealing and trivializing all things private and shameful. The subject matter of the confessional box and the psychiatrist's office is now in the public domain. I have it on good authority that the next season on American network television we and our children will have the opportunity to see a commercial network's first serious experiments with presenting nudity. This will probably not shock anyone, since TV commercials have been offering a form of soft-core pornography for years, as for example the designer jeans commercials. Commercials, too—the one million the average American youth will see in the first 18 years of his or her life at a rate of 1,000 per week—open to youth all of the secrets that once were the province of adults, everything from vaginal sprays to life insurance to the causes of marital conflict. And we must not omit the contribution of news shows, those curious entertainments that daily provide the young with vivid images of adults' incompetence and even madness.

As a consequence of all this, childhood innocence is impossible to sustain, which is why children have disappeared from television. Have you noticed that all the children are now depicted as merely small adults? (I call this the Gary Coleman syndrome.) They are reminiscent of fourteenth-century paintings of children. They are all miniature adults. Watch "Love Boat" or any of the soap operas or family shows or situation comedies, and you will see children whose language, dress, sexuality, and interests are not fundamentally different from those of the adults on the same shows.

Yet, as TV begins to render invisible the traditional concept of childhood, it wouldn't be quite accurate to say that it immerses us in an adult world. Rather, TV uses the material of the adult world as the basis for projecting a new kind of person altogether. We might call this person the adult-child. For reasons that have partly to do with TV's capacity to reach everyone, partly to do with the accessibility of its visual form, partly to do of course with its commercial basis, TV promotes as desirable many of the attitudes that we associate with childishness; for example, an obsessive need for immediate gratification, a lack of concern for consequences, an almost promiscuous preoccupation with consumption. TV seems to favor a population that consists of three age groups: on the one hand, infancy; on the other, senility; and, in between, a group of indeterminate age where everyone is somewhere between 20 and 30 and remains that way until dotage descends.

In this connection, I want to remind you of a TV commercial that sells hand lotion. In this commercial we are shown a mother and a daughter and then challenged to tell which is which. I find this to be a very revealing piece of sociological evidence because it tells us that in our culture, circa 1985, it is considered desirable that a mother should not look older than her daughter; or, that a daughter should not look younger than her mother. Whether this means that childhood is gone or adulthood is gone amounts to the same thing: if there is no clear concept of what it means to be an adult, there can be no clear concept of what it means to be a child.

In any case, however you wish to phrase this transformation taking place in North America especially, and beginning to happen in Europe, it's pretty clear that the behavior, attitudes, desires, and even physical appearance of adults and children are becoming increasingly indistinguishable. There is now virtually no difference, for instance, between adult crimes and children's crimes; and in many states in America, the punishments are now becoming the same. Between 1950 and 1979, the increase among the under- 15-year-old population in what the FBI calls "serious crime" (murder, rape, and so on) exceeds 11,000 percent.

There's also very little difference in dress. The children's clothing industry has undergone a virtual revolution within the past ten or fifteen years; there no longer exists what we once unambiguously recognized as children's clothing. Eleven-year-old boys wear three-piece suits to birthday parties, and 61-year-old men wear jeans to birthday parties. Twelve-year-old girls wear high heels; 52-year-old men wear sneakers; and on the streets of New York, Toronto, and Chicago, you can see grown women wearing little white socks, imitation Mary Janes, and once again miniskirts, that most obvious and embarrassing example of adults imitating and aping the dress of children.

To take another case, children's games, once so imaginatively rich and varied and so emphatically inappropriate for adults, are rapidly disappearing, at least south of the border. Little league baseball and Pee Wee football, for instance, are not only supervised by adults but are modeled, in their organization and emotional style, after big league sports. Junk food, once

suited only to the undiscriminating palates and iron stomachs of the young, is now common fare for adults. Most adults have forgotten that they are supposed to have more developed taste in food than children. If you pay some attention to McDonald's and Burger King commercials, you'll see that this distinction is no longer considered viable.

The language of children and adults has also been transformed; the idea that there may be words adults ought not to use in the presence of children now seems faintly ridiculous. With television's relentless revelation of all adult secrets, language secrets are difficult to guard. It is not inconceivable that in the near future, we'll return to the thirteenth- and fourteenth-century situation in which no words were considered unfit for a youthful ear.

And, of course, with the assistance of modern contraceptives, the sexual appetite of both adults and children can now be satisfied without serious restraint and without mature understanding of the meaning of sex. Here television has played an enormous role, since it not only keeps the entire population in a condition of high sexual excitement, but it stresses a kind of egalitarianism of sexual fulfillment. On television sex is transformed from a dark and profound adult mystery to a product that is available to everyone, like mouthwash or underarm deodorant.

It also remains for me to mention that there has been a growing movement, sometimes called the children's liberation movement, to recast the legal rights of children so that they are more or less the same as adults'. The thrust of this movement, which is opposed to compulsory schooling, resides in the claim that what has been thought to be a preferred status for children (that is, we make them go to school) is in reality only an oppression which keeps them from fully participating in this society (that is, keeps them from becoming instant adults).

All of this means that our culture is providing fewer reasons and opportunities for childhood. But I am not so single-minded as to think that television alone is responsible for this transformation. The decline of the family, the loss of a sense of roots (40 million Americans change residence every year), the elimination through technology of much significance in adult work are other factors. I believe, though, that television creates a communication context which encourages the idea that childhood is neither desirable nor necessary—indeed, that we do not really need children.

In talking about childhood's end, I have not been talking of course about the physical disappearance of children, only the symbolic disappearance; but in fact the physical disappearance is also happening. The birthrate in North America is declining, and has been for a decade, which is why schools are being closed all over the country.

This brings me to the final characteristic of TV that needs mentioning. The idea of children implies a vision of the future. Children are the living messages we send to a time that we will not see. But television is not well suited to communicating a sense of the future or, for that matter, a sense of the past. Television is a present-centered medium; it's a speed-of-light medium. Everything we see on TV is experienced as happening now, which is why we must be told in language across the screen that a videotape we are seeing was made months before. The grammar of television has no analogue to the past and future tenses in language; so it amplifies the present out of all proportion and transforms the childish need for immediate gratification into a way of life. We end up with what Christopher Lasch (1979) has been calling the culture of narcissism: no future, no children, everyone fixed at an age somewhere between 20 and 30.

If what I am saying is true, I can well imagine what this means to people like you. As I said at the beginning. I believe that what I've been describing is disastrous, partly because I value the charm and curiosity and innocence of childhood, partly because I believe that adults need first to be children before they can be grownup. Otherwise, they remain like TV's adults, children all their lives, with no sense of belonging, no capacity for lasting relationships, no respect for limits, no grasp for the future. But, mainly, it is disastrous because as the TV culture obliterates the distinction between child and adult, as it obliterates all social secrets, as it undermines concepts of the future, we seem destined to be moving back toward a medieval sensibility from which literacy had freed us.

In spite of what I said in the beginning, I'm not going to conclude on such a desperate note. Besides, having been breast-fed as an infant, I am an optimist. Let me end by offering this, I hope, more cheerful perspective.

In the fifth century B.C., Athens was on the verge of transforming itself from an oral culture to a writing culture, not unlike what we're doing here in North America, going from a writing culture to an image culture. The great Athenian teacher Socrates feared and mocked the written word; he wrote no books, and were it not for Plato and Xenophon, who did, we'd know almost nothing about him. In one of his most enduring conversations, called the *Phaedrus*, Socrates asserts that oral language, and only oral language, is the most suitable mode for expressing serious ideas, beautiful poetry, and authentic piety. He further claims that writing will result in undermining the capacity for memorizing, in undermining the dialectical process. He has a wonderful line in which he says, "Writing, Phaedrus, forces a student to follow an argument rather than to participate in it." He also says that writing will undermine our concepts of privacy.

Now, in all of these prophecies, Socrates was correct, it turned out just as he said. But what he did not see was what his student Plato did; namely, that writing would create new and wonderful uses for the intellect. So you see, Socrates was right but his vision was limited. Without intending to suggest an unsupportable comparison between me and Socrates, may I end by saying that, although I believe the picture I've drawn for you is accurate, I sincerely hope that my vision, like Socrates' vision, is equally limited and that the television age will turn out to be a blessing. But I doubt it.

A Society That Promotes Drug Abuse: The Effects on Preadolescence

Glenda R. Norwood

Developmental tasks during the middle childhood years include acceptance by one's peer group, a growing sense of self, and a feeling of productivity (Erikson's stage of industry versus inferiority). The media provide children with a standard of success that is unattainable for most—perfect bodies, physical attractiveness, group identity, material wealth, power, and financial success. At the same time, the media also introduce a continuous barrage of "adult" messages (beer commercials, cigarette ads, advertisements for prescription drugs, and so on). Drugs of all varieties are blatantly offered as an answer to "feeling good" and "being one of the gang." On the one hand, we pressure children to be the best and the brightest, and on the other hand, we offer addictive substances when they can't measure up.

Society will not abandon the potent visual messages advanced by media technology. How can we provide a social context for preadolescents that allows them to nurture and judge who they are and who they want to be?

A preponderance of evidence presented by both the professional and the popular press clearly confirms that Americans are experiencing critical drug abuse problems. Drugs of the 1980s range from cocaine to caffeine, vodka to wine. The consequences of this abuse range from shattered individuals to broken families, from warped minds to ruined bodies. The wide variety of drugs available to a user is dramatic and the reason for use by many. Until the appeal and the myths are destroyed, the devastating impact of drugs on young lives will be a continuing crisis.

Youths and adults of the 1960s and 1970s were found to be experimenting with addictive drugs such as marijuana, LSD, cocaine, and a variety of exotically named and labeled "hard drugs." Abuse was flagrant in a subculture that promoted drug use often as a symbol of independence and a reaction against an established society thought to be exploiting youth for its own aims. Uppers, downers, angel dust, speed, and other addictive drugs provided topics for movies, press accounts, conversations, and Sunday sermons. Reference to these drugs and their misuse by children, adolescents, and young adults infiltrated society.

Although "hard drugs" received the majority of attention and press during this time of awareness, alcohol abuse was prevalent. Only in recent years, however, have parents and, belatedly, society and government focused on "just drinking" as a potentially serious form of drug abuse in youth (Savage, 1984). Preadolescent drinking is no longer viewed as normal and harmless experimentation with alcohol, motivated by natural curiosity.

Presently the abuse of prescription drugs in the United States is estimated to account for 75 percent of all drug indices (Bill Press Report, 1984). Prescribed drugs, as opposed to illicit drugs, often are erroneously viewed as a less serious social and health problem, probably because of the notion that a medi-

G. R. Norwood. (1985). A society that promotes drug abuse: The effects on pre-adolescence. *Childhood Education, 61,* 267–271.

cal doctor initially sanctioned their use. But far too often additional, often abusive, circumstances alter the doctor's original intent. Obtaining refills at a number of different pharmacies, the patient may substantially increase recommended dosages. Prescription drugs, painkillers, tranquilizers, and diet pills, often cheaper and easier to obtain than street drugs, are just as deadly for the abuser and wasteful to society as illicit drugs.

Parents are realizing that today's youngsters lead an autonomous and independent life, often secluded from the once-close family unit. In this independence, pseudo-adulthood, drug use often goes unidentified while the problems and abuses compound. All too often remediation or treatment is postponed for two or three years. By the time of intervention and beginning treatment, the consequences of drug abuse for individuals and families can be very serious and often unchangeable (The Chemical People, 1983).

WHY DRUGS ARE ABUSED

Youngsters are now becoming acquainted with drugs at younger ages (The Chemical People, 1983). Research conducted by Nelson ("Parents' Alert," 1983) at Louisiana State University found that by the age of 8 many children were knowledgeable about alcohol. Although the 6- to 10-year age group viewed alcohol consumption as negative, by the age of 12 they were beginning to view it more positively. By 15, many attested to feeling a great deal of pressure to drink alcohol.

Much of the pressure to drink, according to Reagan (1983), is based on recreational reasons. She asserts there is no such thing as a recreational drug and that children who try drugs are exposed to the whole drug culture in which the pressure to try stronger drugs will be greater.

Dr. Negrete (1983), in discussing a historical perspective to understanding the current abuse of drugs, views a distortion of human rights as a strong rationale for drug abuse in the past fifteen years. Civil rights in the 1960s too often were translated by youth to include individual choice in using or not using drugs. Drug abuse and human rights are contradictory; in fact, children have the human right to grow up free of drug dependency.

In analyzing their choice to use drugs, many youths view themselves as autonomously involved in the decision. Actually, many persons are drawn into the results of such a choice: concerned family and friends, taxpayers who pay for policemen's salaries, federally subsidized drug task forces and costs of rehabilitation centers, citizens who travel on the same highway as abusers, and victims of crimes committed by the abuser in supporting the habit. Indeed, a strong argument can be made that one of America's civil rights does not include abusing drugs!

Postman (1981) and Elkind (1982) have concentrated attention on disappearance of childhood from the life cycle. In the past three decades the emphasis appears to focus on babies leaving the crib to become miniature adults, similar to the views of generations of Europeans prior to the sixteenth century. Along with the resurgence of children looking and acting as adults at a younger age comes society's push to accept and even promote more sophisticated behavior at an earlier age. Caught in this frustrated age of development, today's children experiment with behaviors thought to be adultlike with little ability to ascertain the good and bad of such behavior. Elkind believes the pseudo-sophisticated youngster often articulates adult language but is lacking in an understanding of what he or she is verbalizing. Thus, the role modeling of adult behavior encouraged in today's society pressures children to engage in alcohol consumption, smoking, illicit drug use, sexual intercourse, and other roles they perceive to be adult. "Sooner is better" is a message received by our children.

Sadly, today's schools are also caught in the "sooner" idea. Manning (1981) accuses schools of assaulting children by pushing them into developing more quickly than feasible. The push in the last two decades for measuring students' progress has left little time for dealing with children's spontaneous interests and with areas that cannot be measured by tests. The rationale behind pressuring children to achieve beyond their age and normal expectations must be reexamined. Frustrated children become vulnerable to other ways of achieving fulfillment, among them drug abuse.

Elkind (1981) points to television as one of the strongest factors pressuring children to move headlong into adulthood. The medium portrays adolescents as precocious, wise, and insightful beyond their years. There is danger in this message as youngsters become dissatisfied with themselves, and parents and adults begin to accept such mature behavior as the norm. Television presents youth with overt illustrations, says Elkind, of crime, drug abuse, violence, and sexuality. It exposes them to all the world's ills such as war, famine, pollution, political corruption, and unrest. Postman (1980) believes this lack of secrets between adults and children encourages less distinction between the two age groups.

Additionally, the changing family unit of the 1980s has been instrumental in effecting change in childhood's role in society. Many youths are forced into early independence, a fact attributable largely to the growing number of single-parent families, step-families, and families where both parents work. While many such families function productively, children from these homes often experience frustration. Many are alone for long periods of time. Often the parents are burdened with personal concerns that render them incapable of dealing with their children's problems. Such neglected or ignored children often turn to the lure of drugs for escape, excitement, friendships, and a feeling of increased independence.

In contrast to the independent youth just described, adolescents who find themselves playing dependent roles at home and school frequently find they can develop a sense of autonomy by engaging in a youth culture role. Often this involves dressing a certain way, listening to certain music, participating in sports, and dating. Integration into a peer culture is their first major move toward independence from the family. Adolescents often discover that this method of gaining independence does not undermine their parents' values or break the bonds of affection between them and their parents (Fasick, 1984). The key to the outcome of this move toward independence lies, of course, in the type of pursuits in which they engage.

One pursuit gaining popularity among youngsters is the practice of chewing tobacco and dips ("Drug Use and Effects: Tobacco," 1982), in emulation of hero behavior. Researchers are finding this practice may lead to serious gum disorders and eventually cancer of the mouth. Kids likewise experiment with cinnamon oils, gasoline and paint fumes, and other products that result in a potentially dangerous "high" for the user, a risk not recognized by many parents.

A look at contrasting value systems of American youth before and after the 1960s reveals a marked change that lends credence to why today's youth are more susceptible to drug use and abuse. Logan (1983) describes today's youth as a "me"-oriented generation. The pre-1960s concept of how people build technology has now been replaced with the idea of what technology can do for the individual. Logan suggests Erickson's stages of social identity, developed in 1963, may be outdated because of cultural changes that have come about in the past twenty years. In identifying the skills acquired during middle childhood, Erickson firmly linked them to work and productivity. Today's children of that age group, as well as those of later age groups Erickson described, are more interested in pleasure and leisure-type activities than the pre-1960s youth who exhibited a futuristic-oriented outlook with production and work as the focus.

Not only are today's youth less productivity-oriented but they often tend to view failure as synonymous with victimization. Many of today's groups strongly evidence a personal view of themselves as victims. According to Logan, such groups may include minorities, homosexuals, feminists, and the handicapped. Easily linked with such perceived victim groups are drug abusers. One inherent danger perhaps of groups perceiving themselves as victims is the strong possibility of the individual assuming little or no responsibility for personal actions. Children or adolescents who view themselves as victims of race, divorce, poverty, low academic achievement, or any other condition, and then turn to drugs for escape and pleasure, are assuming little responsibility for their actions and futures.

It should be pointed out that Erickson in 1970 readdressed the issue of adolescent identity and its relationship to the prevailing social structure (Emichovich and Gaier, 1983). Further research in the changing social identity stages promises a more thorough understanding in that area of development.

Americans are described as having an obsession with winning. Many have accused sports of replacing sportsmanship with the killer instinct to win. One has only to be a spectator to observe such behavior at a tennis championship match, a major league baseball game, or a college football game. Little League games evidence the same trend of winning at all cost. The 1980 Olympics in Russia brought into the spotlight the use of steroids as a means of producing heavier and stronger athletes with the physical advantage to win (Friedman and Santo, 1984). Winning as the prime objective was also evidenced in the 1984 Los Angeles Olympics. After winning a silver medal, the U.S. Volleyball Team was approached by the media with such questions as "What factors contributed to not bringing home the gold?" implying there was no merit in winning the honored second position.

The need to be first is acted out not only in sports, but in such pursuits as acquiring a job, seeking entrance into prestigious schools, and participating in contests. The emphasis on winning at any price far too often encourages vulnerable youth to do just that. Frequently, abusing drugs may be the price paid; for example, the use of caffeine pills to stay awake all night to study for an exam, diet pills to lose weight to better qualify for the cheerleading contest, painkillers to ward off stress symptoms, "uppers" to experience a rush of needed energy, and "downers" to achieve calmness and relaxation in order to think better.

McDermott's study (1984) found that the parent's attitude toward drug use related to the adolescent's use of drugs. Adolescents who used drugs were more likely to have one or more parents who used drugs. Adolescents who perceived their parents as having a permissive attitude toward drug use were more likely to use drugs. Finally, the parental attitude perceived by the adolescent was as important as, or perhaps more important than, actual parental behavior in determining drug use.

In looking into why youngsters believe they use drugs, as compared to why adults think youths use drugs, Friedman's study (1984) presented contrasting viewpoints for the two groups. The students felt more strongly than the parents that their reasons for drug use were to get high, to feel better, to help get into music, and to help control their anger. The parents' opinions of why youths used drugs were stronger than the students' in the following reasons: curiosity, escape, and peer group use of drugs.

SOCIETAL MESSAGES THAT PROMOTE DRUG USE

Commercial exploitation of drugs by both the media and criminal enterprises succeeds in promoting the use of illicit drugs (Negrete, 1983). The resulting focus on glamour and appeal has infiltrated television, the motion picture industry, recording companies, and rock group performers.

Television commercials continually dose youngsters with messages of beauty if only they will purchase and use kiddie cosmetics such as lip gloss, nail polish, eye shadow, perfumes, and other such glamour aids (Janus, 1982). Magical results, illustrated by before-and-after portraits, make purchasing a final step in achieving maturity. Advertisements for designer jeans depict Brooke Shields provocatively posed in skin-tight pants telling us that nothing comes between her and her Calvins. These sexually referenced messages suggest to youngsters that the child star is a role model of adulthood to be emulated.

Television plays a significant role in alcohol awareness, according to Nelson's research ("Parents' Alert," 1983). Consumption of alcohol was depicted twice per hour in daytime and early-evening programs and three times per hour in late-evening shows. This constant refocusing, whether on alcohol, sex, or illicit drugs, often serves to brainwash one into gradually accepting that idea as part of one's values. The younger and more vulnerable, of course, are more negatively affected. Nelson found a vast number of 4- and 5-year-olds had already developed attitudes and norms regarding alcohol use.

Since their primary goal is to sell a product, advertisers have become adept at sending their messages to the public. Assuming that people will spend money in an attempt to look better, feel better or escape momentarily from their lifestyles, they introduce a product in a way that generally incorporates many of the following goals: a better life, a hero image, acceptance, youthfulness, power, excitement, individualism, ro-

mance, and love. What individual does not secretly desire these results?

Advertisers skillfully use techniques to draw attention to these goals. Color, slogans, beautiful and sexy bodies, irresistible personalities, and out-of-the-ordinary settings are emphasized in subtle and not-so-subtle methods. A shoe advertisement may show someone holding a champagne glass. An airline advertisement may couple a handsome man with a beautiful woman embracing in some luxurious setting, with cups of coffee awaiting their attention. A cigarette advertisement may project an extremely thin female "coming a long way" with suggestions of coming even further if she smokes that brand cigarette. A diet pill advertisement may show a size-one female in designer jeans.

Negrete (1983) discussed youth's susceptibility to such drugs as a dream of moneymakers. There appears to be no limit to how far the greedy will go to make financial gains. Many advertisements address the very young in the manipulations. Indeed, corporations live in fear that children will ridicule them (Blum, 1983).

Our society continually sends signals to the population encouraging drug use. Daily messages to the young include

- *Take a painkiller for a headache.* Lost in the message is the fact that pain is a valuable warning of something amiss. The head may hurt because of intense heat from the sun, an allergic reaction, vision problems, or other health problems that need direct attention rather than band-aid cures.

- *Take a pill to ensure feeling well.* The message that an iron tablet can instantly produce pep and energy substitutes for any consideration of why the individual feels bad. Lack of exercise, irregular eating habits, and other such health factors are overlooked.

- *To guarantee fun at a party, serve alcohol, smoke cigarettes, or use illicit drugs.* Individuals are not given any credit for enjoying meaningful conversation or activity.

- *To relax, drink an alcoholic beverage, coffee, or coke.* One is led to believe relaxing and enjoyment are attained only after alcohol or caffeine usage.

- *Take a pill to sleep.* Overlooked is the fact that insomnia is often the result of more complex conditions such as stress, depression, or lack of proper exercise. These issues need attention before regular sleeping patterns can be attained.

The use of sleeping pills simply prolongs the problem.

- *Take a vitamin for good health.* Overreliance on vitamins as the solution to health problems is widely promoted. Ignored is the value of establishing an eating pattern based on a balanced diet, including fiber essential for proper elimination. The simple joy and sensory pleasure of chewing foods such as an apple may well do as much, or more, for one's daily health as a little flavored pill—and at less cost.

- *To lose weight, take a diet pill.* An easy solution is offered in order to sell a product to those who do not wish to exercise, eat properly, and engage in long-term self-disciplined endeavors.

- *To cope, take a drink.* An instant alcoholic drink is presented as a quick solution for problems, rather than positive means of coping.

- *For skin not as smooth and healthy as desired, use a cosmetic.* The right cream, it is claimed, performs dramatic maximizing and minimizing overnight, thus saving the individual the effort of eating vitamin- and mineral-rich foods and taking extra pains with cleanliness.

- *To be popular and have friends, arrange for alcoholic beverages.* A cadre of fun-loving, happy people sharing a drink appears to solve any loneliness one may experience.

- *To enjoy sports events more fully, engage in beer drinking.* The beer drinker-sportsman linkage, like the America-apple pie concept, is strongly entrenched. One easily could be led to believe drinking beer assures agile, surefooted, balanced, conditioned sportsmen who are looked upon by all as heroes.

CONCLUSION

Weisheit (1983) stated that a social problem is recognized as such only when some groups succeed in bringing it to the public's attention and elicit a demand that something be done. Parents and all adults need to recognize how society is manipulating and brainwashing our future leaders through direct and subliminal messages. A concerted effort must be made to eliminate messages that promote drug use and abuse and to help youth understand how they are being manipulated. The future depends on recognizing the urgent need for action.

Race, Class, Gender, and Schooling

Carl A. Grant

Diversity of peoples in our schools, neighborhoods, and places of employment will continue to increase during the next decade. This pluralism, which has always characterized U.S. society, currently demands that we renew our attention to the effects of race, class, and gender on children's development.

What is it like to go to a school where you are the only person of your race in the class? How do students respond when they realize that none of their teachers or school ad-ministrators is "like them"? Can a child learn effectively when the vocabulary and "language of school" are very different from what he or she hears at home? Because school is an increasingly important place during the middle years, each child deserves to find some support and comfort there. Unfortunately, equitable opportunities for each student will not be ensured until substantial changes are made in curriculum and attitudes.

According to demographic projections, the student population in public schools will soon include one out of four students from families living in poverty; as many as 15 percent of students will be immigrants who do not speak English; and after the year 2000, one out of every three Americans will be nonwhite. Teachers daily encounter concerns related to students' race, class, and gender.

Two examples of teacher-student encounters in schools may help to illustrate this point. Maria's recent lackluster performance in eighth grade is disturbing to her teacher, especially since Maria has been an honor roll student for the last four years. Maria is upset with life and school because she has mixed emotions about whether to follow the customary family tradition of getting married after high school graduation, as her father suggests, or going on to college, like her Aunt Juanita. Juanita tells Maria that the new Chicana women do not live to have babies or please a man but to be their own persons and follow their own dreams. For the teacher to be of *real* assistance to Maria, it is important that she understand the customs and traditions of Hispanic culture. The teacher must see how Hispanics' expectations for Hispanics and females interact to affect Maria.

Paul is a black fourth-grader in inner-city Chicago who has recently dropped out of school and started hanging out with the local gang. After a month, he was picked up and returned to school. When his teacher came to the principal's office to talk with him, she found an insolent, frightened boy. Paul told her that she did not really like him or any of the students in her room. He said that her class was a bore and that the work was "baby stuff" or related to white kids. He suggested that she go teach in her own neighborhood. His teacher was shocked by this verbal attack, perhaps much of it unwarranted. However, she will be better able to relate to Paul if she realizes that his problems are related to race, class, and gender.

Being a poor black male from the inner city carries with it certain ascribed characteristics that may have

C. A. Grant. (1988, December). Race, class, gender, and schooling. *Education Digest, 54* (4), 15–18.

caused Paul to act differently than if he were a poor black *female* or a middle-class black male. Black students may wonder about *their* culture, even if they have one, because they see only fragments of their culture in the school curriculum or on television. Inner-city blacks may see their culture as represented by poverty or by lost dreams and desires. A young black male may see the male role as consisting of a large, sensitive ego, a persistent high value for athletics, and a noncommunicative, risk-taking nature. Because he is poor, he may believe that he is entitled to the glamour he sees on television. He could believe that the only way to get it is to steal it.

There is a need to consider simultaneously the effects of race, class, and gender in an attempt to understand schooling. Paying attention to only one or two of these variables may oversimplify the analysis of their effects and actually perpetuate biases. Furthermore, within an integrated race, class, and gender analysis, it is important to examine how power (politics and privilege), economics (capitalism and classism), and culture (lifestyle, language, and customs) affect students of color on a daily basis.

Race needs to be dealt with from a personal and institutional perspective in school because schools have not welcomed people of color with the same zeal that people of color have demonstrated in their efforts to attend schools. In fact, schools are often guilty of destroying the passion for learning that people of color bring to school. A major problem is keeping students of color *in* school. The dropout rate is staggering (47 percent) and still on the rise. The problem, to some extent, is the fault of the schools and the larger society.

Students often drop out because they do not have much success in school and perceive the discipline system as unfair and the teachers as not particularly interested in them. These perceptions begin at the elementary level. Case studies of effective alternative programs for marginal students (many of whom are of color) clearly show that such students respond positively to schooling that combines a caring relationship and personalized teaching with a high degree of program structure characterized by clear, demanding, but attainable goals.

Education (broadly speaking) is only paying lip service to the educational needs of students of color. Education policies and practices from the 1960s and 1970s were focused mainly on providing or improving access to good-quality schooling for people of color, particularly the poor. During the 1980s, an outpouring of education reform reports has cried out for excellence and equality in education. The cry for "excellence" has received considerable attention, as national educational organizations have recognized some schools for their excellence.

However, the cry for "equity" has received little attention. A colleague and I analyzed nine of the most popular reform reports to determine their attention to race, class, gender, and exceptional students. These reports were examined in areas that have often been a focus of educational research: access to school resources, biases in curriculum, students' language and background, testing procedures, biases in teacher-student interaction, conflicts between student learning styles and dominant teaching styles and staffing patterns.

Two conclusions are important. First, about half the reports do not take race, gender, class, or exceptionality into account. The other half offer an irresponsible and flawed color-blind vision of society. Second, given these patterns, the reports leave much room for educators to reproduce racist, classist, and sexist practices.

MULTICULTURAL EDUCATION

Advocates of multicultural education have reported continually over the past twenty-five years that meaningful attention to racial and cultural diversity does not yet exist in U.S. schools. They argue that curriculum and textbooks have improved somewhat but that further improvement is needed. They also note that teachers' expectations for white students are different from their expectations for students of color, especially for black students, and that teachers of white students may be better prepared than teachers of black or Hispanic students.

Simply put, the relationship of race (with the exception of the white race) to power, economics, *and* culture has never been a part of the core curriculum in schools, and schools are slow to accept multicultural education or make needed changes. Schools should respond by offering students multicultural and social reconstructionist education.

RECONSTRUCTING SOCIETY

By multicultural education, I mean that all elementary schooling should reflect the diverse racial groups in this country. Curriculum, staffing, instruction, testing, etc. should become multicultural. Students are taught about oppression and social inequality in a formal setting. Multicultural and social reconstructionist education prepares students to reconstruct society to better serve the interests of all citizens, especially those who are of color, poor, female, and handicapped.

A reconstructionist approach to education is visionary. Realistic visions and language that inspires hope, although offering sober directions and alternatives, are what is needed to help students of color to take charge of and give meaning to their lives. For example, a recent ethnographic study of an urban junior high school showed that most students of color and low-income white students came to school with optimistic visions, or at least with the anticipation that the school would help them shape their vision for the future. They and their parents placed great trust in the school. Parents believed that the school would put their children on the path to upward mobility and monitor their progress. Students believed that, if they attended class, did their homework, and respected their teachers, their positive future would be ensured.

Neither the students nor their parents were told that their vision of how to fulfill their potential or achieve success was greatly flawed. They were not aware of the fact that the teachers saw them as caught in a cycle of underclass status from which teachers were not preparing them to escape. Students were not aware that the teachers had written them off.

Students were also not informed that once they left the area of the city in which they lived—a community where race relations were exceptionally good—they would probably encounter racism, sexism, and classism. Nor were they taught what to do when they experienced discrimination. In sum, the students were not taught how to analyze their life experiences or how to take charge in order to make changes. School be-

came a part of the process of subordination instead of being an institution for liberation and good-quality education.

Multicultural and social reconstructionist education requires that schools truly serve all students, especially those of color. Its objective is to help students acquire the skills and conceptual frameworks to pursue their own concerns and remove the barriers that prevent them from achieving the best life has to offer.

REALISTIC LEARNING

The elementary school is often the first place outside the home where students learn about race. This learning should not be narrow, but realistic and factual. Students need to be informed as early as possible about race from a cultural, economic, and political perspective. They should be taught to examine how race plays a major role in their daily lives. Teachers of elementary students need to teach from a multicultural perspective. They need to be aware that analyses of classroom life must integrate race, class, and gender to allow teachers to understand students' school life more completely.

Educators must not close their eyes to the dynamic meaning that race brings to the classroom. Color blindness on the part of teachers, if not impossible, is highly improbable. Therefore, teachers need to integrate race and the expanded meaning I have argued for it into their teaching. This will give students—especially students of color—a better opportunity to take charge of their own destinies.

Part Five

ADOLESCENCE

On the roller coaster that is adolescence, teenagers must cope with tremendous physical changes, a newly defined body image, cognitive advances that allow them to ponder possibilities, the search for identity, and new forms of intimacy. Adolescents have not experienced this level of disruption in all domains since infancy. How children weather the years between 12 and 20 depends on biological factors (such as timing of the onset of puberty), previous experiences (sense of autonomy, relationship with parents), and environmental influences (peer group, school, and parental pressures). And the behavior and attitude of individual adolescents are uniquely influenced by culture, gender, and social context.

Uneven and abrupt changes during adolescence often create confusion and internal struggle for some individuals. A girl who reaches puberty earlier than her peers may not yet have the cognitive ability to construct value judgments about her sexual behavior or possess the social maturity to deflect the advances of older boys. Her physical appearance may push her toward decisions she is not prepared or ready to make. In her article, Petersen emphasizes that puberty is not the only hurdle and often not the most traumatic for adolescents. She contends that the timing, and combination of stresses, rather than the intensity of one specific cause, relate to the immediate behaviors and long-term effects on adolescent development. Key contributors may be onset of puberty, transition to a new school (elementary to junior high school), relationship with parents, the need to strongly identify with a peer group, and perception of self.

Significant variability among adolescents is seen in the development of one's self-concept and self-esteem (see the article by Blyth and Traeger). Longitudinal studies point out that although changes in self-image seem to be continuous and stable, the level of self-esteem varies significantly regardless of age. Future research questions should explore which criteria for self-esteem judgments are used at different ages or under different conditions. Self-esteem appears to be less related to age than are the particular events taking place in an adolescent's life. Changing to a new school may affect a teenager's self-image whether he or she is 11 or 15 years old. The research emphasizing continuity reveals that significant changes during adolescence are incorporated gradually into self-image and are not necessarily disruptive. Most adolescents complete their teenage years with a strong self-concept and positive feelings of self-esteem.

On my refrigerator is a sign that reads "ATTENTION TEENAGERS: Leave Home Now While You Still Know Everything." It is a reminder to me and, I hope, to my teenage daughter, that the stage of "adolescent egocentrism" and the assumption that parents get dumber by the minute while peers become omnipresent and all-knowing, will—in time—pass. In reality, of course, teenagers do not have all the information nor do they have the cognitive ability to make decisions about issues as important as starting a family, personal safety, and health. David Elkind (in this section) believes that today's adolescent is pressured by parents (unknowingly), peers, and today's view of children to participate in decisions that are beyond his or her realm of reasonable thought. Our worldview has considered children as becoming increasingly more competent. Unfortunately, we have simultaneously decreased family support (due to work and/or single-parent households) and presented our youth with problems related to drugs, teenage pregnancy, and the HIV (AIDS) virus.

Two characteristics that may increase the vulnerability of adolescence are the "imaginary audience" ("Everyone is always watching what I do and listening to what I say) and the "personal fable" ("It—pregnancy, drugs, accidents, AIDS—will never happen to me"). These characteristics are important tools for carving a new identity. But they can backfire under the pressure of the many decisions adolescents must make.

Adolescents intensely need to belong and to seek identity through peer group membership. Adolescents who don't have other sources of acceptance may become overly dependent on a peer group or feel alienated. Urie Bronfenbrenner suggests we create new models of caring in our families, schools, and communities, in order to counteract feelings of alienation.

Many environmental factors affect development during adolescence. Culture and ethnicity are two that need more attention. Creating a comfortable self-identity is one task of adolescence. It involves reducing the intensity of identification with family and moving out to embrace the values and culture of a peer group. Consider the difficulty of this task if the available peers share few of the behaviors and attitudes of your own family. It can be a terrible shock if the "self," which has been under preparation for more than a decade, doesn't fit and cannot be easily adapted to the idealized self created through an association with peers. Although many teenagers rebel against their parents' attitudes and ideas, they find comfort in knowing that they can easily slide back and forth between the world of parents and peers. For many adolescents from a cultural minority, the sense of having one foot in each of two distinctly different cultures is painful and contradictory. Sung's summary of this conflict as experienced by Chinese youths in New York City makes the bicultural dilemma very clear. In contrast, Williams profiles a young woman cut off from her ethnic heritage by unusual circumstances. As she engages in the developmental process of constructing a self-identity, she finds that a significant piece of her "self" is missing. The significance of our cultural and ethnic past is very powerful. Development can never be viewed in isolation from cultural and ethnic self.

Adolescence encompasses dramatic biological change that is continuously bombarded by significant environmental influences and developmental shifts in cognitive, moral, and social thinking. For most adolescents (and their parents), it is a stage of tremendous challenge and excitement. The exit from childhood and the passage into adulthood offer robust potential for creating unique, balanced, and caring individuals.

Those Gangly Years

A. Petersen

The interplay of social, emotional, physical, and cognitive needs and abilities during adolescence is so intense that it is a challenge to discover what affects an individual when, and how that individual responds to each phenomenon. Although not as potent a determinant of adolescent life as once believed, puberty remains one source of adolescent turmoil. The timing of the onset of puberty affects adolescent behavior and affects boys and girls differently. For example, early maturing boys enjoy their new body image and feel superior. Girls who mature early are less satisfied with their weight and appearance than are later maturing girls. Moods, relationships with parents, interactions with peers, and school achievement are also affected by the onset of puberty.

In addition to physical changes, adolescents deal with transitions to junior high and later to senior high, altered family relations, new feelings and pressures related to peers, and a growing need for independence. How an individual responds to change, and how these life changes combine at any one time, affect the well-being of the adolescent. Differences between coping patterns of males and females become more pronounced during adolescence. For girls, the need to be accepted may overshadow their need for competence. Bright girls often trade high grades for a sense of belonging. The study discussed in the following article only collected data from suburban, white middle-class families. Therefore, it is impossible to know whether outcomes would differ in populations of poor, urban or rural, black, Hispanic, or Asian teenagers. Researchers have a responsibility to investigate developmental patterns of all groups within our diverse society.

"How can you stand studying adolescents? My daughter has just become one and she's impossible to live with. Her hormones may be raging, but so am I!" A colleague at a cocktail party was echoing the widespread view that the biological events of puberty necessarily change nice kids into moody, rebellious adolescents. The view has gained such a foothold that some parents with well-behaved teenagers worry that their kids aren't developing properly.

They needn't worry. My research, and that of many others...suggests that although the early teen years can be quite a challenge for normal youngsters and their families, they're usually not half as bad as

they are reputed to be. And even though the biological changes of puberty do affect adolescents' behavior, attitudes, and feelings in many important ways, other, often controllable, social and environmental forces are equally important.

One 14-year-old, for example, who tried to excuse his latest under-par report card by saying, "My problem is testosterone, not tests," only looked at part of the picture. He ignored, as many do, the fact that, because of a move and the shift to junior high school, he had been in three schools in as many years.

My colleagues and I at Pennsylvania State University looked at a three-year span in the lives of young adolescents to find out how a variety of biological and social factors affected their behavior and their feelings about themselves. A total of 335 young adolescents were randomly selected from two suburban school districts, primarily white and middle to upper-middle class. Two successive waves of these kids were monitored as they moved from the sixth through the eighth grade. Twice a year we interviewed them individually and gave them psychological tests in groups. When the youngsters were in the sixth and eighth grades, we also interviewed and assessed their parents. Just recently we again interviewed and assessed these young people and their parents during the adolescents' last year of high school.

We followed the children's pubertal development by asking them to judge themselves every six months on such indicators as height, pubic hair, and acne in both boys and girls; breast development and menstruation in girls; and voice change and facial-hair growth in boys. We also estimated the timing of puberty by finding out when each youngster's adolescent growth spurt in height peaked, so we could study the effects of early, on-time, or late maturing.

Although we have not yet analyzed all the data, it's clear that puberty alone does not have the overwhelming psychological impact that earlier clinicians and researchers assumed it did. . . . But it does have many effects on body image, moods, and relationships with parents and members of the opposite sex.

Being an early or late maturer (one year earlier or later than average), for example, affected adolescents' satisfaction with their appearance and their body image — but only among seventh- and eighth-graders, not sixth-graders. We found that among students in the higher two grades, girls who were physically more mature were generally less satisfied with their weight and appearance than their less mature classmates.

A seventh-grade girl, pleased with being still childlike, said, "You can do more things — you don't have as much weight to carry around." A girl in the eighth grade, also glad to be a late maturer, commented, "If girls get fat, they have to worry about it." In contrast, an early-maturing girl subsequently commented, "I didn't like being early. A lot of my friends didn't understand." Another girl, as a high school senior, described the pain of maturing extremely early: "I tried to hide it. I was embarrassed and ashamed." However, her discomfort ended in the eighth grade, she said, because "by then everyone wore a bra and had their period. I was normal."

We found the reverse pattern among boys: those who were physically more mature tended to be more satisfied with their weight and their overall appearance than their less mature peers. One already gangling seventh-grade boy, for example, said he liked being "a little taller and having more muscle development than other kids so you can beat them in races." He conceded that developing more slowly might help

"if you're a jockey" but added, "Really, I can't think of why [developing] later would be an advantage." In reflecting back from the twelfth grade, a boy who had matured early noted that at the time the experience "made me feel superior."

For seventh- and eighth-grade boys, physical maturity was related to mood. Boys who had reached puberty reported positive moods more often than their prepubertal male classmates did. Pubertal status was less clearly and consistently related to mood among girls, but puberty did affect how girls got along with their parents. As physical development advanced among sixth-grade girls, their relationships with their parents declined; girls who were developmentally advanced talked less to their parents and had less positive feelings about family relationships than did less developed girls. We found a similar pattern among eighth-grade girls, but it was less clear in the seventh grade, perhaps because of the many other changes occurring at that time, such as the change from elementary to secondary school format and its related effects on friendship and school achievement.

The timing of puberty affected both school achievement and moods. Early maturers tended to get higher grades than later maturers in the same class. We suspect that this may stem from the often documented tendency of teachers to give more positive ratings to larger pupils. Although early maturers had an edge academically, those who matured later were more likely to report positive moods.

As we have noted, among relatively physically mature adolescents, boys and girls had opposite feelings about their appearance: The boys were pleased, but the girls were not. We believe that, more generally, pubertal change is usually a positive experience for boys but a negative one for girls. While advancing maturity has some advantages for girls, including gaining some of the rights and privileges granted to maturing boys, it also brings increased limitations and restrictions related to their emerging womanhood. One sixth-grade girl stated emphatically, "I don't like the idea of getting older or any of that. If I had my choice, I'd rather stay 10." Or, as one seventh-grade boy graphically explained the gender differences, "Parents let them [boys] go out later than girls because they don't have to worry about getting raped or anything like that."

Differences in the timing of puberty also affect interactions with members of the opposite sex. But it takes two to tango, and in the sixth grade, although many girls have reached puberty and are ready to socialize with boys, most boys have not yet made that transition. Thus, as one girl plaintively summed up the sixth-grade social scene, "Girls think about boys more than boys think about girls."

In the seventh and eighth grades, the physically more mature boys and girls are likely to be pioneers in exploring social relations with members of the opposite sex, including talking with them on the phone, dating, having a boyfriend or girlfriend, and "making out." We had the sense that once these young people began looking like teenagers, they wanted to act like them as well.

But puberty affects the social and sexual activity of individual young adolescents both directly and indirectly; the pubertal status of some students can have consequences for the entire peer group of boys and girls. Although dating and other boy-girl interactions are linked to pubertal status, and girls usually reach puberty before boys do, we found no sex differences in the rates of dating throughout the early-adolescent period. When the early-maturing kids began socializing with members of the opposite sex, the pattern quickly spread throughout the entire peer group. Even prepubertal girls were susceptible to thinking and talking about boys if all their girlfriends were "boy crazy."

The physical changes brought on by puberty have far-reaching effects, but so do many other changes in the lives of adolescents. One we found to be particularly influential is the change in school structure between the sixth and eighth grades. Most young adolescents in our country shift from a relatively small neighborhood elementary school, in which most classes are taught by one teacher, to a much larger, more impersonal middle school or junior high school (usually farther from the child's home), in which students move from class to class and teacher to teacher for every subject. This shift in schools has many ramifications, including disrupting the old peer group structure, exposing adolescents to different achievement expectations by teachers and providing opportunities for new extracurricular activities—licit and illicit.

Both the timing and number of school transitions are very important. In our study, for example, students who changed schools earlier than most of their peers, as well as those who changed schools twice (both experiences due to modifications of the school system), suffered an academic slump that continued through eighth grade. Therefore, early or double school transition seemed stressful, beyond the usual effects of moving to a junior high school.

Puberty and school change, which appear to be the primary and most pervasive changes occurring during early adolescence, are often linked to other important changes, such as altered family relations. Psychologist Laurence Steinberg of the University of Wisconsin has found that family relationships shift as boys and girls move through puberty. During mid puberty, he says, conflict in family discussions in-creases; when the conflict is resolved, boys usually become more dominant in conversations with their mothers. (Psychologist John Hill of Virginia Commonwealth University has found that family conflict increases only for boys.) Other research, however, suggests that adolescents wind up playing a more equal role relative to both parents.

In our study, the parents of early-maturing girls and late-maturing boys reported less positive feelings about their children in the sixth and eighth grades than did parents of boys and girls with other patterns of pubertal timing. (These effects were always stronger for fathers than for mothers.) The adolescents, however, reported that their feelings about their parents were unrelated to pubertal timing.

The feelings of affection and support that adolescents and their parents reported about one another usually declined from the sixth to the eighth grades, with the biggest decline in feelings between girls and their mothers. But importantly, the decline was from very positive to less positive—but still not negative—feelings.

Early adolescence is clearly an unusual transition in development because of the number of changes young people experience. But the impact of those changes is quite varied; changes that may challenge and stimulate some young people can become overwhelming and stressful to others. The outcome seems to depend on prior strengths and vulnerabilities—both of the individual adolescents and their families—as well as on the pattern, timing, and intensity of changes.

Youngsters in our study who changed schools within six months of peak pubertal change reported more depression and anxiety than those whose school and biological transitions were more separated in time. Students who experienced an unusual and negative change at home—such as the death of a parent or divorce of parents—reported even greater difficulties, a finding that supports other research. Sociologists Roberta Simmons and Dale Blyth have found that the negative effects of junior high school transitions, especially in combination with other life changes, continue on into high school, particularly for girls.

Many of the negative effects of transitions and changes seen in our study were tempered when adolescents had particularly positive and supportive relationships with their peers and family. The effects of all these early-adolescent changes were even stronger by the twelfth grade than in eighth grade.

Overall, we found that the usual pattern of development in early adolescence is quite positive. More than half of those in the study seemed to be almost trouble-free, and approximately 30 percent of the total group had only intermittent problems during their early teen years. Fifteen percent of the kids, however, did appear to be caught in a downward spiral of trouble and turmoil.

Gender played an important role in how young adolescents expressed and dealt with this turmoil. Boys generally showed their poor adjustment through external behavior, such as being rebellious and disobedient, whereas girls were more likely to show internal behavior, such as having depressed moods. But since many poorly adjusted boys also showed many signs of depression, the rates of such symptoms did not differ between the sexes in early adolescence.

By the twelfth grade, however, the girls were significantly more likely than the boys to have depressive symptoms, a sex difference also found among adults. Boys who had such symptoms in the twelfth grade usually had had them in the sixth grade as well; girls who had depressive symptoms as high school seniors usually had developed them by the eighth grade.

For youngsters who fell in the troubled group, the stage was already set — and the pathways distinguishable — at the very beginning of adolescence. There is an overall tendency for academic decline in the seventh and eighth grades (apparently because seventh- and eighth-grade teachers adopt tougher grading standards than elementary school teachers do). But the grades of boys with school behavior problems or depressive symptoms in early adolescence subsequently declined far more than those of boys who did not report such problems. Thus, for youngsters whose lives are already troubled, the changes that come with early adolescence add further burdens — and their problems are likely to persist through the senior year of high school.

One twelfth-grade boy who followed this pathway described the experience: "My worst time was seventh to ninth grade. I had a lot of growing up to do and I still have a lot more to do. High school was not the 'sweet 16' time everyone said it would be. What would have helped me is more emotional support in grades 7 through 9." In explaining that particularly difficult early-adolescent period he said, "Different teachers, colder environment, changing classes and detention all caused chaos in the seventh to ninth grades."

We did not find the same relationship between academic failure and signs of emotional turmoil in girls as in boys. For example, those seventh-grade girls particularly likely to report poor self-image or depressive symptoms were those who were academically successful. Furthermore, when these girls lowered their academic achievement by eighth grade, their depression and their self-image tended to improve. These effects occurred in many areas of girls' coursework but were particularly strong in stereotypically "masculine" courses such as mathematics and science.

Like the pattern of problems for boys, the girls' pattern of trading grades to be popular and feel good about themselves persisted into the twelfth grade. (Some girls, of course, performed well academically and felt good about themselves both in junior high school and high school.)

We think that for certain girls, high achievement, especially in "masculine" subjects, comes with social costs — speculation supported by the higher priority these particular girls give to popularity. They seem to sacrifice the longer-term benefits of high achievement for the more immediate social benefits of "fitting in." Other studies have revealed a peak in social conformity at this age, especially among girls, and have shown that many adolescents reap immediate, but short-term, social benefits from many types of behavior that adults find irrational or risky.

Our most recent research is focused on exploring further whether the developmental patterns established during early adolescence continue to the end of high school. We are also trying to integrate our observations into a coherent theory of adolescent development and testing that theory by seeing whether we can predict the psychological status of these students at the end of high school based on their characteristics in early adolescence. Other key concerns include discovering early warning signs of trouble and identifying ways to intervene to improve the course of development.

The biological events of puberty are a necessary — and largely uncontrollable — part of growing up. But we may be able to understand and control the social and environmental forces that make adolescence so difficult for a small but troubled group of youngsters. The adolescent's journey toward adulthood is inherently marked by change and upheaval but need not be fraught with chaos or deep pain.

THE PUZZLE OF ADOLESCENCE

At the turn of the century, psychologist G. Stanley Hall dignified adolescence with his "storm and stress" theory, and Anna Freud subsequently argued influentially that such storm and stress is a normal part of adolescence. Ever since, clinicians and researchers have been trying — with only limited success — to develop a coherent theory of what makes adolescents tick.

Psychoanalytic theorist Peter Blos added in the late 1960s and 1970s that adolescents' uncontrolled sexual and aggressive impulses affect relationships with their parents. He suggested that both adolescents and their parents may need more distant relationships because of the unacceptable feelings stimulated by the adolescents' sexuality.

Research conducted in the 1960s showed that not all adolescents experience the storm and stress psychoanalytic theory predicts they should. Many studies, including those of Roy Grinker; Joseph Adelson and Elizabeth Douvan; Daniel Offer; and Albert Bandura, demonstrated that a significant proportion of adolescents make it through this period without appreciable turmoil. These findings suggest that pubertal change per se cannot account for the rocky time some adolescents experience.

Other theories of adolescent development have also been linked to pubertal change. For example, in his theory of how children's cognitive capacities develop, Swiss psychologist Jean Piaget attributed the emergence of "formal operational thought," that is, the capacity to think abstractly, to the interaction of pubertal and environmental changes that occur during the same developmental period.

Some researchers have linked the biological events of puberty to possible changes in brain growth or functioning. Deborah Waber, a psychologist at Boston Children's Hospital, has shown that the timing of pubertal change is related to performance differences between the right- and left-brain hemispheres on certain tasks and to the typical adult pattern of gender-related cognitive abilities: Later maturers, including

most men, have relatively better spatial abilities, and earlier maturers, including most women, have relatively better verbal abilities.

It has also been suggested that pubertal change affects adolescent behavior through the social consequences of altered appearance. Once young adolescents look like adults, they are more likely to be treated as adults and to see themselves that way, too.

Coming also from a social psychological perspective, psychologist John Hill of Virginia Commonwealth University, together with former Cornell University doctoral student Mary Ellen Lynch, have proposed that pubertal change leads parents and peers to expect more traditional gender role behavior from adolescents than from younger children; they suggest that both boys and girls become more aware of these gender stereotypes in early adolescence and exaggerate their gender-related behavior at this age.

Despite all these theories, most studies that look at how puberty affects adolescent development are finding that puberty per se is not as important as we once thought. Puberty does specifically affect such things as body image and social and sexual behavior, but it does not affect all adolescent behavior, and it affects some adolescents more strongly than others. In fact, many studies, like ours, are revealing that other changes in early adolescence, particularly social and environmental ones, are at least as important as biological ones.

The Self-Concept and Self-Esteem of Early Adolescents

D. Blyth and C. Traeger

Self-concept (a descriptive response to the question "Who am I?") and self-esteem (an evaluation of "Who am I?") are two valuable constructs for studying adolescents. Significant changes in physical appearance, relationships with peers and parents, and cognitive abilities dramatically affect changes in one's self-concept ("I'm developing a beard") and self-esteem ("The girls will think my beard is sexy"). Theorists cannot agree on whether self-image changes are discontinuous and qualitative (a major shift in the self-concept) or continuous and quantitative (new ideas about self added on to existing ones).

Research described in the following article demonstrates stability (continuity) in the self-concept during adolescence, indicating that most teenagers weather the changes in self-esteem without serious disruptions. Nonetheless, the rate of change and degree to which changes occur simultaneously appear to affect one's self-image. Change that is very rapid, or two to three changes occurring simultaneously, can adversely affect one's self-esteem. The authors suggest that self-image instability has been overemphasized. However, tremendous variability exists in the self-esteem levels of adolescents.

The conclusions of this article seem to conflict with others (such as "A Society That Promotes Drug Abuse," pp. 115–119) that view adolescence as fraught with conflict, role confusion, and battered self-esteem. What is your opinion of the psychological health of today's adolescents?

Aspects of the self and the self-image have been discussed in a wide variety of theoretical perspectives over the last century. From the pioneering work of James (1890), Cooley (1902), Freud (1923), and Mead (1934) to the more recent formulations by Rosenberg (1965, 1979), the number of different definitions and uses of the terms *self*, *self-image*, and *self-concept* is staggering. As Wells and Marwell (1976) indicate in their excellent review, the self-concept has been a central aspect of psychoanalysis, ego psychology, personality research, sociology, and experimental social psychology. These theoretical perspectives have tended to be imprecise and even contradictory in their use of various self terms. One consequence of this multitude of perspectives and lack of agreement on definitions has been the tendency for the terms to enter into everyday usage, leading to even further imprecision in the way the words are used. Often, people think they know what is meant, but no one means the same thing.

To bring some order to this diversity of complex theories of the self, a number of excellent review articles and books have been written (see, for example, Wells and Marwell, 1976; Wylie, 1974, 1979; Dickstein, 1977). A brief review by Beane, Lipka, and Ludewig (1980) attempts to synthesize what is known about the

D. A. Blyth and C. M. Traeger. (1983). The self-concept and self-esteem of early adolescents. *Theory into Practice*, 22 (2), 91–97. Theme issue on "Early Adolescence." Copyright ©1983 College of Education, The Ohio State University.

Note: The work of the senior author has been supported in part by NIMH grant ROI MH-30739 and a grant from the William T. Grant Foundation.

self-concept which may be of use to educators. From these and other works, it is possible to make several basic distinctions between different aspects of the self.

Perhaps the primary distinction to keep in mind is that between the view of self as agent or process and the view of self as the object of the person's own knowledge and evaluation (Wylie, 1974, p. 1). These views are discussed in two recent books which take differing approaches to the study of the self. Horrocks and Jackson (1972) focus more on the self as a process involving various roles, while Rosenberg (1979), on the other hand, defines the self-image in terms of "the totality of the individual's thoughts and feelings having reference to himself as an object" (p. 7). Although both of these conceptualizations are useful, we shall be primarily concerned with the self-concept as defined by Rosenberg for the duration of this paper. As Rosenberg notes, this view of the self-concept is neither the same as Erickson's (1968) concept of identity nor synonymous with personality, a much broader term. Instead, the self-image is that set of attitudes which one holds about a particular object, namely oneself.

A second key distinction in the literature is that between the self-concept and what is generally referred to as self-esteem (see Beane and Lipka, 1980; Calhoun and Morse, 1977; Dickstein, 1977; and Rosenberg, 1979). This distinction separates those aspects of the self-image which are considered to be basically *descriptive* and nonjudgmental (the self-concept or self-picture) from those aspects or attitudes which can be classified as *evaluations* of the self or the degree of satisfaction with the self (i.e., self-esteem). Along with this distinction between how one describes and evaluates oneself, some authors feel the evaluative or self-esteem aspect is more subject to change due to situational and value influence (Beane and Lipka, 1980; Calhoun and Morse, 1977). Rosenberg (1979), however, argues that two basic motives of the self are the "wish to think well of oneself" (the self-esteem motive) and the "wish to protect the self-concept against change" (the self-consistency motive) (pp. 53–54).

Not everyone finds the distinction between the self-concept and the self-esteem to be viable. Shavelson, Hubner, and Stanton (1976) present an excellent methodological critique which argues that the descriptive and evaluative dimensions are not *empirically* separable. These criticisms notwithstanding, we feel the distinction between self-concept and self-esteem is an extremely useful one. Much of the rest of this article will concentrate on the evaluative dimension since it is the dimension most often measured and is the one which has frequently been thought of as motivating behavior and impacting upon the educational process.

EARLY ADOLESCENCE: A TIME OF CHANGES

In the last ten to twenty years, there has been a growing interest in and awareness of the changes taking place in the first half of the second decade of life—a time which has roughly come to be known as *early adolescence*. . . . All we would like to do is briefly note the nature of some of these changes and their possible implications for the self-concept and self-esteem of the early adolescent.

For most individuals, both males and females, early adolescence is the time during which their bodies undergo the transformation from child to virtually adult stature and proportion. A wide variety of both primary and secondary sexual characteristics develop for the first time during these years. These changes in the body must also become incorporated in early adolescents' views of themselves. Changes in body image and the degree of satisfaction and concern over these changes has been demonstrated most recently by Blyth, Bulcroft, and Simmons (1981) and Simmons, Blyth, and McKinney (in press).

Classical Freudian theory has held that changes associated with pubertal development are quite disruptive and can create serious disturbances in the personality system. Petersen and Taylor (1980) note that there is relatively little support for the view that puberty has direct negative consequences, but a great deal of ambiguity still remains as to what the effects of different aspects of physical development are on the self-image of the early adolescent. For example, Blyth et al. (1981) indicate that there is no significant relationship between self-esteem and the relative onset of puberty for girls but there is a slight positive relationship for boys (early development related to higher self-esteem).

In early adolescence, there is enormous individual variability in when these changes take place and the rate at which they occur. For the most part, these changes are poorly correlated with age and there can be huge differences between individuals in the degree of physical maturity at any point in time during this age range. The rate at which these changes take place is also variable. While considerably more rapid than many of the changes taking place during childhood, they are generally more evolutionary than revolutionary when viewed over time for an individual. These changes are not in themselves likely to account for all the changes in the self-concept of early adolescents which have been noted in the literature.

Another major set of changes which begins to take place in early adolescence has to do with the individual's relationships with his or her significant others such as parents and peers. The process of detaching from parents and getting established among peers can mean major changes in who the individual interacts with most frequently and how that person comes to see him- or herself. Along with these changes in the frequency or intensity of relationships with key others, there may be changes in what these others *expect* of the early adolescent. While Freudian theory has argued that the emotional separation from parents is likely to cause conflict and disturbance, there is little support for the extreme form of this view. The major point is that there may be major changes in both who the early adolescent sees as important and what those individuals expect. Such changes would likely influence the individual's self-concept and may well affect how satisfied one is with oneself.

A third area of change has to do with the developing cognitive abilities of early adolescents. In the last twenty years, there has been an increasing amount of interest within psychology in how people think and how they think about their own thinking abilities. This interest has spread from an interest in how children and adults think about inanimate objects to more recent concerns on how people think about other people (e.g., Hill and Palmquist, 1978) and themselves (e.g., Montemayor and Eisen, 1977; Noppe, 1981; and Bernstein, 1980). Damon and Hart (1982) provide an excellent review of some of the developmental changes in self-perceptions which take place over the first two decades of life. The important point for this discussion is that one cannot assume that attitudes about the self remain qualitatively the same over the life course. In fact, the evidence suggests that as individuals become adolescents, there is an increase in the degree of abstraction used to refer to the self as well as an increase in the use of psychological rather than physical descriptions of the self.

Perhaps this point is made most clearly by Montemayor and Eisen (1977) when they state,

> Self-concept development is not an additive process. Adolescents do not simply add more complex and abstract ideas about themselves to their earlier, childish, concrete conceptions...earlier notions either drop out or are integrated into a more complex picture. (p. 318)

Broughton (1981) takes a somewhat more extreme stance when he argues that there is a qualitative change not only in the content of the self-concept but also in the very form of the self.

A number of important cognitive changes take place during early adolescence and these changes affect how one thinks about oneself in complex ways. While there is not adequate space to do justice to this area, it should be noted that the beginnings of formal operational thought and all it implies is believed to blossom in early adolescence. Future research on the development of the self-concept during the transition from childhood to adolescence will need to more explicitly take into account the changes in how people think about themselves.

A final change which, in our society, usually takes place in early adolescence is the transition from a protective elementary environment to a larger and more complex secondary school environment. Although the impact of this transition into middle or junior high school is discussed in a separate article, it is important to recognize that a major shift in one's ecological setting can have ramifications on the self-concept and the self-esteem of an individual. Work by Simmons, Rosenberg, and Rosenberg (1973), Blyth, Simmons, and Bush (1978), and Simmons, Blyth, Van Cleave, and Bush (1979) have shown that the transition into a junior high school can have a disturbing effect on self-esteem, self-consciousness, and the stability of the self-concept under certain circumstances and particularly for girls.

In concluding this section on some of the changes taking place in early adolescents' lives, we note two factors which may influence the impact of these changes. The two factors are the rate of change a given individual experiences and the degree to which the various changes occur simultaneously. Coleman (1978), in an excellent review article on the state of adolescent theory, articulates the view that virtually none of the changes noted should, in and of themselves, be considered cause for serious disturbance for the average adolescent. Only when two or more of these changes occur simultaneously is the probability for disturbance increased significantly....

Much of the theorizing about self-image development in early adolescence tends to be a simple generalization of the variety of other changes that are faced by the adolescent. It is believed that because the adolescent is going through so many rapid changes, "a restructuring of the concept of self is required in order that these changes may be integrated into the individual's personality" (Dusek and Flaherty, 1981). Most of these general theories of early adolescence stress the issue of discontinuity in the self-concept.

As McCarthy and Hoge (1982) note, a number of theorists have discussed trends in self-image with age. Developmental psychologists have argued both for increasing levels of self-esteem as the child becomes more competent during adolescence (e.g., Long, Ziller, and Henderson, 1968) and also that the adolescent sense of ideal self will grow more rapidly than the real self and lead to a decrease in self-esteem (Zigler, Balla, and Watson, 1972). Erikson (1968) in particular has described the crisis aspects of identity during adolescence. In addition to these more developmental points of view, we find the work by symbolic interactionists in the sociological tradition speaking about the motive to enhance one's self-esteem and the importance of significant others in this process. This tradition tends to predict increased self-esteem unless other factors, such as school environments, intervene (see Simmons et al., 1973; Simmons et al., 1979).

These diverse theoretical perspectives, combined with the multitude of complex changes taking place in early adolescence, suggest that it will be hard to find a simple description of how the self-image develops during this age period.

SELF-IMAGE IN EARLY ADOLESCENCE: RESEARCH TRENDS

Can we piece together a picture of what is happening during the transition from childhood into adolescence from existing research? As Dusek and Flaherty (1981) and Wylie (1974, 1979) have noted, there are a number of difficulties involved in summarizing research in the self-image area. The diversity of instruments, subjects, and the ways in which results have been reported all complicate the task. In spite of these difficulties, we shall note several reviews and a few new studies that have been undertaken in this area.

Wylie (1979) did an extensive review of studies in the self-image area across a wide variety of factors. One of these factors was age. Her conclusion with respect to age trends from late childhood into adulthood indicates that "the bulk of the studies... show no association of age and self-regard scores..." (p. 21). This conclusion was based on studies that met certain methodological criteria and held up across a number of different indicators. Nonetheless, Wylie did note that some of the more idiosyncratic measures provided mixed results with an equal number showing increases, decreases, and no relationship whatsoever between self-esteem and age. The one study which she cited as being perhaps the best executed was a longitudinal study by Bachman and O'Malley (1977) which reported an increase in self-esteem from tenth grade until adulthood. Unfortunately, this study did not begin in childhood or early adolescence. Wylie concluded that the burden of proof for establishing a relationship between age and self-regard must lay on those proposing such a relationship.

Dusek and Flaherty (1981), in an elegantly designed study geared to the issue of continuity and stability in the self-image over the adolescent years (ages 11 through 18), came to a somewhat different conclusion. They found a high degree of continuity in the factors they used to measure the self-concept. From this, they conclude that there is probably not a qualitative change in the self-image as it develops during adolescence. Nonetheless, they note that although

the major changes during pubescence probably do not cause a complete restructuring of the self-concept, there may be considerable individual change. They state, "the most reasonable conclusion to which we may come is that the adolescent's self-concept develops in a basically continuous and stable manner, with change occurring slowly and gradually at the individual subject level" (Dusek and Flaherty, 1981, p. 37). This conclusion, however, is based on semantic differential items which are not specifically geared toward measuring self-esteem. In fact, the specific factor structures which they find persisting throughout adolescence involve dimensions of adjustment, achievement, congeniality, and masculinity.

One important aspect of this study is that none of the three cross-sectional aspects of the study replicated each other. That is, when they looked at different students representing different age groups, the age trends did not appear to be consistent. Although each set suggested turmoil, none of them suggested the same pattern of turmoil. In contrast, by following the same students over time in a longitudinal study, they found a high degree of continuity and a moderate degree of stability in the self-image as they measured it. Dusek and Flaherty conclude that their analysis in part supports Coleman's (1978) focal theory of adolescence, which notes that the changes of adolescence occur gradually and are dealt with separately without much disruption. The authors also note that they might have found more discontinuity in the self-image had they looked at younger children who were not cognitively mature.

In one final study by McCarthy and Hoge (1982), we see yet another somewhat different conclusion. This study looked at junior and senior high school students and followed them for one year using both the Rosenberg and Coopersmith self-esteem scales. They concluded that there is a significant *increase* in self-esteem from grade 7 through 12 but that this increase is relatively small and most likely to be seen only in longitudinal studies. They also found that their cross-sectional data using different students at different ages showed only slight differences and differences which changed direction and magnitude depending on the particular scale and subscale used. One of the major conclusions from this study was that longitudinal studies are most appropriate for studying changes in self-esteem during the adolescent years and that a review of such studies clearly indicates a small but significant increase in self-esteem over time. This research is further supported by our own recent analyses which indicated a general increase in self-esteem from sixth grade through tenth grade for students in an urban school system who were followed for five years (Blyth, Simmons, and Carlton-Ford, 1983).

The preceding review of research on age trends in self-image and self-esteem indicates there probably are no clear-cut age trends which have been proven beyond a shadow of a doubt. In all likelihood, there is a slight *increase* in the self-esteem of youth as they move from early adolescence into later adolescence. There is little support for the view that the self-image is generally disrupted or devalued during early adolescence, although more longitudinal studies started in late childhood are needed before we can eliminate this possibility.

On the issue of stability versus instability, the studies note a high to moderate degree of stability in the self-concept during adolescence. This was also noted recently by Savin-Williams (1983) when he used a variety of methods of measuring different aspects of the self-concept. He found a high degree of stability even from moment to moment during a week when students were asked to describe their self-feelings. Theorists have probably overemphasized the amount of self-image instability which occurs in early adolescence. We need to stop thinking of early adolescence as a time when changes occur so rapidly that it is impossible to maintain a certain degree of stability in how one views oneself. In fact, because of the changes taking place in and around the adolescent, it may be even more important to maintain some basic continuity and stability in one's own self-image.

With all the emphasis on stability and continuity over time, we may well have ignored one of the most important factors which is quite apparent in early adolescence: the tremendous variability in self-esteem and self-image. More important than the relationship between age and self-esteem is the fact that there is a tremendous range in the level of self-esteem, regardless of age. This high degree of variability needs to be stressed more often and dealt with more appropriately in our theorizing. In addition, we need to become aware of the potential changes in the bases upon which self-esteem is evaluated. Are the bases of the judgments about one's self-esteem the same for children? early adolescents? late adolescents? Current evidence from the social cognitive perspective suggests they are not. Further understanding of these changes as they relate to self-esteem changes would be particularly helpful.

Finally, and perhaps most importantly, we must recognize that age in itself is not a cause. All of the studies cited above are looking for a relationship between age and self-esteem. We suggest that a more fruitful line of research and a more productive way of thinking about early adolescence would be to look at the relationship between self-esteem and *the particular*

changes which are taking place in the early adolescents' lives. Such research would emphasize the consequences of change in school environment, the changes in physical development, and the issue of undergoing simultaneous changes in several areas of one's life. A better understanding of the impact of these potential causal agents would greatly advance our understanding of early adolescent self-image. We would include in these changes an examination of sex differences which may develop or be intensified during adolescence (e.g., see Dusek and Flaherty, 1981).

IMPLICATIONS FOR EDUCATORS

From the theory and research discussed above, we shall briefly note three implications of concern to educators dealing with early adolescents. . . . First, many early adolescents are changing cognitively in such a way as to dramatically change the way they see and evaluate themselves. There may be changes in what is of central importance to them—such as a change from wanting to please parents to wanting to be a star athlete. Accompanying these changes is an increasing amount of time devoted to introspection. Early adolescents are bringing themselves into themselves and trying out various roles. We need to understand and facilitate this rather than criticize it as inappropriate or describe it as instability.

A second and equally important aspect of early adolescence is that there are a variety of new significant others involved in helping youths see themselves in different lights. Not only are parents still critically important but peers also enter the picture. Teachers must recognize this change in significant others and also recognize that they may be perceived harshly when compared to students' supportive and warm elementary school teachers. Middle-level educators are asked to be both warm and supportive and yet subject matter competent—a delicate balance that we do not expect of educators at other levels. This balance is particularly critical to early adolescents as they shape their identity. In this regard, early adolescence is an optimal time for parents and other adults to take an active hand in shaping a youth's future.

Finally, the research indicates that the changes taking place in adolescence are not as disruptive as we have been led to believe. These changes are more likely to be sequential than simultaneous in nature for any given individual. This perspective helps to free us from a number of views of adolescence which suggest that it is a time of disturbance and problems. Once we realize that these changes are taking place more slowly and are being incorporated gradually (and successfully) by the majority of early adolescents, it frees us to work with these youth in new ways. It allows educators to be in the business of helping youth find and develop competencies they feel good about rather than being in the business of making people feel good about themselves. We believe our youth do basically feel good about themselves and their abilities in a variety of areas. What we feel less confident about is their feelings about themselves with respect to school and the implications of that lower academic self-image for future achievement and competence. We hope middle-level educators will continue to focus on this area of building competencies upon which positive self-feelings can grow.

Under Pressure

David Elkind

The message bombards us from the television screen, the daily newspapers, and weekly magazines: "It's tough to be a teenager in today's world." The social context of adolescence has been altered dramatically during the last twenty years. The nature of the parent-child relationship has changed; parents are busy working and teenagers are forced to be more independent and "adult." New social dilemmas have arisen—availability of drugs, early sexual relations, exposure to erotic music and videos, the HIV (AIDS) virus, and teen pregnancy. However, the developmental characteristics of adolescents have not changed. Their thinking patterns continue to be egocentric. They are focused on themselves, on what others think of their actions ("imaginary audience") and on their invulnerability ("It won't happen to me"). Will the combination of adolescent egocentric thinking and new social choices and temptations disrupt the normal course of self-identification and increasing, but guided, independence?

In my work with school systems I often meet separately with faculty members, students, and parents. One afternoon a few months ago I spoke with a group of teenagers at a high school. As I generally do during such sessions. I asked the teenagers what sorts of things they felt were stressing them the most. This question isn't intended to start a therapy session or solve problems, but it is a way for young people to hear that other teenagers have many of the same problems as they do.

One girl, who was no more than 13, spoke up. "What bugs me," she said, "is that my boyfriend keeps pressuring me to have sex with him." She then turned to me and asked, "What should I do?"

I answered that if I were in her position, I would say something to the effect that "I like you very much and enjoy being your friend, but if that is the only reason you are friends with me, please find somebody else."

D. Elkind. (1989, Dec.). Teenagers under pressure. *Boston Globe Magazine*: Special Issue, pp. 24 ff.

That evening, after I gave a talk to the high school students' parents, a couple came up to me and introduced themselves as the parents of the girl I had spoken with that afternoon. Apparently she told them about her question and my answer. They were visibly angry. "How dare you say something like that to my daughter," the woman said with considerable venom, "Why you never even asked her whether she loved the boy!"

When I recovered my composure, I explained that if the girl had wanted to engage in sexual activity, she wouldn't have asked for my advice. She asked me, I suggested, because she was looking for some adult support for *not* having sex with her boyfriend.

Unfortunately, this story isn't an isolated one. It reflects a major trend in our society: Young teenagers today are being forced to make decisions that earlier generations didn't have to make until they were older and more mature—and today's teenagers are not getting much support and guidance. This pressure for early decision making is coming from peer groups, parents, advertisers, merchandisers, and even the legal system.

For generations, teenagers have had to make decisions about their behavior: what to wear, whether to smoke or drink, whether to engage in sexual activity. Today, with AIDS, venereal disease, and epidemic drug use, the choices are increasingly risky ones. But unless we understand the pressures today's teenagers are under, at ever-younger ages—and how teenagers think—we can't be much help to them in their decision making.

Since 1975 the number of sixth-graders experimenting with drugs has tripled. This is at least in part a reflection of both peer pressure and the tendency of younger teenagers to copy what the next-older group is doing: About 90 percent of high school students report having experimented with drugs by the time they have left high school.

This combination of older example and peer pressure also helps explain why more young teenagers are sexually active than ever before. The figures are telling: In the 1960s, only about 10 percent of teenage girls were sexually active, but today that figure is closer to 50 percent. Likewise, in the 1960s only about 25 percent of teenage boys were sexually active. Today that number is closer to 65 percent.

You don't have to look far for evidence: At a recent discussion with teenagers on Cape Cod, I was told that boys who were 13 and still virgins were being teased by their friends. I was also told that a month or two of dating is long enough to wait before having sex.

It might be argued that the reason for this increase in early sexual activity is that children are reaching sexual maturity at a much younger age than their peers did a century ago. But the trend toward earlier sexual maturity (as a consequence of better nutrition and better health care) leveled off almost two decades ago. The explanation for all this early sexual activity is our changed social values.

Whether to use drugs and whether to engage in sex aren't the only decisions facing many young teenagers. After a divorce, for example, many children must choose which parent to live with. While it is important for teenagers to make this decision for themselves, the choice is a stressful one, with great potential for damaging relations with one or both parents.

Some business interests are also pushing teenagers into early decision making. A few banks are ready to issue teenagers credit cards with a $1,000 limit. Learning to save money and live on a budget is important, but that's not what's being taught.

And some rock music promoters are eager to push a small number of unnecessarily lascivious "heavy metal" groups to young teenagers without taking responsibility for the kind of fare they're providing. While no one is asking for censorship, there should be some appreciation by the music promoters—those who promote these few bad apples in the rock music barrel—of the inexperience and immaturity of young listeners.

The legal system, too, is struggling with the issue of how much decision-making power young people should have, notably in current cases involving young girls' right to get an abortion without parental notification. In recent years there have been many decisions supporting the constitutional rights of children and youth. But in these decisions the courts may also violate the rights of parents and ignore the needs of the young to be protected from themselves as well as from others.

Ours is the only society in the world that forces teenagers to make so many difficult decisions at such an early age—and gives them so little guidance. Now we're paying the price. When discussing the well-being of young people, health professionals today speak of "the new morbidity."

Fifty years ago, the major cause of death among young people between the ages of 13 and 20 was physical disease, such as polio. Most of the illnesses that accounted for teenage death have since been conquered, and today the majority of teenage deaths are essentially the result of overwhelming stress.

Decision making is stressful, and young people seek relief from stress in the same ways as adults do. Sometimes these escapes end tragically, in death from substance abuse and related accidents, from anorexia, and by suicide. These deaths are the new morbidity.

The new morbidity, however, is only one of the symptoms of the stress experienced by contemporary teenagers. By every measure we have, young people are doing less well today than they did 25 years ago. With more than 1 million teenage pregnancies each year, we have the highest rate of any Western society; twice that of Great Britain, which has the next highest rate.

There has been a 50 percent increase in obesity among children and adolescents in the last twenty years, and young people are doing less well on measures of physical strength and endurance than they did ten years ago. Smoking has increased dramatically among teenage girls, and lung cancer now accounts for more deaths among women than breast cancer. Academic achievement has suffered along with the increase in problem behavior. When compared with youth from other nations, our teenagers routinely score at the bottom academically. Verbal SAT scores, in particular, continue to drop.

How did we come to this deplorable condition? As with all social phenomena, the reasons are complex and not easy to define. Nonetheless, a few major changes in our society and in our ways of thinking about children and youth can be singled out.

Changes in the structure of the American family certainly have played a part. Until the early 1960s, about 90 percent of families were traditional in the sense that the father worked and the mother stayed home to care for the average of 2.5 children. Today only about 10 percent of families are of the traditional sort. As most everyone knows, the majority of today's families are either two-parent working families, single-parent families, or "blended families," made up of a couple and children from more than one marriage. Many of today's parents have few options. To support their families, both parents often have to work outside the home. And because most communities offer little in the way of support systems for parents or children, teenagers must fend for themselves a good deal of the time.

This change in family structure has increased the stress experienced by parents and contributed to a changed conception of children and of youth. Children and young people are now seen as competent to deal with all of life's vicissitudes. Many parents, for example, now take it for granted that infants and young children find it easy to cope with out-of-home care. Adults often assume that their school-age children can deal with the "latchkey" experience. When teenagers come home to an empty house, they are expected to look after themselves.

But child and adolescent competence shouldn't be taken for granted. If circumstances require a parent to work outside the home, there are ways to buffer the stress young people feel. Telling young children how much we miss them, giving latchkey youngsters ways to cope with unexpected events, and providing teenagers with structured activities can help each age group cope with some of the stresses imposed on them by modern family life.

The civil rights movement and the women's movement also have contributed to our new view of children and youth as responsible decision makers. During the 1960s, women and minorities protested that they were not being given credit for their competence and abilities, and they argued that the same was true for minority children and young girls of all races. Recognition of the competence of women and minority groups thus carried with it recognition of the competence of girls and minority children. While children and young people are certainly more competent than we gave them credit for in the past, they are still less able than we might like them to be.

A third factor contributing to the new perception of young people is the extraordinary pace of technological change. Technologies open up new occupations and close others with amazing rapidity. Take, for example, the dictating machine. Regarded as one of our most modern and time-saving innovations a quarter of a century ago, the dictating machine is almost passé today, replaced by laptop computers. School textbooks can barely keep up with scientific developments and are often outdated in five years or less.

When technology changes this quickly, it affects the relationships between adults and youth. For one thing, the knowledge and experience of their elders may have little value for young people growing up in an era in which skills are so quickly outmoded. It often seems that young people are closer—and better able to make use of—new technology than adults are. In some computer firms, for example, there are few employees over 40. Young people appear to be qualified to deal with rapidly changing technology, so we often assume that they are able to make responsible decisions at a very early age.

Yet we have to be careful. Growing up with a technology doesn't mean that young people are necessarily proficient in it. Computers are a good example. Although they are now found in just about every workplace from supermarkets to service stations, computers have yet to be fully incorporated into schools. Computers are complex machines, and we can't expect the majority of elementary or junior high school students to use them as more than word processors or number crunchers. Advanced applications such as programming must wait until most young people have mastered the new abilities that emerge in adolescence.

Understanding these abilities, or rather the young person's inexperience with them, helps explain why inappropriate decision making is so risky in early adolescence. Jean Piaget, the late Swiss psychologist, called the new mental abilities that emerge in adolescence "formal operations." These new operations enable young people to understand historical time and celestial space, grasp simile and metaphor, comprehend algebra and philosophy, construct ideals, and entertain contrary-to-fact possibilities. They make possible the highest level of scientific, philosophical, and religious thinking.

They also enable young people to think about thinking. Young children think, but they don't think about thinking. Formal operations generally develop by age 12 or 13, so most teenagers can imagine that other people have thoughts in their heads, just as they themselves do.

But when thinking about other people's thinking, the young teenager is apt to make a characteristic error. A young person of 12, 13, or 14 is probably experiencing enormous changes in appearance, feelings, and emotions and is preoccupied with his or her metamorphosis. Accordingly, when young teenagers think about other people's thinking, they assume that other people are thinking about the same thing as they're thinking about: namely, themselves. As a consequence, young teenagers construct what I call an "imaginary audience." They believe that everyone is watching them and thinking about them and is deeply concerned with their thoughts and actions. This gives rise, among other things, to the heightened self-awareness and self-consciousness so typical of young teenagers.

The imaginary audience can be a positive motivating force. We all have imaginary audience fantasies of playing a concerto at Carnegie Hall or hitting a grand slam in the World Series. Such fantasies can encourage young people to work toward goals. But the audience can have negative effects as well, making young adolescents particularly vulnerable to peer pressure. The peer group is the most powerful component of the young adolescent's audience, and this is why young adolescents are so bent on conformity in dress, behavior, and language. When young people are required to make decisions about drugs or sexual activity and the audience is in full force, from ages 12 to 14, their decision making will be strongly influenced by what they believe the audience will approve or disapprove of. As young people move into middle and late adolescence, individual friendships supplant the peer group and rob the audience of much of its power.

The influence of the imaginary audience is compounded by another idea young people create in early adolescence, which I call the "personal fable." If everyone is watching you and thinking about you, this idea holds, you must be truly special. Other people may not find the romance of their dreams, but you will. Other people will grow old and die, but not you. The fable, like the audience, has its positive side. We would never drive in Boston or get in an airplane if we didn't believe, deep down, that we are surrounded by a cloak of invulnerability.

But the fable also contributes to more dangerous forms of risk taking. People who smoke, for example, often believe that other people will develop a disease as a result of smoking but not them. Young teenagers believe that other teenagers may get pregnant but not them. Many young teenagers engage in sexual activity and experiment with drugs, then, not because they don't know the risks but because they believe they're immune to the dangers.

The pressure for contemporary teenagers to make important health decisions at an early age thus catches them at a time when they're most vulnerable to peer pressure and risk taking and least responsive to the values and morals of their upbringing. While education about drugs and the risks of sexual activity is important, it simply isn't enough to counter the power of the imaginary audience and the personal fable, both of which are pressuring young people into risk taking.

What can we do? Some things are already being done. At the college and university levels, after many years in which students had wide involvement in educational and administrative matters, the discarded concept of *in loco parentis* is being revived. Many colleges are becoming more strict about on-campus drinking and partying and are providing more university-sponsored activities. Students are accepting these new limits and activities with a certain amount of relief. Without openly acknowledging it, they're pleased that schools are recognizing that they're still not fully grown and can still benefit from rules, limits, and adult-initiated activities. One would hope that high schools might soon begin to emulate the new sense of social responsibility on college campuses.

Likewise, religious organizations are moving back into family ministry, and youth ministry is growing, as is participation in organizations such as 4-H and adolescent scouting. Young people will take the sleaze if we give it to them, but they would prefer positive role models. We need more programs like the one in Atlanta that makes community service part of the high school curriculum, programs that can capture the idealism and generosity of young people. In addition, high schools, which moved away from providing organized activities such as school dances and service clubs, should consider resurrecting these programs.

There is some indication that the media are becoming aware of the need to be more thoughtful about the material they present to impressionable young people. On television, images of teenagers have become more realistic, and TV parents are exerting more authority and control than was shown in shows of the 1970s and early 1980s. In the movie *Big*, the hero decides he doesn't want to stay an adult, despite the attractions of a good job and an alluring girlfriend. When he sees young people at play, he realizes that he doesn't want to skip his childhood.

Parents need to recognize that while young adolescents are competent in many ways, there are many decisions they aren't ready to make on their own. They still need adult guidance, direction, and limit setting. While they may resist and rebel against boundaries, they also appreciate them. Young people are very aware that when we say "no'" we care enough to take the risk of confrontation and battle. As many teen-agers have said to me, speaking about a friend, "I guess his parents really don't love him or they wouldn't let him do that, would they?"

We start preparing our children for adolescence when they are infants. If we are reasonably consistent in our expectations, if we are loving and democratic, yet firm in the standards and limits we set, we give young people an inner sense of who and what they are.

It is this sense of their own personhood that helps young teenagers resist the pressures of the imaginary audience and the personal fable, even when these are at their greatest power. In the end, young teenagers are most likely to make responsible choices when the adults in their lives provide limits, standards, and examples of healthy decision making.

Alienation and the Four Worlds of Childhood

Urie Bronfenbrenner

An adolescent's need to belong is very intense. Adolescents want to be part of a larger whole, and will drastically change behaviors to reach this end. Erik Erikson suggests that over-identification with a peer group is one way to find acceptance and avoid role confusion. Parents, however, are often baffled by the extreme activities of their teenagers as they are initiated into a peer group or clique.

"Breaking away" is part of the process of lessening one's identification with the family. Yet well-known child psychologist Urie Bronfenbrenner maintains that adoles-cents continue to need support and guidance from par-ents, schools, and community. In some cases, attention to the needs of teenagers, and limitations on their activities, have become too lax. Some adolescents become disconnected, and need new kinds of programs and activities to replace a parent-supported neighborhood environment that no longer exists. Bronfenbrenner describes programs in the United States and other countries that can help build an adoles-cent's sense of purpose and belonging.

To be alienated is to lack a sense of belonging, to feel cut off from family, friends, school, or work—the four worlds of childhood.

At some point in the process of growing up, many of us have probably felt cut off from one or another of these worlds, but usually not for long and not from more than one world at a time. If things weren't going well in school, we usually still had family, friends, or some activity to turn to. But if, over an extended pe-riod, a young person feels unwanted or insecure in several of these worlds simultaneously or if the worlds are at war with one another, trouble may lie ahead.

What makes a young person feel that he or she doesn't belong? Individual differences in personality can certainly be one cause, but, especially in recent years, scientists who study human behavior and de-velopment have identified an equal (if not even more powerful) factor: the circumstances in which a young person lives.

U. Bronfenbrenner. (1986, Feb.). Alienation and the four worlds of childhood. *Phi Delta Kappan, 67* (6), 430–436.

Many readers may feel that they recognize the human families depicted in the vignettes that are to follow. This is so because they reflect the way we tend to look at families today: namely, that we see parents as being good or not-so-good, without fully taking into account the circumstances in their lives.

Take Charles and Philip, for example. Both are seventh-graders who live in a middle-class suburb of a large U.S. city. In many ways their surroundings seem similar; yet, in terms of the risk of alienation, they live in rather different worlds. See if you can spot the important differences.

CHARLES

The oldest of three children, Charles is amiable, outgo-ing, and responsible. Both of his parents have full-time jobs outside the home. They've been able to arrange their working hours, however, so that at least one of them is at home when the children return from school. If for some reason they can't be home, they have an arrangement with a neighbor, an elderly woman who lives alone. They can phone her and ask her to look after the children until they arrive. The children have grown so fond of this woman that she is like another grandparent—a nice situation for them, since their real grandparents live far away.

Homework time is one of the most important parts of the day for Charles and his younger brother and sister. Charles's parents help the children with their homework if they need it, but most of the time they just make sure that the children have a period of peace and quiet—without TV—in which to do their work. The children are allowed to watch television one hour each night—but only after they have completed their homework. Since Charles is doing well in school, homework isn't much of an issue, however.

Sometimes Charles helps his mother or father prepare dinner, a job that everyone in the family shares and enjoys. Those family members who don't cook on a given evening are responsible for cleaning up.

Charles also shares his butterfly collection with his family. He started the collection when he first began learning about butterflies during a fourth-grade science project. The whole family enjoys picnicking and hunting butterflies together, and Charles occasionally asks his father to help him mount and catalogue his trophies.

Charles is a bit of a loner. He's not a very good athlete, and this makes him somewhat self-conscious. But he does have one very close friend, a boy in his class who lives just down the block. The two boys have been good friends for years.

Charles is a good-looking, warm, happy young man. Now that he's beginning to be interested in girls, he's gratified to find that the interest is returned.

PHILIP

Philip is 12 and lives with his mother, father, and 6-year-old brother. Both of his parents work in the city, commuting more than an hour each way. Pandemonium strikes every weekday morning as the entire family prepares to leave for school and work.

Philip is on his own from the time school is dismissed until just before dinner, when his parents return after stopping to pick up his little brother at a nearby day-care home. At one time, Philip took care of his little brother after school, but he resented having to do so. That arrangement ended one day when Philip took his brother out to play and the little boy wandered off and got lost. Philip didn't even notice for several hours that his brother was missing. He felt guilty at first about not having done a better job. But not having to mind his brother freed him to hang out with his

friends or to watch television, his two major after-school activities.

The pace of their life is so demanding that Philip's parents spend their weekends just trying to relax. Their favorite weekend schedule calls for watching a ball game on television and then having a cookout in the back yard. Philip's mother resigned herself long ago to a messy house; pizza, TV dinners, or fast foods are all she can manage in the way of meals on most nights. Philip's father has made it clear that she can do whatever she wants in managing the house, as long as she doesn't try to involve him in the effort. After a hard day's work, he's too tired to be interested in housekeeping.

Philip knows that getting a good education is important; his parents have stressed that. But he just can't seem to concentrate in school. He'd much rather fool around with his friends. The thing that he and his friends like to do best is to ride the bus downtown and go to a movie, where they can show off, make noise, and make one another laugh.

Sometimes they smoke a little marijuana during the movie. One young man in Philip's social group was arrested once for having marijuana in his jacket pocket. He was trying to sell it on the street so that he could buy food. Philip thinks his friend was stupid to get caught. If you're smart, he believes, you don't let that happen. He's glad that his parents never found out about the incident.

Once, he brought two of his friends home during the weekend. His parents told him later that they didn't like the kind of people he was hanging around with. Now Philip goes out of his way to keep his friends and his parents apart.

THE FAMILY UNDER PRESSURE

In many ways the worlds of both teenagers are similar, even typical. Both live in families that have been significantly affected by one of the most important developments in American family life in the postwar years: the employment of both parents outside the home. Their mothers share this status with 64 percent of all married women in the United States who have school-age children. Fifty percent of mothers of preschool children and 46 percent of mothers with infants under the age of 3 work outside the home. For single-parent families, the rates are even higher: 53 percent of all mothers in single-parent households who have infants under age 3 work outside the home, as do 69 percent of all single mothers who have school-age children.[1]

These statistics have profound implications for families—sometimes for better, sometimes for worse. The determining factor is how well a given family can cope with the "havoc in the home" that two jobs can create. For, unlike most other industrialized nations, the United States has yet to introduce the kinds of policies and practices that make work life and family life compatible.

It is all too easy for family life in the United States to become hectic and stressful, as both parents try to coordinate the disparate demands of family and jobs in a world in which everyone has to be transported at least twice a day in a variety of directions. Under these circumstances, meal preparation, child care, shopping, and cleaning—the most basic tasks in a family—become major challenges. Dealing with these challenges may sometimes take precedence over the family's equally important child-rearing, educational, and nurturing roles.

But that is not the main danger. What threatens the well-being of children and young people the most is that the external havoc can become internal, first for parents and then for their children. And that is exactly the sequence in which the psychological havoc of families under stress usually moves.

Recent studies indicate that conditions at work constitute one of the major sources of stress for American families.[2] Stress at work carries over to the home, where it affects first the relationship of parents to each other. Marital conflict then disturbs the parent-child relationship. Indeed, as long as tensions at work do not impair the relationship between the parents, the children are not likely to be affected. In other words, the influence of parental employment on children is indirect, operating through its effect on the parents.

That this influence is indirect does not make it any less potent, however. Once the parent-child relationship is seriously disturbed, children begin to feel insecure—and a door to the world of alienation has been opened. That door can open to children at any age, from preschool to high school and beyond.

My reference to the world of school is not accidental, for it is in that world that the next step toward alienation is likely to be taken. Children who feel rootless or caught in conflict at home find it difficult to pay attention in school. Once they begin to miss out on learning, they feel lost in the classroom, and they begin to seek acceptance elsewhere. Like Philip, they often find acceptance in a group of peers with similar histories who, having no welcoming place to go and nothing challenging to do, look for excitement on the streets.

OTHER INFLUENCES

In contemporary American society the growth of two-wage-earner families is not the only—or even the most

serious—social change requiring accommodation through public policy and practice in order to avoid the risks of alienation. Other social changes include lengthy trips to and from work; the loss of the extended family, the close neighborhood, and other support systems previously available to families; and the omnipresent threat of television and other media to the family's traditional role as the primary transmitter of culture and values. Along with most families today, the families of Charles and Philip are experiencing the unraveling and disintegration of social institutions that in the past were central to the health and well-being of children and their parents.

Notice that both Charles and Philip come from two-parent, middle-class families. This is still the norm in the United States. Thus neither family has to contend with two changes now taking place in U.S. society that have profound implications for the future of American families and the well-being of the next generation. The first of these changes is the increasing number of single-parent families. Although the divorce rate in the U.S. has been leveling off of late, this decrease has been more than compensated for by a rise in the number of unwed mothers, especially teenagers. Studies of the children brought up in single-parent families indicate that they are at greater risk of alienation than their counterparts from two-parent families. However, their vulnerability appears to have its roots not in the single-parent family structure as such, but in the treatment of single parents by U.S. society.[3]

In this nation, single parenthood is almost synonymous with poverty. And the growing gap between poor families and the rest of us is today the most powerful and destructive force producing alienation in the lives of millions of young people in America. In recent years, we have witnessed what the U.S. Census Bureau calls "the largest decline in family income in the post-World War II period." According to the latest Census, 25 percent of all children under age 6 now live in families whose incomes place them below the poverty line.

COUNTERING THE RISKS

Despite the similar stresses on their families, the risks of alienation for Charles and Philip are not the same. Clearly, Charles's parents have made a deliberate effort to create a variety of arrangements and practices that work against alienation. They have probably not done so as part of a deliberate program of "alienation prevention"—parents don't usually think in those terms. They're just being good parents. They spend time with their children and take an active interest in what their children are thinking, doing, and learning. They control their television set instead of letting it control them. They've found support systems to back them up when they're not available.

Without being aware of it, Charles's parents are employing a principle that the great Russian educator Makarenko employed in his extraordinarily successful programs for the reform of wayward adolescents in the 1920s: "The maximum of support with the maximum of challenge."[4] Families that produce effective, competent children often follow this principle, whether they're aware of it or not. They neither maintain strict control nor allow their children total freedom. They're always opening doors—and then giving their children a gentle but firm shove to encourage them to move on and grow. This combination of support and challenge is essential, if children are to avoid alienation and develop into capable young adults.

From a longitudinal study of youthful alienation and delinquency that is now considered a classic, Finnish psychologist Lea Pulkkinen arrived at a conclusion strikingly similar to Makarenko's. She found "guidance"—a combination of love and direction—to be a critical predictor of healthy development in youngsters.[5]

No such pattern is apparent in Philip's family. Unlike Charles's parents, Philip's parents neither recognize nor respond to the challenges they face. They have dispensed with the simple amenities of family self-discipline in favor of whatever is easiest. They may not be indifferent to their children, but the demands of their jobs leave them with little energy to be actively involved in their children's lives. (Note that Charles's parents have work schedules that are flexible enough to allow one of them to be at home most afternoons. In this regard, Philip's family is much more the norm, however. One of the most constructive steps that employers could take to strengthen families would be to enact clear policies making such flexibility possible.)

But perhaps the clearest danger signal in Philip's life is his dependence on his peer group. Pulkkinen found heavy reliance on peers to be one of the strongest predictors of problem behavior in adolescence and young adulthood. From a developmental viewpoint, adolescence is a time of challenge—a period in which young people seek activities that will serve as outlets for their energy, imagination, and longings. If healthy and constructive challenges are not available to them, they will find their challenges in such peer-group-related behaviors as poor school performance, aggressiveness or social withdrawal (sometimes both), school absenteeism or dropping out, smoking, drinking, early and promiscuous sexual activity, teenage parenthood, drugs, and juvenile delinquency.

This pattern has now been identified in a number of modern industrial societies, including the United States, England, West Germany, Finland, and Australia. The pattern is both predictable from the circumstances of a child's early family life and predictive of life experiences still to come, e.g., difficulties in establishing relationships with the opposite sex, marital discord, divorce, economic failure, criminality.

If the roots of alienation are to be found in disorganized families living in disorganized environments, its bitter fruits are to be seen in these patterns of disrupted development. This is not a harvest that our nation can easily afford. Is it a price that other modern societies are paying, as well?

A CROSS-NATIONAL PERSPECTIVE

The available answers to that question will not make Americans feel better about what is occurring in the United States. In our society, the forces that produce youthful alienation are growing in strength and scope. Families, schools, and other institutions that play important roles in human development are rapidly being eroded, *mainly through benign neglect*. Unlike the citizens of other modern nations, we Americans have simply not been willing to make the necessary effort to forestall the alienation of our young people.

As part of a new experiment in higher education at Cornell University, I have been teaching a multi-disciplinary course for the past few years titled "Human Development in Post-Industrial Societies." One of the things we have done in that course is to gather comparative data from several nations, including France, Canada, Japan, Australia, Germany, England, and the United States. One student summarized our findings succinctly: "With respect to families, schools, children, and youth, such countries as France, Japan, Canada, and Australia have more in common with each other than the United States has with any of them." For example:

- The United States has by far the highest rate of teenage pregnancy of any industrialized nation—twice the rate of its nearest competitor, England.

- The United States divorce rate is the highest in the world—nearly double that of its nearest competitor, Sweden.

- The United States is the only industrialized society in which nearly one-fourth of all infants and preschool children live in families whose incomes fall below the poverty line. These children lack such basics as adequate health care.

- The United States has fewer support systems for individuals in all age groups, including adolescence. The United States also has the highest incidence of alcohol and drug abuse among adolescents of any country in the world.[6]

All these problems are part of the unraveling of the social fabric that has been going on since World War II. These problems are not unique to the United States, but in many cases they are more pronounced here than elsewhere.

WHAT COMMUNITIES CAN DO

The more we learn about alienation and its effects in contemporary post-industrial societies, the stronger are the imperatives to counteract it. If the essence of alienation is disconnectedness, then the best way to counteract alienation is through the creation of connections or links.

For the well-being of children and adolescents, the most important links must be those between the home, the peer group, and the school. A recent study in West Germany effectively demonstrated how important this basic triangle can be. The study examined student achievement and social behavior in twenty schools. For all the schools, the researchers developed measures of the links between the home, the peer group, and the school. Controlling for social class and other variables, the researchers found that they were able to predict children's behavior from the number of such links they found. Students who had no links were alienated. They were not doing well in school, and they exhibited a variety of behavioral problems. By contrast, students who had such links were doing well and were growing up to be responsible citizens.[7]

In addition to creating links within the basic triangle of home, peer group, and school, we need to consider two other structures in today's society that affect the lives of young people: the world of work (for both parents and children) and the community, which provides an overarching context for all the other worlds of childhood.

Philip's family is one example of how the world of work can contribute to alienation. The United States lags far behind other industrialized nations in providing childcare services and other benefits designed to promote the well-being of children and their families. Among the most needed benefits are maternity and paternity leaves, flex-time, job-sharing arrangements, and personal leaves for parents when their children are ill. These benefits are a matter of course in many of the nations with which the United States is generally compared.

In contemporary American society, however, the parents' world of work is not the only world that both policy and practice ought to be accommodating. There is also the children's world of work. According to the most recent figures available, 50 percent of all high school students now work part-time—sometimes as much as 40 to 50 hours per week. This fact poses a major problem for the schools. Under such circumstances, how can teachers assign homework with any expectation that it will be completed?

The problem is further complicated by the kind of work that most young people are doing. For many years, a number of social scientists—myself included—advocated more work opportunities for adolescents. We argued that such experiences would provide valuable contact with adult models and thereby further the development of responsibility and general maturity. However, from their studies of U.S. high school students who are employed, Ellen Greenberger and Lawrence Steinberg conclude that most of the jobs held by these youngsters are highly routinized and afford little opportunity for contact with adults. The largest employers of teenagers in the United States are fast-food restaurants. Greenberger and Steinberg argue that, instead of providing maturing experiences, such settings give adolescents even greater exposure to the values and lifestyles of their peer group. And the adolescent peer group tends to emphasize immediate gratification and consumerism.[8]

Finally, in order to counteract the mounting forces of alienation in U.S. society, we must establish a working alliance between the private sector and the public one (at both the local level and the national level) to forge links between the major institutions in U.S. society and to re-create a sense of community. Examples from other countries abound:

- Switzerland has a law that no institution for the care of the elderly can be established unless it is adjacent to and shares facilities with a day-care center, a school, or some other kind of institution serving children.

- In many public places throughout Australia, the Department of Social Security has displayed a poster that states, in sixteen languages: "If you need an interpreter, call this number." The department maintains a network of interpreters who are available sixteen hours a day, seven days a week. They can help callers get in touch with a doctor, an ambulance, a fire brigade, or the police; they can also help callers with practical or personal problems.

- In the USSR, factories, offices, and places of business customarily "adopt" groups of children, e.g., a day-care center, a class of schoolchildren, or a children's ward in a hospital. The employees visit the children, take them on outings, and invite them to visit their place of work.

We Americans can offer a few good examples of alliances between the public and private sectors, as well. For example, in Flint, Michigan, some years ago, Mildred Smith developed a community program to improve school performance among low-income minority pupils. About a thousand children were involved. The program required no change in the regular school curriculum; its principal focus was on building links between home and school. This was accomplished in a variety of ways.

- A core group of low-income parents went from door to door, telling their neighbors that the school needed their help.

- Parents were asked to keep younger children out of the way so that the older children could complete their homework.

- Schoolchildren were given tags to wear at home that said, "May I read to you?"

- Students in the high school business program typed and duplicated teaching materials, thus freeing teachers to work directly with the children.

- Working parents visited school classrooms to talk about their jobs and about how their own schooling now helped them in their work.

WHAT SCHOOLS CAN DO

As the program in Flint demonstrates, the school is in the best position of all U.S. institutions to initiate and strengthen links that support children and adolescents. This is so for several reasons. First, one of the major—but often unrecognized—responsibilities of the school is to enable young people to move from the secluded and supportive environment of the home into responsible and productive citizenship. Yet, as the studies we conducted at Cornell revealed, most other modern nations are ahead of the United States in this area.

In these other nations, schools are not merely—or even primarily—places where the basics are taught. Both in purpose and in practice, they function instead as settings in which young people learn "citizenship": what it means to be a member of the society, how to behave toward others, what one's responsibilities are to the community and to the nation.

I do not mean to imply that such learnings do not occur in American schools. But when they occur, it is mostly by accident and not because of thoughtful planning and careful effort. What form might such an effort take? I will present here some ideas that are too new to have stood the test of time but that may be worth trying.

- *Creating an American classroom.* This is a simple idea. Teachers could encourage their students to learn about schools (and, especially, about individual classrooms) in such modern industrialized societies as France, Japan, Canada, West Germany, the Soviet Union, and Australia. The children could acquire such information in a variety of ways: from reading, from films, from firsthand reports of children and adults who have attended school abroad, from exchanging letters and materials with students and their teachers in other countries. Through such exposure, American students would become aware of how attending school in other countries is both similar to and different from attending school in the United States.

But the main learning experience would come from asking students to consider what kinds of things *should* be happening—or not happening—in American classrooms, given our nation's values and ideas. For example, how should children relate to one another and to their teachers, if they are doing things in an *American* way? If a student's idea seems to make sense, the American tradition of pragmatism makes the next step obvious: try the idea to see if it works.

- *Curriculum for caring.* This effort also has roots in our values as a nation. Its goal is to make caring an essential part of the school curriculum. However, students would not simply learn about caring; they would actually engage in it. Children would be asked to spend time with and to care for younger children, the elderly, the sick, and the lonely. Caring institutions, such as day-care centers, could be located adjacent to or even within the schools. But it would be important for young care-givers to learn about the environment in which their charges live and the other people with whom their charges interact each day. For example, older children who took responsibility for younger ones would become acquainted with the younger children's parents and living arrangements by escorting them home from school.

Just as many schools now train superb drum corps, they could also train "caring corps"—groups of young men and women who would be on call to handle a variety of emergencies. If a parent fell suddenly ill, these students could come into the home to care for the children, prepare meals, run errands, and serve as an effective source of support for their fellow human beings. Caring is surely an essential aspect of education in a free society; yet we have almost completely neglected it.

■ *Mentors for the young*. A mentor is someone with a skill that he or she wishes to teach to a younger person. To be a true mentor, the older person must be willing to take the time and to make the commitment that such teaching requires.

We don't make much use of mentors in U.S. society, and we don't give much recognition or encouragement to individuals who play this important role. As a result, many U.S. children have few significant and committed adults in their lives. Most often, their mentors are their own parents, perhaps a teacher or two, a coach, or—more rarely—a relative, a neighbor, or an older classmate. However, in a diverse society such as ours, with its strong tradition of volunteerism, potential mentors abound. The schools need to seek them out and match them with young people who will respond positively to their particular knowledge and skills.

The school is the institution best suited to take the initiative in this task, because the school is the only place in which all children gather every day. It is also the only institution that has the right (and the responsibility) to turn to the community for help in an activity that represents the noblest kind of education: the building of character in the young.

There is yet another reason why schools should take a leading role in rebuilding links among the four worlds of childhood: schools have the most to gain. In the recent reports bemoaning the state of American education, a recurring theme has been the anomie and chaos that pervade many U.S. schools, to the detriment of effective teaching and learning. Clearly, we are in danger of allowing our schools to become academies of alienation.

In taking the initiative to rebuild links among the four worlds of childhood, U.S. schools will be taking necessary action to combat the destructive forces of alienation—first, within their own walls, and thereafter, in the life experience and future development of new generations of Americans.

Bicultural Conflict

B. L. Sung

What if you are an adolescent who needs to establish an identity with a peer group, but acceptance in this group would mean stripping yourself of the belief and value system you have always used? Many teenagers face this dilemma. They are members of the increasing number of cultural minorities who have settled in the United States. In addition to the common trials of the adolescent years, these youth confront enormous "cultural conflict." And no one can construct a positive "ego identity" by negating the previous "self."

Adolescents who are members of cultural minorities are forced to find ways to adapt to an environment that demands their participation in two cultures—it is not an easy task. These adolescents are on the "margins" of two distinct cultures. Families and schools must be sensitive to the stress of this environmental condition.

The moment a child is born, he begins to absorb the culture of his primary group; these ways are so ingrained they become second nature to him. Imagine for a moment how wrenching it must be for an immigrant child who finds his cumulative life experiences completely invalidated and who must learn a whole new set of speech patterns and behaviors when he settles in a new country. The severity of this culture shock is underlined by Teper's (1977, p. 20) definition of culture:

> Culture is called a habit system in which "truths" that have been perpetuated by a group over centuries have permeated the unconscious. This basic belief system, from which "rational" conclusions springs, may be so deeply ingrained that it becomes indistinguishable from human perception—the way one sees, feels, believes, knows. It is the continuity of cultural assumptions and patterns that gives order to one's world, reduces an

infinite variety of options to a manageable stream of beliefs, gives a person a firm footing in time and space, and binds the lone individual to the communality of a group.

This researcher found that language barrier was the most common problem among immigrant Chinese. Language looms largest because it is the conduit through which people interact with other people. It is the means by which we think, learn, and express ourselves. Less obvious is the basis upon which we speak or act or think. If there are bicultural conflicts, these may engender problems and psychological difficulties which may not be immediately apparent but may nevertheless impact on the development of immigrant children.

This chapter highlights some of the cultural conflicts that commonly confront the Chinese child in the home and, particularly, in the schools. Often teachers and parents are not aware of these conflicts and ascribe other meanings or other motives to the child's behavior, frequently in a disapproving fashion. Such censure confuses the child and quite often forces him to

B. L. Sung. (1987). *Chinese Immigrant Children in New York City: The Experience of Adjustment* (Chapter 8, pp. 111-126). New York: Center for Migration Studies.

choose between what he is taught at home and what is commonly accepted by American society. In his desire to be accepted and to be liked, he may wish to throw off that which is second nature to him. This may cause anguish and pain not only to himself but also to his family. A few specific examples of bicultural conflict are presented below to show how everyday occurrences can result in dilemmas for Chinese immigrant children.

AGGRESSIVENESS

In Chinese culture, the soldier or the man who resorts to violence is at the bottom of the social ladder. The sage or gentleman uses his wits, not his fists, so the Chinese child is taught not to fight. The popular American perception is that the ability to fight is a sign of manhood. Thus, some American fathers will give their sons a few lessons in self-defense at the age of puberty. The Chinese parent teaches his son the exact opposite: Stay out of fights (Sollenger, 1968, p. 17). However, when the Chinese child goes to the school playground, he may become the victim of bullies who call him a "sissy." Some teenagers can be tough and cruel. Yet if the child chooses to fight and goes home with a black eye and bruises, his parents chastise him. What is he to do? The unresolved conflict about aggressive behavior is a major problem for Chinese American males. They feel that their masculinity has been affected by their childhood upbringing.

In some instances, teachers or monitors are derisive of the Chinese boys. "Why don't the Chinese fight back?" they exclaim. "Why do they stand there and take it?" This derision only shames the Chinese boys, who feel their courage is questioned. This bicultural conflict may be reflected in the self-hatred of some Asian American male activists who condemn the passivity of their forefathers in response to the discrimination and oppression they endured. Ignorant about their cultural heritage, these activists want to disassociate themselves from such "weakness," and they search for historical instances in which Asians put up a brave but costly and oftentimes futile fight to prove their manhood. The outbreak of gang violence may be another manifestation of the Chinese male's efforts to prove that he is "macho." He may be overcompensating for the derision that he has suffered.

SEXUALITY

In American public schools, sexuality is a very strong and pervasive force. Boys and girls begin noticing each other in the junior highs. At the high school level,

sexual awareness is very pronounced. School is as much a place for male-female association as it is an institution for learning. Not so for the Chinese. Education is highly valued, and it is serious business. Interest in the opposite sex is highly distracting and, according to some old-fashioned parents, is improper. Dating is an unfamiliar concept and sexual attractiveness is underplayed, not flaunted as it is according to American ways.

This difference in attitudes and customs poses a dilemma for Chinese boys and girls. In school, the white, black, or Hispanic girls talk about clothes, makeup, and dates. They talk about brassiere size and tampons. The popular girl is the sexy one who dates the most. She is the envy of the other girls.

For the Chinese girl, this openness is extremely embarrassing. Chinese girls used to bind their breasts, not show them off in tight sweaters. Their attitude toward the opposite sex is quite ambivalent. They feel they are missing something very exciting, yet they will shy away and feel uncomfortable if boys show an interest in them.

Most Chinese parents have had no dating experience. Their marriages were, by and large, arranged by their own parents or through matchmakers. Good girls simply did not go out alone with boys, so the parents are suspicious and apprehensive about their daughters dating, and they watch them very carefully. Most Chinese girls are not permitted to date. For the daring girl who tries to go out against her parents' wishes, there will be a price to pay. It is no easier for Chinese boys. The pressure to succeed in school is even greater than for girls, and parental opposition to dating is even more intense. Yet these children are bombarded by television, advertisements, stories, magazines, and real-life examples of boy-girl attraction. The teenager undergoes puberty and experiences the instinctive urges surging within him or her. In this society they are titillated, whereas in China they are kept under wraps until they are married.

The problem is exacerbated when teachers make fun of Chinese customs and parents. In one instance at one of the Chinatown schools, a young Chinese girl had been forbidden by her parents to walk to school with a young Puerto Rican boy. To make sure that the parents were being obeyed, the grandmother would walk behind the girl as she went to school. Grandma even stayed until her granddaughter went into class, and then she would peer through the window to make sure all was proper before she went home. Naturally, this was embarrassing for the girl, and it must have been noticed by the homeroom teacher. He exploded in anger at the little old lady and made some rather uncomplimentary remarks about this being the United States and Chinese customs should have been left behind in China. This teacher's attitude and remarks could only push the daughter farther from her parents. He should have explained to the girl, or even to the entire class, the cultural values and traditions of her parents, so that the girl could understand how they thought and why they behaved in such a fashion. Putting down the parents and their customs is the worst thing he could have done.

SPORTS

The Chinese attitude about sports is illustrated by an oft-told tale about two Englishmen who were considered somewhat mad. The two lived in Shanghai where they had gone to do business. In the afternoons, they would each take a racket, go out in the hot sun, and bat a fuzzy ball across the net. As they ran back and forth across the court, sweat would pour down their faces, and they would be exhausted at the end of the game. To the Chinese onlookers standing on the side, this was sheer lunacy. They would shake their heads in disbelief and ask: "Why do these crazy Englishmen work so hard? They can afford to hire coolies to run around and hit the ball for them." The Chinese attitude towards sports has changed considerably, but it still does not assume the importance that it enjoys in American life.

In the traditional Chinese way of thinking, development of the mental faculties is more important than development of the physique. The image of a scholar is one with a sallow face and long fingernails indicating that he spent long hours with his books and did not have to do physical labor. Games that require physical prowess such as football and boxing were not even played in China. Kung fu or other disciplines of the martial arts did not call for physical strength as much as concentration, skill, and agility. In the minds of many Chinese, sports are viewed as frivolous play and a waste of time and energy. Add to this the generally smaller physique of the Chinese immigrant student in comparison to his classmates, and we do not find many of them on school teams.

What does this mean to the Chinese immigrant student, especially the boys? On the one hand, they may think that the heavy emphasis upon sports is a displaced value. They may want to participate, but are either too small in stature or unable to devote the practice time necessary to make the school teams. If the "letter men" are the "big wheels," the Chinese student will feel that his kind are just the little guys. But most important of all, an entire dimension of American school life is lost to the Chinese immigrant children.

TATTLING

Should one report a wrongdoing? Should one tell the teacher that a schoolmate is cheating on an exam? Should one report to the school authorities that a fellow student is trying to extort money from him? The American values on this are ambiguous and confusing. For example, in the West Point scandal a few years ago, most of the cadets involved were not cheaters themselves, but they knew about the cheating and did not report it to the authorities. The honor code required that they tell, but the unwritten code among their fellow cadets said that they should not. If they had reported the cheating they would have been socially ostracized.

This bicultural conflict was noted by Denise Kandel and Gerald S. Lesser (1972) in their book *Youth in Two Worlds*, in which their reference groups were Danish and American children. Danish children, like the Chinese, feel duty bound to report a wrongdoing. There is no dichotomy of consequences here. Authorities and peers are consistent in their attitude in this respect, and this consistency helps to maintain social control. The teacher cannot be expected to see everything. Parents cannot be aware of everything their children are doing during the day. If the siblings or schoolmates will help by reporting wrongdoing, the task of teaching the child is shared and made easier for the adults. But when social ostracism stands in the way of enforcing ethnic values, an intense conflict ensues and contributes to the breakdown of social control.

DEMONSTRATION OF AFFECTION

A commonly voiced concern among Chinese children is "My parents do not love me. They never kiss or hug me. They are so cold, distant, and remote." The children long for human warmth and affection because they see it on the movie and television screens, and they read about it in books and magazines. Because their family experiences are so formal and distant, they come to the conclusion that love is lacking. In China, where such behavior is the norm, children do not question it. But in this country, where expressions of affection are outwardly effusive and commonly exhibited, they feel deprived.

This lack of demonstrative affection extends also to the spouse and friends. To the Chinese, physical intimacy and love are private matters never exhibited in public. Even in handshaking, the traditional Chinese way was to clasp one's own hands in greeting. Kissing and hugging a friend would be most inappropriate, and to kiss one's spouse in public would be considered shameless.

Nevertheless, Chinese children in this country are attracted to the physical expressions of love and affection. While they crave it for themselves, they are often unable to reciprocate or be demonstrative in their relations with their own friends and, later on, their own spouses and children because of their detached emotional upbringing.

In the schools, this contrast in cultures is made all the sharper because of the large numbers of Hispanics in the same schools. In general, Hispanics are very outgoing and are not the least bit inhibited about embracing, holding hands, or kissing even a casual acquaintance. The Chinese children may interpret these gestures of friendliness as overstepping the bounds of propriety, but more often than not they wish they could shed their reserve shells and reach out to others in a more informal manner. On the other hand, the aloofness of Chinese students is often wrongly interpreted as unfriendliness, standoffishness, or as a desire to keep apart. If all the students were made aware of these cultural differences, they would not misread the intentions and behaviors of one another.

EDUCATION

That education is a highly prized cultural value among the Chinese is commonly known, and that Chinese children generally do well scholastically may be due to the hard push parents exert in this direction. None of this means, however, that these children do not experience a bicultural conflict regarding education when they see that the bright student is not always the one who is respected in American schools. Labels such as "bookworm," "egghead," and "teacher's pet" are often applied to intelligent students. When parents urge their children to study hard and get good grades, the children know that the payoff may not be social acceptance by their schoolmates. The rewards are not consistent with values taught at home.

Nevertheless, Chinese immigrant high school students indicated in their survey questionnaire that they prized the opportunity to get an education. In fact, they identified the opportunity to get a free education as one of the most important reasons for their satisfaction with their schoolwork—of 143 students who said that they were satisfied with their schoolwork, 135 mentioned this one factor. Education in China, Hong Kong, or Taiwan is attained at great personal sacrifice on the part of the parents and by diligence and industry on the part of the student. In this country, school is free through high school; everyone must go to school

until 16 years of age in New York. It is not a matter of students trying to gain admittance by passing rigorous entrance exams, but a matter of authorities trying to keep dropout rates low that characterizes the educational system here. Since education is free and easy to obtain, it is often taken lightly.

New York academic standards are lower than those in Hong Kong or Taiwan, and the schoolwork is easier. As a result, there is less distinction attached to staying in school or graduating. What the Chinese immigrant students prize highly has less value in the larger society, and again newcomers to this country have doubts about the goals for which they are striving.

THRIFT

Approximately eighteen banks are found within the core of New York's Chinatown. When the Manhattan Savings Bank opened a new branch in October 1977, it attracted to its coffers $3 million within a few months' time. Most of the large banks are aware that Chinatown is fertile ground for the accumulation of capital because the Chinese tend to save more of what they earn than most other ethnic groups in America in spite of the fact that their earnings are small. The savings grow because of two major factors. One is the sense of insecurity common to immigrants, who need a cushion for the uncertainties that they acutely feel. The other is the esteem with which thrift is regarded by the Chinese. A person who is frugal is thought of more highly than one who sports material symbols of success.

The value placed upon thrift poses acute bicultural conflict for Chinese immigrant children who see all about them evidence of an economic system that encourages the accumulation and conspicuous consumption of material possessions. A very important segment of the consumer market is the teenage population. The urge to have stylish clothes, stereos, cameras, hi-fi radios, sports equipment, and even cars creates a painful conflict in the child who is enticed by television and other advertising media, but whose parents reserve a large percentage of their meager earnings for saving in the banks.

In school, the girl who gets money to spend on fashionable dresses and the latest rock records often feels more poised and confident than do her less materially fortunate classmates. She is also admired, complimented, and envied. In the Chinese community, on the other hand, a Chinese girl who spends a lot of money on clothes and frivolities would soon be the object of grapevine gossip, stigmatized as a less-than-desirable prospective wife or daughter-in-law, whereas praises would be sung for the more modestly dressed girl who saved her money.

Chinese students sometimes complain about their parents being "money-hungry." They give their children very little spending money. They do not buy fashionable clothing; rather, they buy only serviceable garments in which the children are ashamed to be seen. The Chinese home is generally not furnished for comfort or esthetics, so when Chinese children visit the homes of their non-Chinese friends and compare them with their own living quarters, they feel deprived and ashamed of their family. They certainly do not want to bring their friends home, and teenagers may themselves stay away from home as much as possible, feeling more comfortable with their peers in clubhouses or on the streets. The contrast in spending attitudes between the underdeveloped economy from which many Chinese immigrants have come and the American economy, which emphasizes mass and even wasteful consumption, is very sharp, and it creates many an unresolved conflict in the immigrant children, who do not realize that cultural differences lie behind it. They may think that their parents value money more than they care for their children, and exhibit this by denying them material possessions that give them pleasure and status in the eyes of their peers.

Credit is another concept foreign to immigrants from the Far East. If one does not have the money, one should not be tempted to buy. Credit is borrowing money, and borrowing should be resorted to only in extreme emergencies. The "buy now, pay later" idea goes against the Chinese grain. So Chinese families postpone buying until they have saved enough to cover the entire purchase price. This attitude is fairly common even when it comes to the purchase of a home. The Chinese family will scrimp and economize, putting aside a large portion of its income for this goal, denying small pleasures for many, many years until the large sum is accumulated. To the Chinese way of thinking, this singleness of purpose shows character, but to the more hedonistic American mind, this habit of thrift may appear asinine or unnecessary.

DEPENDENCY

In her study "Socialization Patterns among the Chinese in Hawaii," Nancy F. Young (1972) noted the prolonged period of dependency of the children commonly found in the child-rearing practices of the Chinese in Hawaii. She wrote,

> Observations of Chinese families in Hawaii indicate that both immigrant and local parents utilize child-rearing

techniques that result in parent-oriented, as opposed to peer-oriented behavior. . . . Chinese parents maximize their control over their children by limiting their experiences with models exhibiting nonsanctioned behavior.

Analyzing and comparing the results of the Chance Independence Training Questionnaire that she administered to six ethnic groups and local (American-born Chinese) as well as immigrant Chinese, Young found the mean age of independence training for American-born Chinese to be the lowest while that for immigrant Chinese [was] the highest (see Table 1).

Immigrant mothers exercise constant and strict supervision over their children. They take their children wherever they go, and babysitters are unheard of. They prefer their children to stay home rather than go out to play with friends. Friends are carefully screened by the mother, and the child is not expected to do things for himself until two years beyond the mean age that a Jewish mother would expect her child to do for himself. On the other hand, American-born Chinese parents expect their children to cut the apron strings sooner than any of the other ethnic groups surveyed.

However, there are areas of dependence and independence in which Young found divergence. The immigrant Chinese child is expected to be able to take care of himself at an earlier age, but he is discouraged from socializing with people outside of the family until a much later age.

The extremes exhibited between the American-born and immigrant Chinese may be indicative of bicultural conflict that the Chinese in this country feel. As children, they may have felt that their parents were overprotective; this was frequently mentioned by the teachers in this study. Evidence of this was observed in elementary schools in the practice of mothers coming to the school from the garment factories during their own lunch hours to feed their children. Many walked their children to and from school, even at the junior high level, but it was not clear whether the parents

Table 1. MEAN AGE OF INDEPENDENCE TRAINING FOR SELECTED ETHNIC GROUPS

Ethnic Stock	Mean Age of Independence Training
Local Chinese (American-born)	6.78
Jew	6.83
Protestant	6.87
Negro	7.23
Greek	7.67
French-Canadian	7.99
Italian	8.03
Immigrant Chinese	8.85

Source: N. F. Young, 1972.

were justifiably afraid for their children's safety from the gangs or whether they were being overprotective. Teachers thought the mothers were smothering the children and restricting their freedom of action. By adolescence, the children must have felt the same. They were chafing against parental control over what they presumed to be their own business, while the parents thought they were merely doing their parental duty. Teachers and parents do not agree on this score; thus parental authority is often undermined by a teacher's scoffing attitude.

RESPECT FOR AUTHORITY

The Chinese value of respect for one's elders and for authority is common knowledge and needs no further elaboration here. Already mentioned is that Chinese immigrant children encountering the disrespect accorded teachers and school authorities for the first time in American classrooms become upset and dismayed. In interviews with students, this concern was voiced frequently.

Challenge against established authority has been a notable feature of youth culture over the past two decades. Parents, teachers, the police, the government, the church—all authority figures in the past—have been belittled and even reviled. Violence against teachers is a leading problem in schools across the nation. If students do not have respect for the teacher, neither will they have respect for the knowledge that the teacher tries to impart. The issue is a disturbing one, not only for the immigrant children but for the entire American society as well.

HEROES AND HEROINES

Who are the people that are praised, admired, looked up to, and revered? This varies with cultures, and the values of a society may be deduced from the type of people who are respected and emulated in that culture. In the United States, the most popular figures are movie, television and stage stars, sports figures, politicians, successful authors, inventors, and scientists, probably in that order. Who are the heroes and heroines of China? Using literature as a guide, they are the filial sons or daughters, the sacrificing mother, the loyal minister, the patriot or war hero who saves his country, and revolutionaries who overthrow despotic rulers and set up their own dynasties. Even in modern-day China, the persons honored and emulated are the self-sacrificing workers who put nation above self.

Priests, ministers, and rabbis once commanded prestige in this country, but the status of these men of God has declined. In China, monks or priests have always occupied lowly positions. In contrast to the United States, in China actors were "riff-raff." Women did not act in the theater, so men had to play the female roles. Western influence has brought about changes in the pseudo-Chinese cultures of Hong Kong and Singapore where stage performers and movie stars are now popular and emulated.

As a rule, Chinese heroes and heroines were people of high moral virtues, and they set the standards of conduct for others. In this country, the more sensational the exposé of the private lives of our national leaders or entertainment figures, the more our curiosity is aroused. How movie stars retain their popularity despite the relentless campaigns to expose them is very difficult for someone not brought up in the United States to comprehend. An old adage says, "No man is a hero to his valet." Yet, the very fact that American heroes and heroines survive and thrive on notoriety and self-confession can only mean that the American people secretly admire such behavior. One might say Chinese heroes are saints; American heroes are sinners.

INDIVIDUALISM

Dr. Francis L. K. Hsu, noted anthropologist, has written extensively about individualism as a prominent characteristic of American life. According to D. Hsu (1960, 1972) the basic ingredient of rugged individualism is self-reliance. The individual constantly tells himself and others that he controls his own destiny and that he does not need help from others. The individual-centered person enjoins himself to find means of fulfilling his own desires and ambitions.

Individualism is the driving force behind the competitiveness and creativity that have pushed this nation forward. Loose family ties, superficial human relationships, little community control, and weak traditions have given the individual leeway to strike out on his own without being hindered by sentimentality, convention, and tradition. Self-interest has been a powerful incentive.

In contrast, Dr. Hsu contends, the Chinese are situation-centered. Their way of life encourages the individual to find a satisfactory adjustment with the external environment of men and things. The Chinese individual sees the world in relativistic terms. He is dependent upon others and others are dependent upon him. Like bricks in a wall, one lends support to the other and they all hold up the society as a whole. If even one brick becomes loose, the wall is considerably weakened; interlocked, the wall is strong. The wall is the network of human relations. The individual subordinates his own wishes and ambitions for the common good.

Dr. Kenneth Abbott, in his book *Harmony and Individualism*, also points out that Western ideas of creativity and individualism are not accented in Chinese and must be held within accepted norms. One of the reasons for this is the importance ascribed to maintenance of harmony. Harmony is the key concept in all relationships between god(s) and man and between man and man. It is the highest good.

To the Chinese, the sense of duty and obligation takes precedence over self-gratification (it is not uncommon to find Chinese teenagers handing over their entire paychecks to their parents for family use or for young Chinese males to pursue a course of study chosen for them by their parents rather than one of their own choosing). Responsibility toward distant kin is more keenly felt by the Chinese than by Americans. Honor and glory accrue not only to the individual but to all those who helped him climb the ladder. This sense of being part of something greater than oneself gives the Chinese a feeling of belonging and security in the knowledge that they do not stand alone. On the other hand, individual freedom of action is very much restricted.

The foregoing are but examples of the many areas of bicultural conflicts that confront a newcomer to these shores. In sum, they are:

- Chinese children are brought up to refrain from aggressive behavior, whereas the masculine image in this country often stresses the macho type. Chinese males are particularly troubled by this bicultural conflict.

- Sexual attractiveness is expressed subtly according to Chinese custom, whereas it is stressed according to American customs. This is an area of special concern for the high school-age Chinese American female.

- Sports are a consuming pastime for the American people, whereas it takes a back seat to scholastic achievement for the Chinese.

- Chinese children feel that they are duty-bound to report wrongdoing; yet tattling is a serious offense in the eyes of their American peers.

- Chinese children in this country are attracted by the physical expressions of love and affection customary here, but they are inhibited by their less demonstrative upbringing. At the same time, they may question their parents' love in light of the more overt affection they observe among their peers' parents.

- Education and scholastic achievement are not as highly valued in the United States as they are in China.

- Thrift is a worthy character trait according to the Chinese way of thinking, whereas conspicuous consumption is favored in the United States. The two ways of thinking are incompatible and cause conflict for Chinese children.

- Immigrant Chinese parents do not encourage early independence in their children. They discourage their children from socializing outside the family until a much later age than do other ethnic groups.

- Immigrant Chinese children find it hard to accept the lack of respect for authority—especially toward teachers—among their peers in school.

- Chinese heroes and heroines tend to be persons of high moral caliber. American idols tend to be entertainment figures, sports stars, or persons who have achieved tangible success in terms of wealth and material attainment. The more sensational the private lives of these people, the more they attract public attention.

- The Chinese try to fit themselves into the scheme of things whereas the American way is based on individualism.

- Such better-known examples of cultural conflict as respect for elders, modesty and humility, male superiority, and others have been omitted here because they have been dealt with at length elsewhere.

MARGINALITY

There are two divergent trains of thought regarding cultural conflict. Robert E. Park first coined the term "marginal man" for this predicament. Park, in the *International Encyclopedia of the Social Sciences* (1968, vol. 4, p. 427) stressed that "marginal men are—precisely because of their ambiguous position from a cultural, ethnic, linguistic, or sociostructural standpoint—strongly motivated to make creative adjustments in situations of change, and in the course of this adjustment process, to develop innovations in social behavior." However, the evidence is not clear. Marginal individuals are more prone to succumb to anomie and thus become carriers of social disorganization rather than creative change. Everett Stonequist, in his work

The Marginal Man (1937, pp. 3–4, 8), brings out the latter viewpoint. He wrote,

> The marginal personality is most clearly portrayed in those individuals who are unwittingly initiated into two or more historic traditions, languages, political, loyalties, moral codes, or religions. This occurs, for instance, as a result of migration. . . .
>
> When the standards of two or more social groups come into active contrast or conflict, the individual who is identified with both groups experiences the conflict as an acute personal difficulty or mental tension. . . .
>
> So the marginal man. . .is one who is poised in psychological uncertainty between two (or more) social worlds; reflecting in his soul the discords and harmonies, repulsions and attractions of these worlds, one of which is often "dominant" over the other; within which membership is implicitly if not explicitly based upon birth or ancestry (race or nationality); and where exclusion removes the individual from a system of group relations.

Adults tend to perceive their marginality as a sense of wanting to be accepted members of a group or groups and conversely a sense of exclusion from such groups. Children, on the other hand, perceive their marginality as a dilemma. They are faced with a situation where courses of action are diametrically opposed or radically different. They do not see the dilemma as rising from cultural differences; they just see it as an impasse. The choices are painful and more often than not immobilizing. Not having the maturity to evaluate or modify their courses of action or to adjust their values, they do nothing; the [vacuum] of their indecision or their inability to decide is extremely uncomfortable.

For Chinese immigrant children who live in New York's Chinatown or in the satellite Chinatowns, these conflicts are moderated to a large degree because there are other Chinese children around to mitigate the dilemmas that they encounter. When they are among their own, the Chinese ways are better known and better accepted. The Chinese customs and traditions are not denigrated to the degree that they would be if the immigrant child were the only one to face conflict on his or her own. Even so, teachers and parents should be made aware of these conflicts to avoid exacerbating the differences and to inculcate in both the Chinese and non-Chinese a healthy respect for cultural differences.

Robert Park's sanguine outlook, however, leads us to expect that discomfort, generated by the conditions of the marginal state, may lead to new forms of adaptive behavior more in tune with the changed environment in a new homeland. To him, marginality is the soil from which creative change sprouts.

Looking for Linda:
Identity in Black and White

B. E. Williams

*Developing a sense of self, a self-identity, and knowing who
one is—these are the important tasks of adolescence. Sense
of self is inextricably tied to cultural and ethnic heritage,
interactions with parents, other appropriate adults, and
peers. When Linda, the young woman profiled in the following article, began to seek her self-identity, she was missing the substantive ingredient of her ethnic heritage. She
could not cement together the pieces of a stable and positive
sense of self because she lacked significant relationships
with people of her ethnic group.*

*We live in an increasingly pluralistic society, yet social
institutions such as schools, human service agencies, and
social policies continue to deny the significance of ethnicity.
Every child must consistently have access to information,
relationships, and opportunities that enable him or her to
form a holistic self—one that represents and values all dimensions of the individual.*

This century has seen many advances in the institutional care of children. Warehousing has given way to
humane and frequently sophisticated approaches.
Most state welfare systems speak freely of "indi-
vidualized care," "appropriate placement," "levels of
care," and many other such phrases. However, Washington (1982) asserts that, by and large, social workers
have shown too little interest in ethnicity as an essential influence on practice and criticizes schools of social
work for producing graduates who devise intervention for the ethnic poor without grasping the significance of ethnicity and without adjusting for it. A
melting-pot view of social practice can produce the
erroneous assumption that techniques are automati-
cally translatable from one ethnic or minority group to
another, without adequate understanding of modifications that may be necessary to meet special needs.

Although social work has always given lip service
to cultural pluralism, the latent goals of social work

intervention have often been to assimilate minority
groups to a single middle-class standard (Hunt and
Walker, 1978). Social work has, with some justification,
been criticized as an instrument of conservative policies (Longres, 1982). Those providing the services are
beholden to the majority because these services derive
legitimacy and funding from them. The services exist
only to the extent that the more affluent and powerful
are willing to mandate and support them through
taxes and philanthropic contributions. Furthermore,
social workers have traditionally come from the ranks
of the majority or upwardly mobile.

Although many forms of exclusion and discrimination exist in this country, none is so pervasive, so
deeply rooted, persistent, and intractable as that
based on color (Hopps, 1982). To deny that it is the
basis for much of today's oppression only evades the
problem.

Much of the time, professional social work has
self-consciously tried to be color blind in dealing with
children of minority groups. This may ease the con-
science, but the unconscious biases and the mores of

B. E. Williams. (1987, May–June). Looking for Linda: Identity in black and white. *Child Welfare*, 66 (3), 207–216.

the system make themselves felt. Stehno (1982) points out that the differences in the placement and treatment of minority youths and white youths by social service systems are still clearly visible, with black children underrepresented in the more sophisticated treatment facilities, such as group homes and residential treatment centers. Even when these children do make it to these settings, any lack of cultural awareness and understanding may well work to their detriment. Turning a blind eye to color and pretending that it does not exist denies core identity in any person. Simply "changing" the orientation of a child, though it may be satisfying to the worker and apparently successful, cannot be anything but harmful in the end.

Germain (1978, 1979) clearly explicates the importance of the person's ethnic identity system and credits it with imparting knowledge, values, and attitudes through cultural processes. These in turn mediate the individual's interaction with the various environmental systems, influencing the level of coping, and further interactions. As has been stressed in the literature, the explicit aim of social work intervention is to help the client maximize social functioning (Washington, 1982). This necessitates learning a great deal about a client's cultural identity and supporting its values. To ignore this is to produce conflicts that may not be readily apparent in the overt adjustment of the child, but may result in scarring at a more profound level. The following case exemplifies this principle.

THE DREAM

Linda was upset. The houseparent told the social worker at the Home that Linda seemed distracted, out of sorts and "not her usual cheerful, well-organized self" that morning. Before school she requested an interview later in the day with the social worker because she had something "very important" to discuss, so it was no surprise when Linda appeared mid-afternoon in the clinical director's office, having left school early. But the purpose of Linda's session was a surprise. She wanted to talk about a dream she had had the previous night—a very disturbing dream, like none she had had before, or at least none that she remembered. In fact, she had taken time to write the dream down during a lull at school, so that she would not forget any part of it (although at this time she felt it was unforgettably seared in her brain). This was the dream:

It all started the summer before (according to Linda's dream). She met a nice boy at the beach. The other kids at the Home, the houseparents, the director, really liked her new boyfriend. The couple went everywhere together and she felt the "world smiling" on them as they fell in love. Although she knew that she was going to miss the Home, with the staff's blessing she decided to marry him in the fall. It was a happy marriage, with Linda learning to cook, keep house, and do "wifely" things. Everything was wonderful except she knew that her family would not approve of him, so she put off telling them of the marriage. Then she discovered she was pregnant. From the beginning she had mixed feelings about the pregnancy and found herself sad and happy at the same time. The husband seemed completely happy, but she just couldn't seem to reconcile herself to the approaching birth. The crux of the dream came when she was about six months pregnant and showing quite a bit. It was early in the morning and her young husband had gone to work. She went into the bathroom to wash up and began thinking about how she was going to be forced to tell her parents. A feeling of overwhelming depression swamped her and she began to cry bitter tears. She raised her eyes to the mirror to look at her swollen body and tear-streaked face. As she confronted her image in the mirror, she suddenly realized why she was so reluctant to tell her folks and what was so sad about the pregnancy. In the mirror her skin was white—she was white and the boy she had married in her dream was black. The child she carried would not belong to either race (as she perceived it) and would have no home. She cried for her "bastard baby" (her words) and for herself with her white face. She knew then that she was "white" and that there was no home for her, either. In fact, at that point she even repudiated the love her black husband professed for her.

Linda woke up sobbing, depressed, and alarmed. The dream was so vivid she examined her flat stomach and tried to figure out who and where her husband was. Dragging herself out of bed, she went to the bathroom mirror (the same one in her dream) to examine herself. With disbelief and still groggy from sleep, she stared at the black face reflected.

BACKGROUND CASE MATERIAL

Linda was a 17-year-old black girl who had been a resident of the Home for almost two years at the time of the dream. In school she was a senior, approaching graduation and facing termination of current living arrangements. The residents were welcome to stay in placement during the summer following high school graduation, working and saving money for a start in the "adult" world. They had to make plans to leave by mid-August. Linda was a ward of the court and the state juvenile justice system, which had agreed to continue monetary support for placement until that time. She had been in the care of various agencies since childhood, but with the advent of her 17th birthday, she was essentially free to go where she wanted.

There had been no contact with the family, in spite of repeated attempts on the director's part to encourage their participation. Linda reported that distance was the reason they would not come. As near as could be ascertained by the staff, they had written two letters during her stay. She was encouraged to call them at Christmas and again when she was approaching graduation. There was no response. The question arose as to how welcome she would be should she return to her hometown to work. She made the decision to remain in the vicinity.

Linda first came to the attention of the authorities on a dependent and neglect charge against the parents. The family lived in a border town where Mexican-Americans constituted the majority of the citizens. Black families were few and far between and black foster families practically nonexistent. So, although things were never really satisfactory, she was left in her own home for some years with a white caseworker keeping close tabs on the situation. Linda became very fond of her child welfare worker, who seemed to be the only bright spot in her existence. The worker dearly loved Linda and constantly took her on outings. The contrast with her neglectful and abusing mother was stark.

At school Linda did well with her white teachers. Because she was very bright and verbal, as well as frequently being the only black child in the classroom, she attracted the attention of well-meaning teachers who gave her a lot of time and attention. Many hours after school and on weekends were spent in various activities to which school personnel invited her. All of her role models were white, and it was obvious that she was not participating in what little black community there was. And no one wanted her to. She had become everyone's pet project and they were accepting her as "one of us" and not perceiving her as a member of the black community. It was almost as though her daily brief periods at home were interludes in her real life in the white world.

When she grew to adolescence and went out of the neighborhood school into a central high school, she knew well how to navigate the white world. Although the opportunity for a choice of black friends broadened considerably, Linda chose not to associate with them, making friends among the "liberal" white teenagers. Her caseworker resigned, and another took her place. The new worker had heard such good things about Linda—what a rewarding case she was and what progress she was making under child welfare auspices—that she was immediately favorable. Linda

never felt as close to her as to the initial one, but apparently made the transition smoothly.

At 15 Linda made her first "mistake." In solidly with the middle-class white teenagers who were trying their wings and their parents' patience, she began to experiment with drugs. Although she really didn't like drugs, she bought, sold, and used with the best of them. And they were caught. The other children were given probation and placed in the custody of their parents. Linda was sent to the detention center by shocked child welfare workers who had "done their best." Once at the receiving center, however, the workers could not forget what an exemplary child she had been and pleaded for treatment rather than a detention facility. The decision was "a child in need of supervision," rather than a psychiatric or juvenile delinquency case. Removing her from the home community seemed to offer the best solution, and she was sent across the state to a residential facility that had an excellent track record in the care of adolescents.

Linda was only the second black girl in the history of the Home. Welcomed with open arms by the staff, she immediately became a favorite. Likable, intelligent, friendly, and apparently happy to be there, her winning ways made the other girls appear surly. The staff was concerned that she might not be happy at the neighborhood high school, which had been integrated by means of crosstown busing. Fear of "contamination" by the discontented black students in the population prompted the decision to take her downtown every day to the central high school. A good socioeconomic mix, this was the only "naturally" integrated school in town. She was encouraged (as were all the children) to make friends and bring them home for supper or other activities at the Home. She did make friends—all white—and also soon had several white teachers whom she really liked. The staff was happy; Linda seemed to have settled in.

It should be noted that the staff of the facility was without exception white. A training site for the local state university graduate school of social work, even the social work interns were white. The board members, the physicians who furnished medical care, and the benefactors of the nonprofit institution were white, as was the surrounding neighborhood. How well Linda fit and what a credit she was to the Home always pleased the staff. Not so the two black boys in one of the boys' cottages. By comparison, they were always into some devilment and maintained close ties with their "irresponsible families." It seemed as if every time they went home for a visit, they came back obstreperous. Linda, however, always spent her holidays with a staff member and conducted herself with both liveliness and good manners.

DISCUSSION

Black psychiatrists Grier and Cobbs (1968) have denied the existence of positive self-esteem among blacks, while Foster and Perry (1982) point out that the prevailing view of blacks has been that they suffer from negative self-esteem manifested in feelings of self-hate and a lack of self-actualizing behavior. Oppressive social and economic conditions, racism and discrimination, in combination with an attempt to identify with the values of the dominant white society, have contributed in a large measure to this negative self-image. Undeniably, color is a tag that is difficult to dispense with. Blacks become members of a highly visible victim group, thus lacking an inconspicuous avenue of escape from their disempowered status (Maguire, 1980). Pinderhughes (1976) emphasizes that the most severely victimized adopt values of autonomy and isolation as a defense against the stresses that overwhelm them. Their autonomy is not based on growth and self-actualization, however, but on a feeling that they have been abandoned, are now alone, and cannot expect help from anyone. One of the best-known defenses against powerlessness is that of identifying with the aggressor (Pinderhughes, 1979).

It does not take a complicated analysis of Linda's dream to recognize a psyche under stress. Stehno (1982) writes that the minority child's sense of well-being is developed in interaction with the inner, nurturing environment before he or she is directly confronted with the hostile wider society. This forms patterns of close involvement, including frequent interactions among and exchange of help with kin (McAdoo, 1982). Social workers must realize that individuals do not learn their coping behaviors or their mores, social drives, or values from the larger society. Children learn a particular culture and a particular moral system only from those people with whom they have close contact and who exhibit that culture in frequent relationships with them (Washington, 1982). Perceptual experiences, shared symbols, oral traditions, feelings, and sentiments that make up ethnicity are learned and constitute the individual's nurturing environment (Davis, 1948).

What is the result when that nurturing environment is not that of the child's own family, or not even within the appropriate ethnic group? Linda, though remaining in her own home until age 15, was separated psychologically from her cultural heritage much earlier. A review of her childhood reveals only essentially negative relationships with her family and essentially nonexistent relationships with a broader black community. Every helping or positive relationship was established with the white community. At no time in her 17 years did Linda become involved with a warm, caring, or powerful black role model. All power and all goodness appeared to be vested in the majority-controlled systems with which she interacted—child welfare, schools, juvenile justice, the Home.

Linda's family and ethnic group became merely shadow persons, existing in the background of the satisfying world that stroked her. Her lack of interest in and contact with them during her placement contrasted strikingly with the attachment and identification the other children, both black and white, had with their origins. And this was encouraged by those helping her. She was a satisfying case, quickly picking up the required behavior, excelling in the prescribed ways, warmly attached to her caseworkers and teachers, appreciative of and seemingly satisfied with the living arrangements at the Home. The houseparents particularly enjoyed having her because they did not have to compete with her family, who stayed out of their way, literally and psychologically. Each step away from a cultural identity earned her points. However, the color of her skin remained the same. Clark's assertion (1965) never was more true than in Linda's case: "It is still the white man's society that governs the Negro's image of himself."

Linda's dream brought to consciousness her dilemma. She was a creature of both worlds and citizen of neither. The "bastard child" within her was tragically not welcome in her family and her dual black-white identity would not serve her well in the wider world to which she was going. Her poignant cry to the caseworker, "Don't you understand? I looked in the mirror and *I was white!*" chilled her listener.

CONCLUSIONS

The issues raised by this case are not unique to Linda. Although she graphically illustrates the extreme, thousands of minority children who enter the child care system each year are subjected to variations on the theme. During the past twenty years, many minority planners and social workers have devoted attention to strategies for improving services to minority youth. One of the suggested plans involves the formation of minority-controlled agencies to serve minority children. Although theories of minority specialists in child development tend to support this thrust, there has been insufficient research to support the argument that this type of agency is any more effective than, say, special outposts of larger white agencies (Stehno, 1982). Due to the scarcity of such institutions, it is doubtful that we have the luxury of waiting until the experimental data can be assimilated. Steps must be taken now to ensure that those children we serve do not become our victims.

Billingsley and Giovannoni (1972) suggested three strategies for improving services to minority children: (1) help agencies that provide services mainly to white children to improve their work with minority children, through a better understanding of cultural factors; (2) maintain the provision of services in both the private and public sectors; and (3) go with the idea of developing new, minority-controlled services when feasible.

Although biculturality—the holding of values from and the ability to function in two worlds—is an adaptive mechanism, the strengthening of the majority assimilation to the detriment of personal identity does the child little service. Treatment should be directed not only to strengthening the family structure, but to reinforcing the group, community, and extrafamilial social systems in order to give the child more effective support (Pinderhughes, 1982). Over and over we must emphasize the importance of the ethnic group in working with these children. To cut them off from their cultural community is to deny them not only their heritage, but their present identity. Black consciousness and positive self-valuation may be bolstered by both formal institutions and organizations such as the family, church, and fraternal groups, and by informal associations, including friendships and social relationships (Walsh, 1975). A better understanding of positive self-valuation among blacks and the factors contributing to these attitudes might help practitioners in fields like education, mental health, and social welfare as they design and implement programs (Foster and Perry, 1982). For instance, practitioners aware of the strengths that could be drawn from a black family would build on this as a major support system and draw on it as a resource to be integrated into the planning and structuring of social welfare programs. More attention might be focused on a systematic assessment of the role of the family and other community support systems in fostering blacks' valuation of themselves. Attacking the problem of internalized self-defeating values and behavioral tendencies requires skill in the role of counselor, because it involves dealing with personality formation and such phenomena as spoiled identities, traits of victimization, and fatalism (Longres, 1982). Therapists who work with the black client must be well differentiated and understand the concept of countertransference. It is necessary that they understand the true nature of their participation in the victim system, and if white, acknowledge themselves as benefactors of the system that oppresses their clients.

Color, ethnicity, and culture cannot be blithely ignored in planning for these children. It will not go away and no matter how insulated the cocoon in which we protectively wrap them, in the end the butterfly emerges the predestined hue. This was agonizingly clear to Linda as she stood on the threshold of adulthood. She had the coloration of the adult butterfly, but she did not know how to fly. In terms of the future survival for people of color in an unfriendly environment, this is an issue that must weigh heavily on those who are concerned about it (Hopps, 1982).

Linda left the Home after high school graduation, three months post dream. Although the clinical director had a new awareness of the issues, little was possible in the remaining time. Contacts were established with middle-class blacks in the community to try to provide support for her after her discharge, but Linda felt uncomfortable with them. Until the last she clung to the safety of the Home and then, cut adrift, she disappeared. An unconfirmed rumor had her attending the state university and living with a white boy. The juvenile justice system closed the case, the child welfare agency declared her grown, and the Home placed her records in the "successful" file.

How long?

APPENDIX: READING AND WRITING ABOUT CHILD DEVELOPMENT

READING FOR MEANING

Reading is a daily activity. You probably read a wide variety of material—newspapers, menus, novels; and you read for a range of reasons—information, entertainment, understanding new ideas. There are different levels of reading comprehension, which are based upon your abilities and the purpose of the reading exercise. The instruction booklet for a new camera is read for literal meaning. You want to know how to work the camera. You read the words as they are written without trying to interpret underlying meaning or thinking about why the author expends so much effort explaining lighting factors and so little time discussing types of film. The purpose of reading an instruction booklet is information.

However when reading articles on developmental issues, you are concerned with more than the simple translation of the words on the page. Why has the author written this article? Who is the intended audience? How did the author accumulate this information and come to these conclusions? What is the author's interest? Bias? Theoretical perspective? How does this information fit with what you already know about development? And most importantly, how can you come to "own" this information? Can you use it to support your own ideas? Can you apply it to other areas of development?

As a student of human development, "owning the information" is the purpose of reading text. "Owning" is the process of being introduced to new ideas, thinking about them in relation to what you already know, and acting on them by applying them to new situations or existing ideas.

A simple analogy of the process of owning information is learning to ride a bike. Remember, if you can, someone (mom, dad, or an older sibling) explaining to you in words how to ride a bike. "Sit on the seat, put your hands on the handle bars, put your feet on the pedals, find your balance, and go!" As you listened, many questions and feelings may have raced through your mind. "If I put both feet on the pedals, I will fall down." "What happens if I can't stop?" "What do you mean by balance and how do I find it?" You were interpreting instructions through the lens of what you already knew about your abilities and bike riding. You were "reading between the lines" and inferring what might happen if you followed the directions as given. Finally you combined the literal instructions with your interpretation of that information, climbed on the bike, and applied your understanding of this new knowledge. It took time, but with adjustments in the application of your interpretation of how to ride a bike, you mastered the task. Now (and forever) you own the information and ability that enables you to ride a bike. The process of reading a child development article for specific content is similar to learning to ride a bike.

Strategies for Reading Child Development Articles

Because students know how to read (decode words), they often do it without thinking about it. After receiving a poor grade on an exam or paper, students often complain to professors: "I don't know how this happened. I read the chapter three times." Merely reading the words on the page is not sufficient for learning.

Strategy #1 Acquaint yourself with the article before you read it. Who is the author? Is he or she a practitioner, a researcher, or a professional writer? Skim the article and read the headings. What are the main concepts the author will describe? Study the charts or graphs if there are any. What kind of information do they give you? Read the last paragraph which often summarizes the main points of the article. (This is not a suspense novel so you don't have to worry about ruining the surprise ending.) Ask yourself how the author came to these conclusions. What else do you need to know before you accept them as true?

Strategy #2   Decide how you can relate your own experiences to the article you are reading. Michael Lewis's article, "Emotional Development in the Young Child," describes how emotions are observed and charted in very young children. Have you ever watched an infant's facial expression change from happy to apprehensive to upset? What does that look like? How do we know—can we know—whether the infant is experiencing a true emotion? What is your emotional profile? Can your friends and family "read" your emotions easily? Do the intensity and/or frequency of certain emotions change over time? What do you already know about the development of emotions?

Strategy #3   Begin reading the article and read between the lines. What is the author's view of development? Is he or she a behaviorist, maturationist, or interactionist? Michael Lewis discusses emotional expression as an important clinical tool when assessing cognitive development and temperament profiles. What are other implications? What information do you give another person when you express emotion? Michael Lewis also mentions individual differences as related to emotional development. He links differences to levels of cognitive development. Are there differences that result from cultural and ethnic origins? Are Hispanics more expressive emotionally and Asians more reserved? Can we observe differences in the youngest infants of each culture?

Strategy #4   Analyze and evaluate content as you read. Where and how did the author obtain the information? Can the ideas expressed and conclusions drawn be generalized for all populations? Do they match your experiences and what you already know about the topic? If not, where are the differences? What questions would you like to ask the author? Often an article will not give you adequate details about the research methods used to gather data. But you need to question the method and the validity of the findings nonetheless.

Strategy #5   Apply the new information you are reading to a situation you know well. For example, do you know or might you observe an infant who is beginning to express true joy through smiles and gurgles? How do toddler behaviors change once they learn to be ashamed or guilty about actions like smearing chocolate pudding on the table? What difficulties might a child face if she or he did not acquire certain emotions at certain times? Is the description of emotional development similar to other patterns of behavior such as cognitive or physical development?

Reading for content is more than decoding the words on the page. It requires additional effort and thought. If you practice reading critically with the determination to connect new content with your own experiences and knowledge base, you will reap the benefits of greater understanding and "ownership" of new ideas.

WRITING REACTIONS TO CHILD DEVELOPMENT ARTICLES

You may be asked to respond to reading assignments through a written assignment. You want to be able to demonstrate your "ownership" of the topic in question. As an early childhood educator, there is one sight that is immediately discouraging to me—walking into a classroom of young children and seeing twenty-five renditions of a Halloween pumpkin that look exactly alike. This tells me that each child has wasted his or her time taking someone else's idea and reproducing a mirror image. There is no inkling of the unique thoughts and abilities of the child reflected in the product. Making pumpkins has been a rote exercise, not a learning experience.

College professors experience a similar reaction when they receive a pile of student papers that all read alike. Professors know that only minimal learning occurs when a student parrots back information contained in an article or text. The teacher's purpose in requiring responsive writing assignments is to discover how each student interprets and applies the information given. Students must find a voice that enables them to demonstrate their "ownership" of new information.

Strategies for Writing Assignments

Strategy #1   What is the purpose of this paper? What is being asked of you? What kind of information does the audience (teacher) want? It is critical to think through the criteria of the task before you begin to write. What information is important to share in this paper? Be selective. Relating every new bit of information you learned from the article is usually *not* the best way of demonstrating your level of understanding. Once you have decided which key concepts will be included, organize these ideas in a logical, sequential manner.

Strategy #2   Select and organize key concepts, supporting/related ideas. Develop detailed examples to illustrate your points. Cluster your ideas in an outline or graphic format before writing. You want to convince the reader that you understand the content of this article on three levels: literal comprehension, interpretation, and application. Key concepts (such as the relationship between emotional and cognitive development) may be supported by other ideas found in the article or ideas and experiences you have had that relate to the topic. You might question the degree of influence between cognitive development vs. environmental factors such as parents' responses to demonstrations of intense emotion. Use concepts described in the article to extend your ideas ("I agree with this viewpoint and here are some examples that support that view") and to confront your own thinking on the issue ("I don't agree with what has been said and here are some examples that support my opinion"). One important goal of a reaction paper is to build a good case—identify key concepts, support them with related ideas, and use detailed examples to document your conclusions.

Strategy #3   Revise—Proofread—Revise—Proofread. The current literature on writing process is emphatic that writing is a multi-step process. Written assignments are not "one shot, pen stops, you're done" products. Written assignments take time. Revising and proofreading are critical to the final product.

Revise your paper by re-focusing on the purpose. Have you written what you intended to write? Have you met the required criteria? Have you demonstrated your ability to comprehend, interpret, and apply new information? Be critical. You can be your own best friend if you learn to scrutinize your own writing.

When you proofread your paper, get into the shoes of your intended audience. Read your paper as if your are reading it for the first time. Is all the necessary information clearly stated so that the reader can follow your ideas and understand the connections between them? It is, of course, difficult to jump out of your own perspective and examine your work from another point of view. Therefore, ask someone to proofread your paper for you. Let your proofreader know the purpose of your paper—what you are trying to get across. Also share any concerns you have about clarity and organization. Insist that your proofreader review your paper with an honest and critical eye. A proofreader who wants to please you rather than analyze your work will not be helpful to you.

Once your paper has been carefully proofread, consider the comments and suggestions offered. Revise your paper again, incorporating the necessary changes. And proofread again.

IN CONCLUSION

The articles in this book of readings have been selected to offer a diversity of ideas, and a variety of viewpoints. The articles represent a range of sources and intended audiences. The variation will stimulate you to raise questions and debate conflicting ideas. In many of the articles it will be easy for you to relate the information to your own experiences and point of view. However, there are some articles, such as "Looking for Linda," that may require you to stretch your own repertoire of experience or draw on analogous situations in order to incorporate new information into your own, personal realm of understanding.

Read the articles as an active, thinking participant. Insist on making the content meaningful to you by connecting your own personal experiences. Part of the excitement of studying child development is that we were all once children and most of us interact with young children during our lives. Use this knowledge base to validate and extend your learning.

REFERENCES AND NOTES

PART I INFLUENCES IN DEVELOPMENT

Ryan, "Giving Birth in America"

1. American College of Obstetrics and Gynecology (1988), Report of a 1987 survey of ACOG's membership. Washington, DC: ACOG.
2. Ibid.
3. Progress toward achieving the 1990 objectives for pregnancy and infant health (1988), *Morbidity and Mortality Weekly Report, 37,* 405.
4. Ibid.
5. B. Guyer, L. A. Wallach and S. L. Rosen (1982), Birth-weight-standardized neonatal mortality rates and the prevention of low birth weight: How does Massachusetts compare with Sweden? *New England Journal of Medicine, 306,* 1230.
6. E. Lieberman et al. (1987), Risk factors accounting for racial differences in the rate of premature birth, *New England Journal of Medicine, 317,* 743.
7. J. R. Bragonier, I. M. Cushner, and C. J. Hobel (1984), "Social and personal factors in the etiology of preterm birth," in F. Fuchs and P. Stubblefield (eds.), *Preterm Birth: Causes, Prevention and Management* (New York: Macmillan), p. 64.
8. U.S. General Accounting Office (1987), *Prenatal Care: Medicaid and Uninsured Women Receive Insufficient Care,* GAO/HRD-87-137 (Washington, DC: U.S. GAO).
9. Bragonier, Cushner, and Hobel (1984).
10. U.S. Department of Health and Human Services (DHHS), Public Health Service (1981), *Consensus Development Conference on Cesarean Childbirth* (Bethesda, MD: U.S. DHHS).
11. N. Gleicher (1984), Cesarean section rates in the United States: The short-term failure of the National Consensus Development Conference in 1980, *Journal of the American Medical Association, 252,* 3273.
12. K. O'Driscoll, M. Foley, and D. MacDonald (1984), Active management of labor as an alternative to cesarean section for dystocia, *Obstetrics and Gynecology, 63,* 485.
13. DHHS (1981).
14. K. O'Driscoll, M. Foley, and D. MacDonald (1984).
15. K. J. Leveno et al. (1986), A prospective comparison of selective and universal electronic fetal monitoring in 34,995 pregnancies, *New England Journal of Medicine, 315,* 615.
16. U.S. Congress, Office of Technology Assessment (OTA) (1988), *Infertility: Medical and Social Choices,* OTA-BA-358 (Washington, DC: U.S. Government Printing Office).
17. P. C. Steptoe and R. G. Edwards (1978), Birth after reimplantation of a human embryo, *Lancet, 2,* 366.
18. U.S. Congress, OTA (1988).
19. Instruction on respect for human life in its origin and on the dignity of procreation (1987, Mar. 11), *New York Times,* p. A14.
20. S. Elias and G. J. Annas (1988), *Noncoital Reproduction in Reproductive Genetics and the Law* (Chicago: Year Book Medical Publishers), p. 222. Ethics Committee of the American Fertility Society (1986), Ethical considerations of the new reproductive technologies, *Fertility and Sterility, 46* (3), Supplement. American College of Obstetricians and Gynecologists, Committee statement: Ethical issues in human in vitro fertilization and embryo placement (Washington, DC: ACOG.)

Cole, "Infants at Risk"

Als, H. (1982). Towards a synactive theory of development: Promise for the assessment of infant individuality. *Journal of Infant Mental Health, 3* (4), 229–243.

Als, H., and Duffy, F. (1983). *The Behavior of the Premature Infant: A Theoretical Framework for a Systematic Assessment.* New York: Elsevier Press.

Boland, M., Allen, T., Long, G., and Tasker, M. (1988, Nov.–Dec.). Children with HIV infection: Collaborative responsibilities of the child welfare and medical communities. *Social Work,* 504–509.

Brazelton, T. B. (1984). *The Neonatal Behavioral Assessment Scale.* 2nd ed. Philadelphia: Lippincott.

Brown, E., and Cole, J. (1989, Feb.). Narcotic withdrawal syndrome in neonates. *Ab Initio* (Boston, MA), *1* (1).

Chasnoff, I., Griffin, G., MacGregor, S., Derkes, K., and Burns, K. (1989). Temporal patterns of cocaine use in pregnancy. *Journal of the American Medical Association, 261* (12), 1741–1744.

Cole, J. (1985, Apr.). Infant stimulation reexamined. *Neonatal Network Journal,* 24–30.

Cole, J., Begish-Duddy, A., Judas, M., and Jorgensen, K. (In press). Changing the NICU environment: The Boston City Hospital model. *Neonatal Network Journal.*

Cole, J., and Frappier, P. (1985, Nov.–Dec.). Infant stimulation reassessed: A new approach to providing care for the preterm infant. *Journal of Obstetrics, Gynecology, and Neonatal Nursing,* 471–477.

Fulroth, R., Phillips, B., and Durand, D. (1989, Aug.). Perinatal outcome of infants exposed to cocaine and/or heroin in utero. *American Journal for Disease in Children, 143,* 905–910.

Greenspan, S., and Greenspan, N. (1985). *First Feelings: Milestones in the Emotional Development of Your Baby and Child.* New York: Viking.

Haith, M. (1980). *Rules That Babies Look By.* Hillsdale, NJ: Erlbaum.

Illsley, R., and Mitchell, R. (1984). *Low Birthweight: A Medical, Psychological and Social Study.* New York: Wiley.

Klaus, M., and Klaus, P. (1986). *The Amazing Newborn.* Reading, MA: Addison-Wesley.

LaRue-Jones, C., and Lopez, R. (1989, Oct. 2). Components report on drug abuse. In G. Hill (Ed.), *Report of the Expert Panel on the Content of Prenatal Care,* Vol. 2. Washington, DC: U.S. Department of Health and Human Services.

Miller, J., and Carlton, T. (1988, Nov.–Dec.). Children and AIDS: A need to rethink child welfare practice. *Social Work,* 553–555.

Mirochnick, M., Meyer, J., Cole, J., and Zuckerman, B. (Forthcoming.) Circulating catecholamine in cocaine-exposed neonates. Boston City Hospital, Boston, Massachusetts.

Nugent, J. K. (1981). The Brazelton Neonatal Behavioral Assessment Scale: Implications for intervention. *Pediatric Nursing 7* (3), 18–21.

Prechtl, H. (1977). Neurological examination of the full term newborn infant (2nd ed.). *Clinics in Developmental Medicine* (vol. 63). Philadelphia: Lippincott.

Regan, A. Personal communication, 1989. Boston City Hospital, Boston, Massachusetts.

Tronick, E., and Lester, B. (1985). *Infant Stimulation: Pediatric Round Table, Number 13.* New Brunswick, NJ: Johnson and Johnson.

Turkewirtz, G., and Kenny, P. (1985). The role of developmental limitation of sensory input on sensory/perceptual organization. *Journal of Developmental Behavioral Pediatrics, 6,* 302–306.

Ultmann, M., Belman, A., Ruff, H., Novick, B., Cone-Wesson, B., Cohen, H., and Rubenstein, A. (1985). Developmental abnormalities in infants with AIDS and ARC. *Developmental Medicine and Child Neurology, 27,* 563–571.

Wolff, P. (1974). The causes, controls, and organization of behavior in the neonate. *Psychological Issues, 45,* 237–242.

PART II   INFANTS AND TODDLERS

Acredolo and Goodwyn, "Symbolic Gesturing in Language Development"

Bates, E. (1979). Intentions, conventions, and symbols. In Bates, E., Benigni, L., Bretherton, I., Camaioni, L., and Volterra, V. (Eds.), *The Emergence of Symbols: Cognition and Communication in Infancy.* New York: Academic Press.

Bates, E., Benigni, L., Bretherton, I., Camaioni, L., and Volterra, V. (Eds.) (1979). *The Emergence of Symbols: Cognition and Communication in Infancy.* New York: Academic Press.

Bates, E., Bretherton, I., Shore, C., and McNew, S. (1983). Names, gestures and objects: The role of context in the emergence of symbols. In Nelson, K. (Ed.) *Advances in Child Development and Behavior.* New York: Academic Press.

Ekman, P., and Freisen, W. V. (1969). The repertoire of nonverbal behavior: Categories, usage, and coding. *Semiotica, 1,* 49–98.

Ferrier, L. (1978). Word, context, and imitation. In Locke (Ed.), *Action, Gesture, and Symbol.* New York: Academic Press.

Goldin-Meadow, S., and Feldman, H. (1975). The creation of a communication system: Study of deaf children of hearing parents. *Sign Language Studies, 8,* 225–234.

Goldin-Meadow, S., and Feldman, H. (1979). The development of language-like communication without a language model. *Science, 197,* 401–403.

Holmes, K. M., and Holmes, D. W. (1980). Signed and spoken language development of a hearing child of hearing parents. *Sign Language Studies, 28,* 239–254.

Nelson, K. (1973). Structure and strategy in learning to talk. *Monographs of the Society for Research on Child Development, 173,* 1–135.

Nelson, K. (1974). Concept, word, and sentence: Interrelations in acquisition and development. *Psychol. Rev., 81,* 267–285.

Peirce, C. S. (1932). In Jartshorne and Weiss, *Collected Papers.* Cambridge: Harvard University Press.

Prinz, P. M., and Prinz, E. A. (1979). Simultaneous acquisition of ASL and spoken English in a hearing child of a deaf mother and hearing father: Phase I—early lexical development. *Sign Language Studies, 25,* 282–296.

Volterra, V., and Taeschner, T. (1977). The origin and development of child language by a bilingual child. *Journal of Child Language, 5,* 311–326.

Werner, H., and Kaplan, B. (1963). *Symbol Formation.* New York: Wiley.

Lewis, "Emotional Development in the Young Child"

1. C. Darwin (1872), *The Expression of Emotions in Man and Animals* (Chicago, University of Chicago Press).

2. S. S. Tomkins (1963), *Affect, Imagery, Consciousness*. Vol. 2: *The Negative Affects* (New York: Springer).

3. P. Ekman, W. V. Friessen (1978), *The Facial Action Coding System (FACS)* (Palo Alto, CA: Consulting Psychologists Press).

4. C. E. Izard (1971), *The Face of Emotion* (New York: Appleton).

5. M. Lewis, and J. Brooks (1974), Self, other, and fear: Infants' reactions to people, in M. Lewis, and L. Rosenblum (eds.), *The Origins of Fear: The Origins of Behavior*, 2nd ed. (New York: Wiley).

6. J. Brooks, and M. Lewis, (1976), Infants' responses to strangers: Midget, adult and child, *Child Development*, 47, 323–332.

7. K. M. S. Bridges (1932), Emotional development in early infancy, *Child Development*, 3, 324–334.

8. P. H. Wolffe (1963), Observations on early development of smiling, in B. M. Foss (ed.), *Determinants of Infant Behavior*, Vol. 2 (New York: Wiley).

9. W. K. Berg and K. M. Berg, (1979), Psychophysiological development in infancy: State, sensory function and attention, in J. D. Osofsky (ed.), *Handbook of Infant Development* (New York: Wiley).

10. J. B. Watson, and R. Rayner (1970), Conditioned emotional reactions, *Journal of Experimental Psychology*, 311–314.

11. M. R. Gunnar, (1980), Control, warning signals and distress in infancy, *Developmental Psychology*, 16, 281–289.

12. C. Stenberg, J. Campos, and R. Emde (1983), The facial expression of anger in seven-month-old infants, *Child Development*, 54, 178–184.

13. M. Lewis (1986), Origins of self knowledge and individual differences in early self recognition, in A. G. Greendwald, J. Suls (eds.), *Psychological Perspective on the Self*, 3rd ed. (Hillsdale, NJ: Erlbaum), pp. 55–78.

14. M. Lewis, M. W. Sullivan, C. Stanger, et al. (1989), Self development and self-conscious emotions, *Child Development*, 60, 146–156.

15. A. H. Buss (1980), *Self Consciousness and Social Anxiety*, San Francisco: Freeman.

16. M. L. Hoffman (1975), Altruistic behavior and the parent-child relationship, *Journal of Personal and Social Psychology*, 31, 937–943(a).

17. M. Lewis (1986), Thinking and feeling—The elephant's tail. In C. A. Maher, M. Schwebel, and N. S. Fagley (eds.), *Psychological Perspective on the Self*, 3rd ed. Hillsdale, NJ: Erlbaum.

18. M. Lewis and J. Brooks-Gunn (1979), *Social Cognition and the Acquisition of Self*. New York: Plenum Press.

19. J. Brooks-Gunn and M. Lewis (1982), Affective exchanges between normal and handicapped infants and their mothers. In T. Field, and A. Fogel (eds.), *Emotion and Early Interaction* (Hillsdale, NJ: Erlbaum), pp. 161–188.

20. T. Field and A. Fogel (eds.) (1976), *Emotion and Interaction: Normal and High Risk Infants* (Hillsdale, NJ: Erlbaum).

21. A. Thomas and S. Chess (1977). *Temperament and Development* (New York: Brunner-Maze).

22. W. B. Carey (1972), Clinical applications of infant temperament, *Journal of Pediatrics*, 81, 823–828.

23. J. Wotobey and M. Lewis (In press), Individual differences in the reactivity of young infants, *Developmental Psychology*.

24. M. Lewis (1979), The development of attention and perception in the infant and young child, in W. M. Cruickshank and D. P. Hallahan (eds.), *Perceptual and Learning Disabilities in Children*, 2nd ed. (Syracuse, NY: University Press).

25. S. B. Crockenberg (1981), Infant irritability, mother responsiveness and social support, influence on the security of infant-mother attachment, *Child Development*, 52, 857–865.

Honig, "Compliance, Control, and Discipline"

Ainsworth, M.D.S., Bell, M. V., and Stayton, D. J. (1971). Individual differences in strange-situation behavior of one year olds. In H. R. Schaffer (Ed.), *The Origins of Human Social Relations*. London: Academic Press.

Beckwith, L. (1972, June). Relationships between infants' social behavior and their mothers' behavior. *Child Development*, 43 (2), 397–411.

Bishop, B. M. (1951). Mother-child interaction and the social behavior of children. *Psychological Monographs*, 65 (11), 328.

Chapman, M., and Zahn-Waxler, C. (1982). Young children's compliance and non-compliance to parental discipline in a natural setting. *International Journal of Behavioral Development*, 5, 81–94.

Clarke-Stewart, K. A., VanderStoep, L. P., and Killian, G. A. (1979, Sept.). Analysis and replication of mother-child relations at two years of age. *Child Development*, 50 (3), 777–793.

Eimer, B. N., Mancuso, J. C., and Lehrer, R. (1981, Feb.). A constructivist theory of reprimand as it applies to child rearing. Paper presented at the Eleventh Annual Interdisciplinary UAP-USC Piagetian Theory and the Helping Professions Conference. Los Angeles, California.

Erickson, M. F., and Crichton, L. (1981, April). Antecedents of compliance in two-year-olds from a high-risk sample. Paper presented at the Biennial Meeting of the Society for Research in Child Development, Boston, Massachusetts.

Forehand, R. L., and MacMahon, R. J. (1981). *Helping the Non-Compliant Child: A Clinician's Guide to Parent Training*. New York: Guilford.

George, G., and Main, M. (1979, June). Social interactions of young abused children: Approach, avoidance and aggression. *Child Development*, 50 (2), 306–318.

Gordon, T. (1970). *Parent Effectiveness Training*. New York: Wyden.

Hay, D. F., and Rheingold, H. L. (1983). The early appearance of some valued social behaviors. In D. L. Bridgeman (Ed.), *The Nature of Prosocial Development: Interdisciplinary Theories and Strategies*. New York: Academic Press.

Hetherington, E. M., Cox, M., and Cox, R. (1978). Stress and coping with divorce: A focus on women. In J. Gullahorn (Ed.), *Psychology and Transition*. New York: Winston.

Hoffman, M. L. (1970). Moral development. In P. H. Mussen (Ed.), *Carmichael's Manual of Child Psychology*, 3rd ed. New York: Wiley.

Hoffman, M. L. (1975). Moral internalization, parental power, and the nature of parent-child interaction. *Developmental Psychology, 11*, 228–239.

Holden, G. W. (1983, Feb.). Avoiding conflict: Mothers as tacticians in the supermarket. *Child Development, 54* (1), 233–240.

Holzman, M. (1974). The verbal environment provided by mothers for their very young children. *Merrill-Palmer Quarterly, 20*, 31–42.

Honig, A. S. (1982a, March). Infant-mother communication. *Young Children, 37* (3), 52–62.

Honig, A. S. (1982b, July). Prosocial development in children. *Young Children, 37* (5), 51–62.

Honig, A. S. (1985). Discipline tips for teachers. *New York Early Education Reporter, 31* (2), 4–5.

Honig, A. S., and Wittmer, D. S. (1981, April). Caregiver interaction and sex of toddler. Paper presented at the Biennial Conference of the Society for Research in Child Development. Boston, Massachusetts.

Honig, A. S., and Wittmer, D. S. (1982). Teachers and low-income toddlers in metropolitan day care. *Early Child Development and Care, 10* (1), 95–112.

Honig, A. S., and Wittmer, D. S. (Spring 1985). Toddler bids and teacher responses. *Child Care Quarterly, 14* (1), 14–29.

Howes, C., and Olenick, M. (1984, April). Family and child care influences on toddler's compliance. Paper presented at the Annual Meeting of the American Educational Research Association, New Orleans, Louisiana.

Kopp, C. B. (1982). Antecedents of self-regulation: A developmental perspective. *Developmental Psychology, 18*, 199–214.

Kuczynski, L. (1983). Reasoning, prohibitions, and motivations for compliance. *Developmental Psychology, 19*, 126–134.

Landauer, T. K., Carlsmith, J. M., and Lepper, M. (1970, Sept.). Experimental analysis of the factors determining obedience of four-year-old children to adult females. *Child Development, 41* (3), 601–611.

Londerville, S., and Main, M. (1981). Security attachment, compliance, and maternal training methods in the second year of life. *Developmental Psychology, 17*, 289–299.

Lytton, H. (1979). Disciplinary encounters between young boys and their mothers and fathers: Is there a contingency system? *Developmental Psychology, 15*, 256–268.

Lytton, H. (1980). *Parent-Child Interaction: The Socialization Process Observed in Twin and Singleton Families*. New York: Plenum Press.

Lytton, H., and Zwirner, W. (1975). Compliance and its controlling stimuli observed in a natural setting. *Developmental Psychology, 11*, 769–779.

Main, M., and Weston, D. R. (1981, Sept.). The quality of the toddler's relationship to mother and father: Related to

conflict behavior and the readiness to establish new relationships. *Child Development, 52* (3), 932–940.

Martin, J. A. (1981). A longitudinal study of the consequences of early mother-infant interaction: A microanalytic approach. *Monographs of the Society for Research in Child Development, 46* (3), No. 190.

Matas, L., Arend, R. A., and Sroufe, A. L. (1978, Sept.). Continuity of adaptation in the second year: The relationship between quality of attachment and later competence. *Child Development, 49* (3), 547–556.

McLaughlin, B. (1983). Child compliance to parental control techniques. *Developmental Psychology, 19*, 667–673.

Minton, C., Kagan, J., and Levine, J. A. (1971, Dec.). Maternal control and obedience in the two-year-old. *Child Development, 42* (6), 1873–1894.

Olson, S. L., Bates, J. E., and Bayles, K. (1984). Mother infant interaction and the development of individual differences in children's cognitive competence. *Developmental Psychology, 20*, 166–179.

Rubenstein, J. L., Howes, C., and Boyle, P. (1981). A two-year follow-up of infants in community-based day care. *Journal of Child Psychology and Psychiatry, 22*, 209–218.

Schaffer, H. R. (1984). *The Child's Entry into a Social World*. Orlando, FL: Academic Press.

Schaffer, H. R., and Crook, C. K. (1979, Dec.). Maternal control techniques in a directed play situation. *Child Development, 50* (4), 989–996.

Schaffer, H. R., and Crook, C. K. (1980). Child compliance and maternal control techniques. *Developmental Psychology, 16*, 54–61.

Shure, M. B., and Spivak, G. (1979). *Problem Solving Techniques in Child Rearing*. San Francisco: Jossey-Bass.

Siegal, M., and Rablin, J. (1982). Moral development as reflected by young children's evaluation of maternal discipline. *Merrill-Palmer Quarterly, 28*, 499–509.

Smith, C. A. (1982). *Promoting the Social Development of Young Children: Strategies and Activities*. Palo Alto, CA: Mayfield.

Stayton, D. J., Hogan, R., and Ainsworth, M.D.S. (1971, Oct.). Infant obedience and maternal behavior: The origins of socialization reconsidered. *Child Development, 42* (4), 1057–1069.

Sroufe, L. A. (1979). The coherence of individual development. *American Psychologist, 34*, 834–841.

Wetstone, H. S., and Friedlander, B. Z. (1973, Dec.). The effect of word order on young children's responses to simple questions and commands. *Child Development, 44* (4), 734–740.

Wolfgang, C. H. (1977). *Helping Aggressive and Passive Preschoolers Through Play*. Columbus, OH: Merrill.

Wolfgang, C. H., and Glickman, C. D. (1980). *Solving Discipline Problems*. Boston: Allyn & Bacon.

Ziajka, A. (1981). *Prelinguistic Communication in Infancy*. New York: Praeger.

McBride and DiCero, "Separation"

DeMeis, D. K., Hock, E., and McBride, S. L. (1986). The balance of employment and motherhood: Longitudinal study of mothers' feelings about separation from their first-born infants. *Developmental Psychology, 22,* 627–632.

Field, T., Gewirtz, J. L., Cohen, P., Garcia, R., Greenberg, R., and Collins, K. (1984). Leavetakings and reunions of infants, preschoolers, and their parents. *Child Development, 55,* 628–635.

Frankel, D. G., and Roer-Bornstein, D. (1982). Traditional and modern contributions to changing infant-rearing ideologies of two ethnic communities. *Monographs of the Society for Research in Child Development, 47* (4, Serial No. 196).

Hayghe, H. (1986, Feb.). Rise in mothers' labor force activity includes those with infants. *Monthly Labor Review,* 43–45.

Hock, E. (1984). The transition to day care: Effects of maternal separation anxiety on infant adjustment. In R. C. Ainslie (Ed.), *The Child and the Day Care Setting.* New York: Praeger.

Hock, E., and Clinger, J. B. (1981). Infant coping behaviors: Their assessment and their relationship to maternal attitudes. *Journal of Genetic Psychology, 138,* 231–243.

Hock, E., DeMeis, D., and McBride, S. (1988). Maternal separation anxiety: Its role in the balance of employment and motherhood in mothers of infants. In A. Gottfried and A. Gottfried (Eds.), *Maternal Employment and Children's Development: Longitudinal Research.* New York: Plenum.

Hock, E., McBride, S., and Gnezda, T. (1989). Maternal separation anxiety: Mother-infant separation from the maternal perspective. *Child Development, 60,* 793–802.

Hofferth, S., and Phillips, D. (1987, Aug.). Child care in the United States, 1970–1995. *Journal of Marriage and the Family,* 559–571.

Humphry, R. (1985). Colic in infancy and the mother-infant relationship. Unpublished doctoral dissertation, Ohio State University, Columbus.

Kagan, J. (1984). *The Nature of the Child.* New York: Basic Books.

Kotelchuck, M. (1972). The nature of the child's tie to his father. Unpublished doctoral dissertation, Harvard University.

Lester, B., Kotelchuck, M., Spelke, E., Sellers, M., and Klein, R. (1974). Separation protest in Guatemalan infants: Cross-cultural and cognitive findings. *Developmental Psychology, 10,* 79–85.

Mahler, M., Pine, R., and Bergman, A. (1975). *The Psychological Birth of the Human Infant.* New York: Basic Books.

McBride, S. L., and Belsky, J. (1988). Characteristics, determinants, and consequences of maternal separation anxiety. *Developmental Psychology, 24* (3), 407–414.

Pitzer, M. (1985). A study of maternal separation anxiety in working mothers of second-born infants. Unpublished doctoral dissertation, Ohio State University, Columbus.

Public Agenda Foundation (1983). *Survey: Work in the 1980's and 1990's.* New York: Public Agenda Foundation.

Spelke, E., Zelazo, P., Kagan, J., and Kotelchuck, M. (1973). Father interaction and separation protest. *Developmental Psychology, 9,* 83–90.

Lauter-Klatell, "How Do I Say, 'Let's Play'?"

Atwater, J., and Morris, S. K. (1984, Aug.). An analysis of toddlers' social behavior in a day care setting. Paper presented at the annual American Psychological Association meeting, Toronto, Ontario, Canada. (ERIC Document Reproduction Service No. ED 253 320)

Becker, J. (1977). A learning analysis of the development of peer-oriented behavior in nine-month-old infants. *Developmental Psychology, 13* (5), 481–491.

Brenner, J., and Mueller, E. (1982). Shared meaning in boy toddlers' peer relations. *Child Development, 53,* 380–391.

Eckerman, C., Whatley, J., and Kutz, S. (1975). Growth of social play with peers during the second year of life. *Developmental Psychology, 11,* 42–49.

Lauter-Klatell, N. (1983). *A comparison of social interaction patterns in same-age and mixed-age dyads.* Unpublished doctoral dissertation, Boston University.

Rubenstein, J., and Howes, C. (1976). The effects of peers on toddler interaction with mother and toys. *Child Development, 47,* 597–605.

PART III   PRESCHOOL DEVELOPMENT

Schickedanz, "Young Children Can Learn Some Important Things When They Write"

Bissex, G. (1980). *GNYS AT WRK: A Child Learns to Read and Write.* Cambridge, MA: Harvard University Press.

Ehri, L. C., and Wilce, L. S. (1980). The influence of orthography on readers' conceptualization of the phonemic structure of words. *Applied Psycholinguistics, 1,* 371–385.

Liberman, I. Y., Shankweiler, D., Fischer, F. W., and Carter, B. (1974). Explicit syllable and phonemic segmentation in the young child. *Journal of Experimental Child Psychology, 18,* 201–212.

Mann, V. (1986). Phonological awareness: The role of reading experience. *Cognition, 24,* 65–92.

Read, C. (1975). *Children's Categorization of Speech Sounds in English.* Urbana, IL: National Council of Teachers of English.

Schickedanz, J. (1990). *Adam's Righting Revolutions: A Six-year Case Study of One Child's Writing Development.* Portsmouth, NH: Heinemann Educational Books.

Roedell, "Developing Social Competence in Gifted Preschool Children"

Abroms, K. I. (1983). Affective development. In M. B. Karnes (Ed.), *The Underserved: Our Young Gifted Children* (pp. 118–143). Reston, VA: Council for Exceptional Children.

Abroms, K. I., and Gollin, J. B. (1980). Developmental study of gifted preschool children and measures of psychosocial giftedness. *Exceptional Children, 46,* 334–341.

Combs, M. L., and Slaby, D. A. (1977). Social skills training with children. In B. Lahey and A. Kazdin (Eds.), *Ad-*

vances in Clinical Child Psychology (Vol. 1, pp. 161–201). New York: Plenum.

Elardo, P., and Cooper, M. (1977). *AWARE*. Menlo Park, CA: Addison-Wesley.

Gallagher, J. J. (1958). Peer acceptance of highly gifted children in elementary school. *Elementary School Journal, 58*, 465–470.

Hollingworth, L. C. (1942). *Children Above 180 IQ, Stanford-Binet*. Yonkers-on-Hudson, NY: World Book.

Lewis, M., Young, G., Brooks, J., and Michalson, L. (1975). The beginning of friendship. In M. Lewis and L. A. Rosenblum (Eds.), *Friendship and Peer Relations* (pp. 27–66). New York: Wiley.

O'Shea, H. (1960). Friendships and the intellectually gifted child. *Exceptional Children, 26*, 327–335.

Roedell, W. C. (1978). Social development in intellectually advanced children. In H. B. Robinson (chair), *Intellectually Advanced Children: Preliminary Findings of a Longitudinal Study*. Symposium presented at the Annual Convention of the American Psychological Association, Toronto.

Roedell, W. C. (1984). Vulnerabilities of highly gifted children. *Roeper Review, 6*, 127–130.

Roedell, W. C., Jackson, N. E., and Robinson, H. B. (1980). *Gifted Young Children*. New York: Teachers College Press.

Shwedel, A. M., and Stoneburner, R. (1983). Identification. In M. B. Karnes (Ed.), *The Underserved: Our Young Gifted Children* (pp. 17–39). Reston, VA: Council for Exceptional Children.

Silverman, L. K. (In preparation). *Gifted Education*. St. Louis, MO: C. V. Mosby.

Slaby, R. G., and Roedell, W. C. (1982). The development and regulation of aggression in young children. In J. Worell (Ed.), *Psychological Development in the Elementary Years* (pp. 97–149). New York: Academic Press.

Spivack, G., and Shure, M. B. (1974). *Social Adjustment of Young Children*. San Francisco: Jossey-Bass.

Tannenbaum, A. J. (1983). *Gifted Children: Psychological and Educational Perspectives*. New York: Macmillan.

Terman, L. M. (1925). *Genetic Studies of Genius: Mental and Physical Traits of a Thousand Gifted Children* (Vol. 1). Stanford, CA: Stanford University Press.

Whitmore, J. R. (1980). *Giftedness, Conflict, and Underachievement*. Boston: Allyn & Bacon.

deYoung, "Disclosing Sexual Abuse"

Arieti, S. (1976). *Creativity: The Magic Synthesis*. New York: Basic Books.

Bernstein, B. E., Claman, L., Harris, J. C., and Samson, J. (1982, Feb.). The child witness: A model for evaluation and trial preparation. *Child Welfare, 61* (2), 95–104.

Bernstein, B. E., and Claman, L. (1986, Mar.–April). Modern technology and the child witness. *Child Welfare, 65* (2), 155–163.

Brant, R. S. T., and Tisza, V. B. (1977, Jan.). The sexually misused child. *American Journal of Orthopsychiatry, 47* (1), 80–90.

Chance, J. E., and Goldstein, A. G. (1984). Face-recognition memory: Implications for children's eyewitness testimony. *Journal of Social Issues, 40* (1), 69–85.

Cohen, R. L., and Harnick, M. A. (1980). The susceptibility of child witnesses to suggestion. *Law and Human Behavior, 4* (4), 201–210.

Conte, J. R., and Berliner, L. (1981, Dec.). Sexual abuse of children: Implications for practice. *Social Casework, 62* (10), 601–607.

de Jong, A. R. (1985, May). The medical evaluation of sexual abuse in children. *Hospital and Community Psychiatry, 36* (5), 509–512.

deYoung, M. (1981, May). Promises, threats and lies: Keeping incest secret. *Journal of Humanics, 9* (1), 61–71.

deYoung, M. (1982a). *The Sexual Victimization of Children*. Jefferson, NC: McFarland.

deYoung, M. (1982b, Spring). Innocent seducer or innocently seduced? The role of the child incest victim. *Journal of Clinical Child Psychology, 11* (1), 56–60.

Farrell, M. K., Billmore, M. E., Shamroy, J. A., and Hammond, J. G. (1981, Jan.). Pubertal gonorrhea: A multidisciplinary approach. *Pediatrics, 67* (1), 151–153.

Ferenczi, S. (1949). Confusion of tongues between adults and the child. *International Journal of Psychoanalysis, 30* (2), 225–230.

Finkelhor, D., and Browne, A. (1985, Oct.). The traumatic impact of child sexual abuse: A conceptualization. *American Journal of Orthopsychiatry, 55* (4), 530–541.

Freud, A. (1965). *Normality and Pathology in Childhood*. New York: International Universities Press.

Fritz, G. S., Stoll, K., and Wagner, N. N. (1981, Spring). A comparison of males and females who were sexually molested as children. *Journal of Sex and Marital Therapy, 7* (1), 54–59.

Jersild, A. T. (1968). *Child Psychology*. Englewood Cliffs, NJ: Prentice-Hall.

Kaplan, S. L., and Kaplan, S. J. (1981). The child's accusation of sexual abuse during a divorce and custody struggle. *Hillside Journal of Clinical Psychiatry, 3* (1), 81–95.

Marin, B. V., Holmes, D. L., Guth, M., and Kovac, P. (1979). The potential of children as eyewitnesses: A comparison of children and adults in eyewitness tasks. *Law and Human Behavior, 3* (3), 295–306.

Meiselman, K. C. (1978). *Incest: A Psychological Study of Causes and Effects with Treatment Recommendations*. San Francisco, CA: Jossey-Bass, 1978.

Melton, G. B. (1981). Children's competency to testify. *Law and Human Behavior, 5* (1), 73–85.

Melton, G. B. (1985). Sexually abused children in the legal system: Some policy recommendations. *American Journal of Family Therapy, 13* (1), 61–66.

Nelson, K. E. (1971). Memory development in children. *Psychonomic Science, 25* (3), 346–348.

Peevers, B. H., and Secord, P. F. (1973). Developmental changes in attribution of descriptive concepts to persons. *Journal of Personality and Social Psychology, 27* (1), 120–128.

Phillips, J. L. (1981). *Piaget's Theory: A Primer*. San Francisco: Freeman.

Rholes, W. S., and Ruble, D. N. (1984). Children's understanding of dispositional characteristics of others. *Child Development, 55* (4), 550–560.

Rosenfeld, A. A., Nadelson, C. C., and Krieger, M. (1979, April). Fantasy and reality in patient reports of incest. *Journal of Clinical Psychiatry, 50* (4), 159–164.

Singer, D., and Reveson, T. (1978). *How a Child Thinks.* New York: New American Library.

Summit, R. C. (1983). The child sexual abuse accommodation syndrome. *Child Abuse and Neglect, 7* (2), 177–193.

Varendonck, J. (1911). The testimony of children in a famous trial. *Archives de Psychologie, 11* (1), 129–171.

Whipple, G. M. (1911). The psychology of testimony. *Psychological Bulletin, 8* (3), 307–309.

Wigmore, J. H. (1975). *Evidence in Trials at Common Law.* Boston, MA: Little, Brown.

PART IV   MIDDLE CHILDHOOD

Kamii, "Why Big Bird Can't Teach Calculus"

Dantzig, T. (1967). *Number: The Language of Science.* New York: Free Press.

Flavell, J. H. (1985). *Cognitive Development.* 2nd ed. Englewood Cliffs, NJ: Prentice-Hall.

Kamii, C. K. (1985). *Young Children Reinvent Arithmetic: Implications of Piaget's Theory.* New York: Teachers College Press.

Kamii, C. K. (1986, Aug.). Place value: An explanation of its difficulty and implications for the primary grades. *Journal for Research in Childhood Education, 1,* 75–86.

Kamii, M. (1982). Children's graphic representation of numerical concepts: A developmental study. (Doctoral dissertation, Harvard University Graduate School of Education, 1982). *Dissertation Abstracts International, 43,* 1478A.

Kline, M. (1972). *Mathematical Thought from Ancient to Modern Times.* New York: Oxford University Press.

Piaget, J. (1965). *The Child's Conception of Number.* New York: Norton.

Resnick, L. B., and Ford, W. W. (1981). *The Psychology of Mathematics for Instruction.* Hillsdale, NJ: Erlbaum.

Ross, S. H. (1989). Parts, wholes, and place value: A developmental view. *Arithmetic Teacher, 36* (6), 47–51.

Wilder, R. C. (1968). *Evolution of Mathematical Concepts: An Elementary Study.* New York: Wiley.

Postman, "The Disappearance of Childhood"

Lasch, C. (1979). *The Culture of Narcissism.* New York: Norton.

Mankewicz, F., and Swerdlow, J. (1979). *Remote Control.* New York: Ballantine.

Plumb, J. H. (1971). The great change in children. *Horizon, 13* (1), 7.

Tuchman, B. (1978). *A Distant Mirror.* New York: Knopf.

Norwood, "A Society That Promotes Drug Abuse"

Bill Press Report. (1984, Aug.). Channel 11, 5 P.M. Newscope, Atlanta, Georgia.

Blum, A. (1983, Mar.). An inside look at cigarette and alcohol pushers. Presentation at P.R.I.D.E. Drug Conference, Hilton Inn, Atlanta, Georgia.

The Chemical People. (1983, Nov.). Television Production, Metropolitan Life Foundation, Northbrook, Illinois.

Drug Use and Effects: Tobacco. (1982, Sept.). *Drug Abuse Update.*

Elkind, D. (1981, Nov.–Dec.). All Grown Up and No Place to Go. *Childhood Education, 58* (2), 69–73.

Elkind, D. (1982, Jan.). The hurried child. *Instructor, 91* (5), 40–45.

Elkind, D. (1982, Mar. 16). Are we making our children grow up too fast? *Family Circle,* pp. 119–121.

Emichovich, C. H., and Gaier, E. L. (1983, Winter). Ideology and idealism in early adolescence. *Adolescence, 18* (72), 787–797.

Fasick, F. A. (1984, Spring). Parents, peers, youth culture and autonomy in adolescence. *Adolescence, 19* (73), 143–157.

Friedman, A. S., and Santo, Y. (1984). A composition of attitudes of parents and high school students regarding cigarettes, alcohol, and drug use. *Journal of Drug Education, 14* (1), 37–51.

Janus, S. (1982, June 22). The death of innocence. *Awake, 63* (12).

Logan, R. D. (1988, Winter). A reconceptualization of Erickson's identity stage. *Adolescence, 18* (72), 943–946.

McDermott, D. (1984, Spring). The relationship of parental drug use and parents' attitudes concerning adolescent drug use to adolescent drug use. *Adolescence, 19* (73), 89–97.

Manning, M. A., and Manning, G. (1981, Nov.–Dec.). The school's assault on childhood. *Childhood Education, 58* (2), 84–85.

Negrete, J. (1983, Mar.). Overview of World Health Organization Addiction Research Foundation Report. Presentation at P.R.I.D.E. Drug Conference, Hilton Inn, Atlanta, Georgia.

Parents' alert. (1983, Feb.). *ACEI Exchange, 51* (6).

Postman, N. (1981, Nov.–Dec.). Disappearing childhood. *Childhood Education, 58* (2), 66–68.

Reagan, N. (1983, Jan.–Feb.). The first lady talks about drug abuse. *American Education* (U.S. Department of Education), *19* (1) 2–4.

Savage, T. V. (1984, Jan.–Feb.). Investigating the social aspects of alcohol use. *Health Education, 15,* 49–50.

Weisheit, R. A. (1983, Fall). The social context of alcohol and drug education: Implications for program evaluation. *Journal of Alcohol and Drug Education, 29* (1), 72–81.

PART V   ADOLESCENCE

Blyth and Traeger, "The Self-Concept and Self-Esteem of Early Adolescents"

Bachman, J. G., and O'Malley, P. M. (1977). Self-esteem in young men: A longitudinal analysis of educational and occupational attainment. *Journal of Personality and Social Psychology, 35,* 365–380.

Beane, J. A., and Lipka, R. P. (1979, Aug.). Enhancing self-concept/esteem in the middle school. *Middle School Journal, 4,* 20–27.

Beane, J. A., and Lipka, R. P. (1980). Self-concept and self-esteem: A construct differentiation. *Child Study Journal, 10,* 1–6.

Beane, J. A., Lipka, R. P., and Ludewig, J. W. (1980, Oct.). Synthesis of research on self-concept. *Educational Leadership,* pp. 80–89.

Bernstein, R. M. (1980). The development of the self-system during adolescence. *Journal of Genetic Psychology, 136,* 231–245.

Blyth, D. A., Bulcroft, R., and Simmons, R. G. (1981). The impact of puberty on adolescents: A longitudinal study. Presentation at the Annual Meeting of the American Psychological Association, Los Angeles.

Blyth, D. A., Simmons, R. G., and Bush, D. (1978). The transition into early adolescence: A longitudinal comparison of youth in two educational contexts. *Sociology of Education, 51,* 149–162.

Blyth, D. A., Simmons, R. G., and Carlton-Ford, S. (1983). The adjustment of early adolescents to school transitions. *Journal of Early Adolescence, 3* (1).

Broughton, J. M. (1981). The divided self in adolescence. *Human Development, 24,* 13–32.

Calhoun, G., Jr., and Morse, W. C. (1977). Self-concept and self-esteem: Another perspective. *Psychology in the Schools, 14,* 318–322.

Coleman, J. C. (1974). *Relationships in Adolescence.* London: Routledge & Kegan Paul.

Coleman, J. C. (1978). Current contradictions in adolescent theory. *Journal of Youth and Adolescence, 7* (1), 1–11.

Cooley, C. H. (1902). *Human Nature and the Social Order.* New York: Scribners.

Damon, W., and Hart, D. (1982). The development of self-understanding from infancy through adolescence. *Child Development, 53,* 841–864.

Dickstein, E. (1977). Self and self-esteem: Theoretical foundations and their implications for research. *Human Development, 20,* 129–140.

Dusek, J. B., and Flaherty, J. F. (1981). The development of self-concept during the adolescent years. *Monographs of the Society for Research in Child Development, 46* (4) (Serial No. 191).

Erikson, E. H. (1968). *Identity, Youth, and Crisis.* New York: Norton.

Freud, S. (1961 [1923]). *The Ego and the Id.* Standard edition, vol. 19. London: Hogarth.

Hill, J. P., and Palmquist, W. J. (1978). Social cognition and social relations in early adolescence. *International Journal of Behavioral Development, 1,* 1–36.

Horrocks, J. E., and Jackson, D. W. (1972). *Self and role—A theory of self-process and role behavior.* New York: Houghton Mifflin.

James, W. (1980). *Principles of Psychology* (Vol. 1). New York: Holt.

Long, B. H., Ziller, R. C., and Henderson, E. H. (1968). Developmental changes in the self-concept during adolescence. *School Review, 76,* 210–230.

McCarthy, J. D., and Hoge, D. R. (1982). Analysis of age effects in longitudinal studies of adolescent self-esteem. *Developmental Psychology, 18,* 372–379.

Mead, G. H. (1934). *Mind, Self, and Society.* Chicago: University of Chicago Press.

Montemayor, R., and Eisen, M. (1977). The development of self-conceptions from childhood to adolescence. *Developmental Psychology, 13,* 314–319.

Noppe, I. C. (1981). Age and cognitive-developmental factors in the development of self-conceptions. Paper presented at biennial meetings of the Society for Research in Child Development.

Petersen, A., and Taylor, B. (1980). The biological approach to adolescence: Biological change and psychological adaptation. In J. Adelson (ed.), *Handbook of Adolescent Psychology.* New York: Wiley.

Rosenberg, M. (1965). *Society and the Adolescent Self-Image.* Princeton, NJ: Princeton University Press.

Rosenberg, M. (1979). *Conceiving the Self.* New York: Basic Books.

Savin-Williams, R. (1983). Conceiving or misconceiving the self: Issues of self-esteem in adolescents. *Journal of Early Adolescence, 3* (1).

Shavelson, R. J., Hubner, J. J., and Stanton, G. C. (1976). Self-concept: Validation of construct interpretations. *Review of Educational Research, 46,* 407–441.

Simmons, R. G., Blyth, D. A., and McKinney, K. L. (1983). The social and psychological effects of puberty on white females. In J. Brooks-Gunn and A. Petersen (Eds.), *Girls at Puberty.* New York: Plenum.

Simmons, R. G., Blyth, D. A., Van Cleave, E., and Bush, D. (1979). Entry into early adolescence: The impact of school structure, puberty and early dating on self-esteem. *American Sociological Review, 44,* 948–967.

Simmons, R. G., Rosenberg, F., and Rosenberg, M. (1973). Disturbance in the self-image at adolescence. *American Sociological Review, 38,* 553–568.

Wells, L. E., and Marwell, G. (1976). *Self-Esteem: Its Conceptualization and Measurement* (Vol. 20). Beverly Hills, CA: Sage Library of Social Research.

Wylie, R. C. (1974). *The Self-Concept: A Review of Methodological Considerations and Measuring Instruments* (Vol. 1). Rev. ed. Lincoln: University of Nebraska Press.

Wylie, R. C. (1979). *The Self-Concept: Theory and Research on Selected Topics* (Vol. 2) Rev. ed. Lincoln: University of Nebraska Press.

Zigler, E., Balla, D., and Watson, N. (1972). Developmental and experimental determinants of self-image disparity in institutionalized and noninstitutionalized retarded and normal children. *Journal of Personality and Social Psychology, 23,* 81–87.

Bronfenbrenner, "Alienation"

1. Urie Bronfenbrenner (1984, May 4). New worlds for families, paper presented at the Boston Children's Museum.

2. Urie Bronfenbrenner (1986), The ecology of the family as a context for human development, *Developmental Psychology*, 22(6), 723–742.

3. Mavis Heatherington (1981), Children of divorce, in R. Henderson (ed.), *Parent-Child Interaction* (New York: Academic Press).

4. A. S. Makarenko (1967), *The Collective Family: A Handbook for Russian Parents* (New York: Doubleday).

5. Lea Pulkkinen (1982), Self-control and continuity from childhood to adolescence, in Paul Baltes and Orville G. Brim, (eds.), *Life-Span Development and Behavior*, Vol. 4 (New York: Academic Press), pp. 64–102.

6. S. B. Kamerman (1980), *Parenting in an Unresponsive Society* (New York: Free Press); S. B. Kamerman and A. J. Kahn (n.d.), *Social Services in International Perspective* (Washington, DC: U.S. Department of Health, Education, and Welfare); and Lloyd Johnston, Jerald Bachman, and Patrick O'Malley (1985), *Use of Licit and Illicit Drugs by America's High School Students—1975–84* (Washington, DC: U.S. Government Printing Office).

7. Kurt Aurin, personal communication (1985).

8. Ellen Greenberger and Lawrence Steinberg (1986), *When Teenagers Work* (New York: Basic Books).

Williams, "Looking for Linda"

Billingsley, A., and Giovannoni, J. M. (1972). *Children of the Storm: Black Children and American Child Welfare.* New York: Harcourt Brace Jovanovich.

Clark, K. B. (1965). *Dark Ghetto.* New York: Harper & Row.

Davis, A. (1948). *Social Class Influence Upon Learning.* Cambridge, MA: Harvard University Press.

Foster, M., and Perry, L. R. (1982, Jan.). Self-valuation among blacks. *Social Work*, 27 (1), 60.

Germain, C. B. (1978, Dec.). General systems theory and ego psychology: An ecological perspective. *Social Service Review*, 52, 535–549.

Germain, C. B. (1979). *Social Work Practice: People and Environment.* New York: Columbia University Press.

Grier, W. H., and Cobbs, P. M. (1968). *Black Rage.* New York: Basic Books.

Hopps, J. G. (1982, Jan.). Oppression based on color. *Social Work*, 27 (1), 3–4.

Hunt, C. L., and Walter, L. (1978). *Ethnic Dynamics: Patterns of Intergroup Relations in Various Societies.* Holmes Beach, FL: Learning Publications.

Longres, J. F. (1982, Jan.). Minority groups: An interest-group perspective. *Social Work*, 27 (1), 12.

Maguire, D. C. (1980). *A New American Justice.* Garden City, NY: Doubleday.

McAdoo, H. P. (1982, Jan.). Demographic trends for people of color. *Social Work*, 27 (1), 16.

Pinderhughes, C. (1976). Black personality in American society. In M. M. Smythe (Ed.), *Black American Reference Book*, Englewood Cliffs, NJ: Prentice-Hall.

Pinderhughes, E. B. (1979, July). Teaching empathy in cross-cultural social work. *Social Work*, 24 (7), 312–316.

Pinderhughes, E. B. (1982, Jan.). Family functioning of Afro-Americans. *Social Work*, 27 (1), 94.

Stehno, S. M. (1982, Jan.). Differential treatment of minority children in service systems. *Social Work*, 27 (1), 39–45.

Walsh, E. J. (1975). *Dirty Work, Race and Self-Esteem.* Ann Arbor, MI: Institute of Labor and Industrial Relations, University of Michigan-Wayne State University.

Washington, R. O. (1982, Jan.). Social development: A focus for practice and education. *Social Work*, 27 (1), 104–105.

INDEX